Atlin

Where Everyone Knows
Your Dog's Name

Bradford D. Smith

Fathom Publishing Company
Anchorage, Alaska

ISBN 978-1-888215-82-3 Hardcover
ISBN 978-1-888215-81-6 Paperback
ISBN 978-1-888215-83-0 e-book
Library of Congress Control Number 2021919315
Printed in United States of America

ISBN 978-1-888215-46-5 Paperback
Printed in Canada

Cover design and area maps
  Jacques Polomé, Jacques Polomé Design, Perth, Australia.

Publisher's Cataloging-in-Publication data
Names: Smith, Bradford D., author.
Title: Atlin : where everyone knows your dog's name / Bradford D. Smith.
Description: Includes bibliographical references and index. | Anchorage,
   AK: Fathom Publishing Company, 2021.
Identifiers: LCCN: 2021919315 | ISBN: 978-1-888215-82-3 (hardcover) |
   978-1-888215-81-6 (paperback) | 978-1-888215-83-0 (ebook)
Subjects: LCSH Smith, Bradford D.–Childhood. | Atlin (B.C.)–Biography.
   | Atlin (B.C.)–Social life and customs. | Atlin (B.C.)–History. |
   BISAC BIOGRAPHY & AUTOBIOGRAPHY / Personal Memoirs |
   BIOGRAPHY & AUTOBIOGRAPHY / Cultural, Ethnic & Regional /
   General | BIOGRAPHY & AUTOBIOGRAPHY / Historical
Classification: LCC F1087 .S65 2021 | DDC 917.11/092–dc23

bradfordsmithauthor.com

fathompublishing.com
Fathom Publishing Company
P.O. Box 200448
Anchorage, Alaska 99520-0448
Telephone /Fax 907-272-3305

Dedication

To the loving memory of my mother, Diane Solie Smith.

To my sons, John Frost and Taylor Smith,
to my beautiful and smart granddaughters,
Delilah and Daisy Tannura
and to my amazing wife and partner in life,
Zandra Holt.

Table of Contents

Articles by Diane Solie Smith

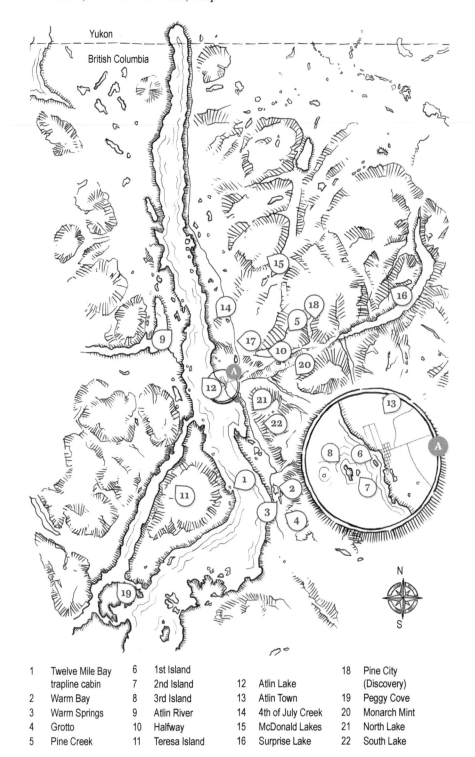

1	Twelve Mile Bay trapline cabin	6	1st Island			18	Pine City (Discovery)
2	Warm Bay	7	2nd Island	12	Atlin Lake	19	Peggy Cove
3	Warm Springs	8	3rd Island	13	Atlin Town	20	Monarch Mint
4	Grotto	9	Atlin River	14	4th of July Creek	21	North Lake
5	Pine Creek	10	Halfway	15	McDonald Lakes	22	South Lake
		11	Teresa Island	16	Surprise Lake		

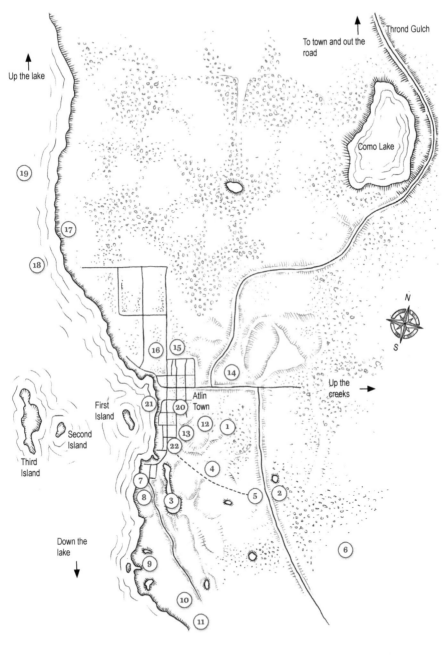

1	Skating ponds	7	Rope swing	13	Sliding hill	18	Canoe St. Bernard
2	Black Rocks	8	Mine shaft	14	Pete and John's		incident
3	Slough	9	Mike's Channel		horse corrals	19	Where the truck sank
4	Short cut	10	Keith and Julie's	15	Campground	20	Courthouse
5	Dump	11	Mouth of Pine	16	Mineral Springs	21	*M/V Tarahne*
6	On the mountain	12	Alkali Flats	17	Red Bluffs	22	School

Acknowledgments

First, I want to thank my mother, Diane Solie Smith, for her many contributions to this book. Her amazing prose from long ago is prominently featured and her beautiful photos populate the pages. Her artwork graces every chapter head. Most of all, I'm thankful for her grand example and for inspiring me to be a better human being. Rest in Peace, Mom.

I wish to thank the following people for putting up with my random and often obscure questions pertaining to Atlin's past minutia. Helen Smith, Clive Aspinal, Arthur Mitchell, Caroline Moore, Terry Milos, and Rob Shaw.

Without the amazing gift of a box of old Atlin newspapers, this book would be lesser for it. Thank you, Carol and Bill Boyko.

I have to extend a huge thank you to my life-long friend Randy Green who is okay with being my fall guy.

Thanks to Terry Milos and Martin Blakesley for including me in their writing processes and encouraging mine. Without that support and motivation, completion of this project would have been in doubt.

Thanks to Randy Green, Wade Jackson, Marla Thombleson, Carol Boyko and Kendall Merry for suffering through earlier iterations of the book and providing me with much needed feedback.

Last, but importantly not least, I want to thank Connie Taylor and the gang at Fathom Publishing. Without their knowledge and constructive input, this book would be a shell of what it has become.

Introduction

As a young boy growing up in Northern Canada in the 1960s and 70s, life was a perpetual adventure; an astonishing journey that most of us were not aware we were taking.

Nestled amongst soaring mountains, ensconced in a tiny cove on the eastern shore of the vast and beautiful Atlin Lake, sits the small town of Atlin, British Columbia.

Summer view of Atlin Mountain and its distinct rock glacier, mid-2000s. In our wildest dreams, we never imagined climbing it with a snow machine, but now there's an annual race to the top of the rock glacier and back down. I don't think my 1980 Elan 250 Ski-Doo would have made it. Photo by Caroline Moore.

Â Tlèn is the Tlingit word for great water. Atlin Lake is fed by gold-rich creeks, lazy rivers and meandering streams all filling the colossal mother of the mighty Yukon River. Surrounded by thousands of miles of unspoiled wilderness and steeped in rich gold rush history, Atlin was our home.

Once a thriving, bustling, gold field camp of thousands, it had recently been left grasping at a fading existence. After surviving its mid-century near demise, only a dozen years later by the mid-1960s, Atlin was on the verge of a rebirth, a modern boom. At the time, the word "town" may have been an exaggeration—village or hamlet are possibly better descriptions. Nevertheless, "community" was the word that defined it. Community in its purest sense was at its core; it was its essence, its immortality and its salvation. Atlin was the center of our universe, our playground of epic proportions, our family, our classroom, and our mother.

In the late 1960s, it consisted of a couple-hundred kindred souls: miners, hunters, trappers, merchants, First Nations people, artists, adventurers, big-game guides and oddballs—they were all proud to call Atlin home. These same people possessed a passionate and dogged determination to see Atlin survive and even thrive again.

At the height of the Cold War, when young men were dying in the jungles of Southeast Asia, while nations were fought over and divided in the Middle East, and the entire world cowered under the threat of nuclear annihilation, we were fishing and camping, riding our bikes and snaring rabbits. We vaguely heard what was happening on the "Outside" as we called it, and when we did it wasn't relevant and didn't seem real to us. We didn't get the news, per se, but occasionally we heard our parents or teachers talking about the communists or the war. Mostly, we didn't pay attention. While other kids watched the Vietnam War explode its Technicolor guts across their TV screen every night, we were building forts and hunting grouse.

We lived in the "North." The "North" was as much a vague reference to whatever wasn't the "South" as any geographical destination or compass direction. In those times, not a lot of attention was paid to delineating the borders between Alaska and the Yukon or Northern British Columbia; it was simply the North. Canada has plenty of "north," but this was our North. People who lived in the North, lived; people who lived in the South, existed. That was our philosophy. We knew living where we did made us different, better, special. We had no idea why and probably never spent a second thinking about or caring if it was true. It just was.

Atlin reached near-death throes in the 1950s when the population sunk to its lowest since the gold rush, dipping to around seventy-five residents; but in the mid-1960s it doubled in size, and then by the mid-1970s, it doubled again. Atlin was in vogue once more. The back-to-nature movement was in full swing and Atlin's spectacular beauty, wonderful heritage, and even its isolation made it perfect for many. The town offered a chance to completely change one's life, to escape the crowded drudgery of the city and to save your family from a life of insignificance. It provided a chance to raise your children in a safe place. All these things brought people. In Atlin, you had a direct say in your community, you could mold it to reflect your desires and values, and it was a place where you weren't a faceless number but rather an integral cog in the daily workings of your community—you mattered.

This story combines my mother's depictions of everyday Northern living from the time and my recollections of growing up in small town Northern Canada.

Atlin: Many Things to Many People
Atlin News Miner 1972
Diane S. Smith

Atlin is a youngster in the eyes of history. A scant seventy-two years old, it was founded when a prospector's pan first held tiny particles of Pine Creek gold and men swarmed to grab a share of the wealth. Atlin boomed when the horse was king in the world of transportation and when muscle, sweat and curses were the major forces behind earth-renting operations that gouged gold from the streams. Atlin enjoyed a boisterous youth then settled into a declining middle age.

Atlin has always been many things to many people. Most of the first stampeders saw it only as a place to make a fast buck, a place to grab for the brass ring before drifting on to the next strike. But many of the early gold seekers found it suited them as a place to settle down. For them it was right for building homes, raising families and becoming established in the community way of life. These were Atlin's real founding fathers. An unfortunate few found it a point of no return, a place of shattered dreams and lost hope. Others fell victim to a northern nature's fatal sword. For some, Atlin became the end of the road but for many others, it was the end of the rainbow.

The ones who stuck it out through the lean years are the ones to whom the latter-day pioneers owe tribute. They were the stubborn ones who kept Atlin on the map when an economy based on gold production sagged disastrously and it was often a challenge to keep body and soul together. A unique combination of the "Atlin Spell" and the tough perseverance of these settlers kept the town quietly alive while others faded into history.

Atlin waited while the world outside passed through decades of war and prosperity, then into a time of restlessness born of overcrowding and a singular dedication to materialistic pursuits. Atlin became a little quieter and emptier while clinging to the hope another boom would occur, but unaware it would be quite different from the first.

The village has a charm, now rare. An old-fashioned atmosphere prevails that is balm to a victim of the plastic and chrome world to the south. Here the new log buildings blend amiably with the old false fronts. The sound of horse bells and the clop, clop of hooves is heard in the streets. A Malamute's wail may rent the still night and whirring chopper blades may cut crystal clear air, but the mind-numbing din of factory and traffic do not exist.

Atlin offers solace to the harried spirit worn ragged by the push/pull of the city. It offers vast miles of surrounding wilderness for the sportsman, the nature lover, or loner who simply wants room in which to think.

Atlin lacks many amenities, but the inconvenience of outhouses and water storage barrels is offset by an easygoing air. Time is available to exchange a yarn over a cup of coffee or to listen to the tinkle of the ice along the lakeshore. Time is also available to skin a moose or to help a neighbor to start a frozen truck. Time is very likely Atlin's newfound wealth, discovered and highly prized by the new pioneers who harbor vivid memories of the mad hatter pace of other places.

Atlin is also a place in which to change the course of a life. People come here searching for new surroundings, new friends and new adventures. The town draws those who have jogged

Looking southeast, Atlin is in the foreground, Teresa Island in the background with Torres Inlet on the right, 2019. Photo by Caroline Moore.

themselves from old worn ruts and are now experiencing the joys and pitfalls of trying something entirely different.

Here an electrical technician operates a grocery store, an iron worker owns a new hotel, a man who worked in broadcasting sales and public relations at a Toronto radio station has a small motel and has just begun gold mining, while his wife, a former media director with an ad agency, prepares to open an art gallery. A registered nurse, a telephone operator and a draftsman have gift and craft stores. A young couple with degrees in psychology and education have opened a general store. A former die cutter has been a cook at a hunting camp, fought forest fires, dug graves, worked at construction and is currently driving truck at the highway department—a mixed bag, to be sure, but in all cases certainly a change. For a few city-bred young people, Atlin has been a place to try a Tom Sawyer-type of existence denied them in an urban childhood. It is a place for them to experience life in the bush and to try a little living off the land. Some newcomers are doing things long dreamed of, like running a trapline, driving a dog team, working a placer claim, building a log house.

As in the early days, many people of many skills, professions and talents are gathering here and blending into

Atlin in January, taken south of town, facing north, 2018. The Alkali Flats are to the right and flank the town. Photo by Clive Aspinall.

the community. Each adds to the continuity and continuing life of a busy, rejuvenated Atlin. And each finds that Atlin has a special meaning for them.

———

Part I —Ways and Means

The Atlin Inn, constructed by the White Pass Company in 1917 was completed in thirty-five days by sixty men for a cost of twenty thousand dollars. Only open for eighteen years, it was a luxury establishment catering to the very wealthy traveler from around the globe. The building was torn down for salvage in 1968 and the pieces live on in many of today's homes and businesses.

Chapter One

Greatest Place and Time

Even at a very young age we carried pocket knives wherever we went. Our parents didn't see anything wrong with it; in fact, they bought them for us. We took them to school and the teachers were fine with it. We used them for whittling, carving small boats, making bows and arrows, slingshots, and spears. We gutted our fish, skinned small animals, cut rhubarb and fishing line, opened cans, cleaned our finger nails and made shavings for fire starter. It was hard to imagine not having one. We were also responsible and mostly safe with them, aside from the odd game of stretch or chicken. Don't tell.

It was never unusual to see three or four pre-teen boys walking through town, each carrying a BB gun over their shoulder, an event that might cause a stir these days. Day-long grouse or squirrel hunting trips were a great way to spend a summer day and contribute to the household larder. My mom made a delicious grouse breast and dumpling dish. Some people ate squirrels, but that far north they're pretty skinny, so mostly they went to the dog pot, but the skins were worth a dollar if fleshed, stretched and dried properly. Hey, that's five comic books.

1

Gold panning on Spruce Creek, one of Atlin's gold-rich creeks, has yielded thousands of ounces over the years and is still mined to this day, 1972.

Our entertainment didn't come in one-size-fits-all, neat, shiny packages—we had to look for it and invent it. We found it in what others might see as mundane and ordinary places and objects. A dried rhubarb stalk, or clump of dirt became swords, spears, blow guns and grenades. A piece of rope became a swing or bridge or lasso. Willows became bows, arrows and slingshots. Logs were turned into rafts and teeter totters and forts.

We climbed trees and tried to travel from one to another, pretending we were monkeys or Tarzan. If we could find a limber enough sapling, we climbed to the top and tried to get it to bend, gently lowering us to the ground. We called them elevators, although many of us had yet to experience a real elevator. My friend climbed about twenty feet (6m) up a young birch tree one day. He got to the point where his weight started to bend the tree, but instead of gently lowering him, the top of the tree snapped off and he plunged to the ground. Lucky for him it was marshy, and aside from the wind being knocked out of him, he was fine.

We made obstacle courses with hidden traps and tripwires and tried to get our unsuspecting friends to follow us through them. We climbed to the roofs of all the old abandoned buildings and some occupied ones. It became a challenge to figure out how to get on them without a ladder and without getting caught. I remember scaling the Old Kershaw Hardware building, hiding behind the parapet wall and throwing snowballs at unsuspecting passersby.

We were the kind of kids who had snare lines for rabbits and squirrels and who hunted grouse and ptarmigan with slingshots. By the time we were ten, we could use and sharpen a chainsaw, drive a Ski-Doo, shoot a rifle and mush a dog team. Some of us could drive a stick shift and some had killed their first moose. We were all pretty good with a bow and arrow and we were deadly with a rock.

Throwing rocks was second nature, something we did every day. We threw them at cans, bottles, birds, mean dogs and quite often each other. Believe it or not, we even had semi-organized rock fights. A group of us met down at the forestry dock, and half of us hid behind the dock and the other half behind a jumble of boulders approximately fifty feet (15m) away. The beach provided an unlimited supply of ammo. The battle often ended with someone getting hurt, but never seriously. I still carry a scar on my wrist

I'm playing on one of the abandoned steam shovels before it was brought to town to be in the museum collection, 1970.

from where, in mid-throw, I was struck by a particularly sharp projectile. The truth was not what I told my mother, mind you. I don't remember the fib I told, but I'm sure it was less interesting than the truth. Although we got a knot on our head or a cut here or there, we continued to do it because it was fun, or we were stupid ... either way, it happened (seems like a theme emerging).

We all carried matches because we never knew when we might need to light a fire to dry out before we got hypothermia or a whooping from Mom, and yes, we understood hypothermia. We knew how to find or make a shelter and how to keep our sense of direction when there weren't landmarks. We could identify edible berries, mushrooms and plants. We knew how to skin animals and cook over a fire. We had nicknames like Rat, Duck, Mouse, Gringo and Snorg and Beans and Skipper and Wieners. We were rough and tumble kids with wild imaginations and fearless spirits.

We wore Ski-Doo boots and mukluks in the winter, gumboots (rubber) in the spring, and Bulldog runners in the summer. We all wore blue jeans and jean jackets with western-style shirts with snaps. When it got hot in the summer, Mom cut the legs off a pair of my ratty jeans to make shorts and I wore an undershirt. We all wore wool socks year-round, usually with our big toe sticking through. In the winter we never took off our long johns, and we dried our boot liners every night by the stove and sometimes on the heat registers in the back of the classroom at school. That was the same place we stored our gym clothes, thus contributing to the lovely bouquet of odors wafting through our classrooms.

We bought our clothes at the General Store or at Hudson's Bay in Whitehorse, or Mom ordered them out of the Simpson Sears or Sears Roebuck Catalogues. Clothes were mended and patched, socks were darned and nothing was thrown away. If you outgrew something, it was passed down to someone else until it couldn't be mended or patched anymore. Then it became a rag or quilt or even chinking for log cabins. Nothing was wasted.

Chapter Two

Where We Came From

Mom was born in Everett, Washington, in 1931 to Daniel and Offie Solie. With older brother Gordon, the Solies soon moved to Bremerton, Washington, where Mom grew up on the shores of Puget Sound. Her father, Daniel, a building contractor, constructed much of the civilian housing for the Puget Sound Naval Ship Yard. Daniel built the family home on the high banks of Puget Sound with a pristine view, access to the beach and surrounded by Douglas Fir trees. The Solie family lived a modest but comfortable life, even throughout the depression and war years. Mom led an independent childhood with ten years between her and Gordon, and with him away most of her teen years, fighting in World War II, she spent much of her time alone. With her dog Lucky in tow, she explored the beaches and forest around her home. She was an accomplished sailor, swimmer, hunter and fisher. She excelled at downhill skiing and enjoyed exploring the ancient forests of the Olympic Peninsula.

A feminist before it was accepted and a free thinker at the start, Mom always felt she didn't quite fit the mold, the societal blueprint set out for young ladies of the day.

Mom with her first dog, Lucky, 1943. They explored the woods and waters of Puget Sound together.

After high school, she entered Olympic Junior College, and then went on to the University of Washington where she first majored in fine arts, then engineering. She was in college during a time when those that returned from World War II were taking advantage of the education afforded them through the GI Bill. Mom found herself surrounded by serious, no-nonsense adults. This played a big part in the reasoning behind shifting from fine arts to engineering.

While many of her peers were starting families, Mom went to work as a draftsman at the Puget Sound Naval Ship Yard, a civilian working for the United States Navy. The only woman in an office full of men, she quickly became adept at fitting in with the guys.

As a young boy growing up watching World War II movies, I was fascinated with her stories of excursions into the bowels of America's most famous aircraft carriers and battleships. At that time, many were being re-fitted and commissioned for action in the Yellow Sea during the Korean conflict. She went places on those ships no woman had been before. I remember her telling me she was assigned a guide, supposedly to keep her from getting lost, but more to run ahead and warn the crew that a woman was coming. Mom worked extensively on redesigning and upgrading the steam catapult system on the Essex class aircraft carriers like the USS Yorktown and the USS Intrepid.

From childhood, she was fascinated with Alaska and the Yukon's Klondike Gold Rush. The rich history and harsh environs appealed to her sense of adventure. She read voraciously anything she could find: books by Jack London and Rex Beach and Robert Service's poetry beguiled her and awakened an intense yearning. She dreamed of the Klondike, the fur traders and explorers, and, above all, the women who survived and even prospered in the North against insurmountable odds. Finding few peers that shared her interest, she kept her desires to herself, hoping one day to follow her heroes northward.

Mom in Flatty, her tiny sailboat, Puget Sound, Washington, 1949.

Mom met and married her first husband at the shipyard, and they had one son, Daniel, named after his grandfather. Mom reveled in the challenge of managing career, marriage and motherhood. As usual, taking the path less traveled was her inclination. To make a long story short, Mom divorced at a time when such things were derided, to say the least. But rather than enduring a life of misery, and with the belief that something greater awaited, she ended a dysfunctional relationship at a time when it wasn't what women did. After an acrimonious custody battle, Daniel, eleven, chose to stay with his father.

Her mother had recently passed, her marriage had ended, and it was made obvious that there was to be no place for her, a woman, in the family construction business. Heartbroken, her life uncertain and yearning for change, the lure of the North, forever niggling in the recesses of her mind, surged to the forefront. Not one to let the bastards keep her down, she decided to act on it. Like many of those early pioneers that spoke to her from the pages of those dusty old books, she too felt there was nothing to lose—so why not follow her dream?

Franklin Street downtown Juneau, Alaska, 1963. Only four short years since becoming a state, Juneau was still buzzing with excitement. Originally home of the Auke and Taku Tribes, Juneau was named after a white man, Joe Juneau, who discovered gold in what's now called Gold Creek with partner Richard Harris.

At thirty-two years old, she applied for and landed a job in Juneau, Alaska, as draftsman for the United States Coast Guard. This was it: her dream fulfilled. At last, she would join her idols and venture north. Once again, the only woman in the boys club, she had no problem fitting in and was quickly liked and respected.

Juneau still had that aura of a gold field camp in those days, but it was a combination of fishermen, loggers and miners who were the colorful rogues and rapscallions of the day. Juneau, the capital of America's newest state, was a place where you could leave your money on the bar while you danced and where the state's first governor was seen dressed as Santa, drunkenly singing Christmas carols outside the Red Dog Saloon, accompanied by a chorus of stray huskies.

Arriving shortly before the 1964 Good Friday earthquake, she quickly found herself inundated with work as the Coast Guard was on full alert for the next several years. The 9.2 magnitude quake caused severe damage to Alaska's infrastructure and the ensuing tsunami reached as far as California. With unlimited overtime and the hectic atmosphere of the office, it wasn't long before she became restless and constantly reminded of the similarities of her previous life. Juneau gave her a sense of what the North was about and she enjoyed the people and their independent spirits, but she couldn't help thinking there was more.

During this time, she met my dad, Edwin Davis Smith, a superintendent for the Alaska Juneau Power Company and a contractor for the Coast Guard. In his words, he was a glorified light bulb changer for the Coast Guard. With a background in iron working, he was hired to change the bulbs in the Loran navigation towers along Alaska's rugged coastline, including the Port Clarence Tower, the tallest man-made structure in Alaska, which reached a height of 1350 feet (410m).

Dad started life in Kentucky, and like my mom, he didn't feel he fit into the accepted norms of the time—high school, marriage, kids, and work at the steel mill, a job that had killed his father at an early age. Wanting something different, right after high school he joined the Army and in short time found himself fighting in Korea. The Army taught him demolitions and he became an explosives expert.

I asked him one time why he didn't continue that trade in civilian life. He mumbled something about how much he liked his fingers. Apparently finding demolitions too dangerous, he decided iron working was a much safer vocation. From the skyscrapers of New York City's skyline to the Mackinaw Bridge in Michigan, to Seattle's high rises and on to the DEW Line (Distant Early Warning), he crossed the United States and Canada looking for his next adventure, eventually landing in Juneau, where among other things, he helped erect the state museum and the federal building. His stint building the enormous geodesic domes that housed the radar for the DEW Line gave him his first taste of what life in the North entailed and he was immediately hooked.

The DEW Line was a series of radar stations strung across the top of North America, Greenland and Iceland, as well as Alaska's Aleutian Island Archipelago. It was erected in the 1950s to warn against the approach of Russian bombers and is now defunct as satellites replaced it.

Like my mom, my dad was enticed by the North's freedoms and boundless opportunities for anyone willing to work hard. The type of man that could quickly master most anything he came across, his

Downtown Dawson City, 1963. Dawson was the epicenter of the Klondike Gold Rush, after George and Kate Carmack with Skookum Jim and Dawson Charlie discovered gold in nearby Rabbit Creek, later called Bonanza Creek, in 1896. Dawson City grew from a First Nations fish camp to a population of 40,000 virtually overnight.

jack-of-all trades approach fit well in the North, a place where jobs can be few and often diverse.

Mom was attracted to this rugged man of congenial disposition and they soon married and I was born. They were both in their early thirties, and I was somewhat of a surprise but also the push that got them thinking about moving to a smaller, quieter corner of the North, where they could raise me and live a less-conventional life, free of big-city stress and worries.

In 1965, they decided, in their words, that "they needed to get away from the rat race of the city." Keep in mind, at the time Juneau had a population of approximately five thousand. While I was only a few months old, they took a long trip through Alaska and the Yukon searching for a new place to call home. Having fallen in love with Dawson City and determining it held their future, it was only on a whim they decided to make the long, dusty trip to Atlin. The rest, as they say, is history. My mom said Dawson disappeared from her mind as they came around that last corner of the Atlin Road and in front of her loomed the sharp, snow-capped peaks and distinct rock glacier of Atlin Mountain, and stretched out before it, the deep-blue, crystal-clear waters of Atlin Lake. The little village perched on the shore of the great lake, sequestered neatly in a small bay and protected by three islands, looked like a picture postcard, and as they later learned, it had been, and continued to be, the subject of many postcards.

Both my parents were history buffs and, like Dawson, Atlin's history was vibrant, exciting and still tangible—they could see it in the many false-front buildings, the impressive lake boats hauled out on shore in front of town, and the once-grand hotels, crumbling but still commanding attention. Unlike Dawson, Atlin has the magnificent lake, and a multitude of impressive mountains—overall, scenery on a par not rivaled for thousands of miles, if at all. Strolling through the quiet streets, it was easy for my parents to see and feel how it had been during its heyday. On a quiet summer night, if you were still enough, you just might hear a ragtime tune wafting down Pearl Avenue and fading away between the Globe Theater and Garrett's store.

They camped on a flat gravel bar beside Pine Creek while exploring the surrounding countryside and meeting Atlin's many colorful denizens. My whole life I listened to my mom tell people about washing my stinky (not the word she used) diapers in that ice-cold creek. After camping two weeks, they left satisfied. They had found their new home and were determined to become citizens.

Liza the cow enjoying a sunny day on Pearl Avenue. The Globe Theater is the nearest building on the right, was built in 1917 by Edwin Pillman. It was completely refurbished by the Atlin Historical Society and opened for movies and events.

Atlin's lakefront, summer 1967. The M/V Tarahne, center, the bow of the SS Scotia, left; and the SS Atlinto, far right, were used to haul passengers and freight. The Tarahne and the Atlinto are saved and restored. The Scotia was too rotten to be moved and it was burned in place.

Looking north on Atlin's First Street, summer 1967. The building on the right was built by Jules Eggert and served as his jewelry store. It is the third store he built on this site, losing the first two to the town fires of 1900 and 1914. The clock was for advertisement and works intermittently.

Aerial view of Atlin, the M/V Tarahne on the shoreline and First, Second and Third Islands with Atlin Mountain in background, 2018. Atlin Mountain is part of the Coastal range and is 6,712 feet (2,046m). Photo by Caroline Moore.

Chapter Three

What We Did There

Two years later in the spring of 1967, with their 1957 GMC pickup truck loaded with all their belongings, including a camper, a trailer, a boat, four dogs, two cats and a toddler, the Smiths arrived in Atlin without a clue of what they would do or where they would live. This was indicative of many people moving to Atlin around that time. It took two long, bumpy, and flat-tire ridden return trips to the Haines ferry dock to eventually stockpile everything they owned in their new hometown. The Skagway to Carcross Road would not open for another eleven years, so vehicle travel went through Haines. A trip of roughly six hours today was a two-to-three-day feat in those days depending on conditions. Skagway to Atlin can easily be accomplished in a leisurely three-hour drive today.

Not long after arriving, my parents found themselves the proud owners of The Kootenay, a historic ten-room hotel with a restaurant and bar. At that time, it was Atlin's longest-running business. They also purchased the town's historic courthouse complete with living quarters, solving both the income and habitation questions.

The third Kootenay Hotel as it looked in the summer of 1967 when my parents purchased it from Bunn and Mavis Shaw, ending a fifty-seven-year ownership by Mavis' family. A little over a year later, a chimney fire would rage out of control and, like its two predecessors, this Kootenay Hotel would also succumb to fire. Photo by Rob Shaw.

They quickly made the Old Courthouse livable and we moved in that fall. With a slim budget, they spent that winter renovating and repairing The Kootenay in time for its grand reopening in spring. I might mention that neither had any experience running a hotel, restaurant or bar.

Their new purchase was, in fact, the third Kootenay Hotel. The first was merely a bunkhouse and saloon built in 1899, which burned to the ground a year later on Christmas Eve of 1900 during Atlin's first town fire.

The second Kootenay was quickly built, but in a much grander fashion than its humble predecessor. A ballroom, gymnasium, kitchen and dining hall were added. An early photo shows the ballroom sporting an enormous crystal chandelier. This Kootenay changed hands more than once before being purchased by John Roxborough, an adventurer from Ireland who arrived in Atlin following the 1898 gold strike.

The second Kootenay Hotel was lost in the town fire of 1914. It was the deadliest fire in Atlin history and wiped out the downtown core. There was total destruction between First and Third from

A chimney fire spelled the end of the third Kootenay Hotel. It burned to the ground on a frigid November night in 1968. Photo by Clive Aspinall.

Munroe Avenue to Pearl Avenue, a distance of four blocks. An estimate of the total damage was set at one million dollars at 1914 prices.

In the determined spirit of the time, John Roxborough, with his sons William and Robert, built again, as did other Atlin businesses. This, the third version of The Kootenay, was a modest structure with only ten guest rooms, a large bar and a quaint dining room. Much of the furnishings and mill work were made by local craftsmen.

After John passed away, William and his wife Anais became chief proprietors. Robert's wife Olive died at a young age and William and Anais raised a number of Robert's thirteen children. William and Anais forever became known as Auntie and Uncle to all they knew. After Uncle passed, Auntie handed the reins to her niece and nephew, Mavis and Bunn Shaw, who ran it up until my parents purchased it in 1967. At that time, The Kootenay was the longest continually-run business in Atlin's history.

I have only a few memories of The Kootenay. I remember my parents did theme dinners. Mexican night was complete with

After The Kootenay burned, Atlin was left without a café, so my parents rented the Moose Hall and reopened the Kootenay Café in that location.

serapes, sombreros and maracas. On Italian night, the tables were covered in red and white checkered tablecloths with Chianti bottle candle holders. My most vivid memory of The Kootenay was watching it burn to the ground from my parents' bedroom window that cold November night in 1968, and believe it or not, I remember surveying the rubble heap the next day with my dad. Mostly it was the smell that I remember and the melted coins we found—for some reason they fascinated me.

The Kootenay Café lived on for a little over a year, housed in the Moose Hall building. It was closed upon the opening of the Trappers Café in the log gas station and garage my dad built on the site of The Kootenay.

I'm not sure if the phoenix has a finite number of reincarnations, but it is for certain the Old Kootenay's ended at three, well ... almost, three-and-a-half, maybe.

My father had a dream that ended up bordering on obsession to provide the town with yet another Kootenay Hotel, and his was to be the grandest of them all. He deemed the current location too small for his ambitious dream, so he built the garage and gas station with room for a small café on the original site. I'm guessing this was to

Dad working on the foundation of what would briefly be the fourth Kootenay Hotel, 1971. Built on a much bigger lot across the street from the third Kootenay that burned down a little over a year after my parents bought it. My dad was able to complete a ten-unit hotel with a café and a bar.

gain capital for the much larger project, as we didn't seem to own it long, if at all.

Soon a larger, more prestigious piece of land was purchased across the street, and the foundation for the next Kootenay was poured. The plans for this version were a two-story log structure with twenty guest rooms, a large dining room with a view of the lake, and a saloon.

At the cost of a bankruptcy and the beginning of the end of a marriage, he was somehow able to get one story completed, housing a bar, a small café, and ten rooms. For a very brief time it was called The Kootenay. The next owners changed the name to the Atlin Inn and through many different owners and many years, it eventually became the two-story, twenty-room establishment my father dreamed it would.

That winter after The Kootenay burned down was a lean one. My dad tried his hand at trapping by dog team as well as buying and selling furs. That same winter he and a friend poached a moose out of season to help with the food bill. The moose tasted like spruce boughs and was as tough as shoe leather. They ended up grinding the whole moose into hamburger, and only by adding beef fat was it rendered "edible." Needless to say, I haven't liked spruce-flavored meatballs ever since.

The next summer, with time in excess, Mom opened The Discovery Shop, at first calling it the Bottle Shoppe because that was about all it contained—old bottles. It was in the judge's small chambers on the lower floor of the Old Government Building/Courthouse that we called home.

Years before, Mom had majored in commercial art at the University of Washington. Then, to avoid becoming another starving artist, she had switched to engineering and that led to a career in drafting. In her words, "I learned a lot about plans and forgot a lot about art." But the yen to putter around with arts and crafts never completely disappeared, and The Discovery Shop was reason to try out some long-suppressed ideas. That first fling at shop business made one thing clear—Atlin visitors needed a place to browse and ask questions. Most people weren't interested in old bottles, but they were interested in Atlin.

By the following summer, my parents had put together a rustic museum in the courtroom adjacent to the shop. Through their own scavenging, and others, plus many donations, the fledgling museum was expanding rapidly. The museum brought in a lot of visitors, and Mom became the reluctant curator of what would later become an award-winning collection of relics and antiquities representing Atlin's gold rush days and First Nations' culture and heritage.

Eventually, the museum was turned over to the town when a historical society was formed under the deft guidance of Shirley Connolly, Norah Smith, Jan Harvey, my mother and many others.

My dad was determined to build a new hotel, but while exploring financial options, he found himself with a variety of jobs that included moving a historic building across town, building the two-story log garage I previously mentioned, trapping, and helping plumb in the water and sewer system for the new school buildings, first having to thaw the frozen ground by lighting fires to melt the ice. This technique would later serve him well in his brief stint as a grave digger. Please keep in mind, a couple of years before, my mom had been a draftsman for the United States Coast Guard and my dad had been a superintendent of a power company!

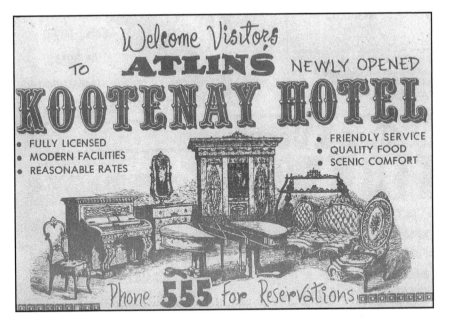

Advertisement from the newspaper, the Atlin News Miner *in 1970. Three-digit phone numbers were so much easier.*

Diane Solie Smith founded the Atlin Museum along with her husband, Ed. They turned it over to the Historical Society. Originally published in the Atlin News Miner. Photo by Tom Kirkwood.

Chapter Four

This Old House

My parents bought the Old Courthouse for $3,500 in 1967. Proud owners of the biggest structure in town, they quickly set about repairing and restoring. That summer as they readied the old girl for our first winter, we lived in the backyard in our camper.

One of the first things my dad did was paint the ball that's attached to the top of the flagpole that sits on the top of the tower. An afterthought for an ironworker, but it impressed some, and it helped introduce us to the town. Teetering atop a flimsy ladder leaning against an almost seventy-year-old wooden pole, more than six stories above the street, with a bucket of gold paint in one hand and a brush in the other, was his way of introducing the Smith family to Atlin.

He never really understood the fear of heights and he believed exposure was the best cure. When I was five, he had me up on the roof while he did repairs to the previous repairs, and as that didn't seem to fully cure me from my "imagined malady," he later took me up telephone poles on his shoulders. I guess it worked as, eleven years later, I found myself precariously perched on top of my old

The Courthouse opened in the summer of 1900. Its presence cemented Atlin as the center of mining and government in the area. It was originally located one block east and was moved in the 1950s to this location. The sign in the foreground is the first Discovery Shop sign in 1970.

house cursing him for using difficult-to-remove ring nails where he'd done his repairs. I was then employed as a carpenter's assistant and roofer. We had the job of re-shingling the building.

By the next year, the Old Government Building was showing off a new blue-with-white-trim paint job, new glass panes, insulation, and it no longer had a leaky roof. My mom deemed the new paint scheme a big hit, as a number of homes around town soon sported close variations of the same thing. Emulation is the best form of flattery, but most likely it was the color on sale at Beaver Lumber in Whitehorse over that summer.

A fifty-foot (14m) square structure that housed a courtroom and judges' chamber, a gold commissioner's office and an apartment on the second floor. Horses having a snooze in the shade of the Old Courthouse, 1972. Photo by *Terry Milos.*

This Old House
Atlin News Miner 1973
Diane S. Smith

It was impossible to resist the 1900 vintage edifice. One look at Atlin Lake from the ten-foot-high (3m) living room window and a glance of the tower soaring fifty feet (18m) above the street had us instant victims of its austere charm. So it was that summer day nearly six years ago when we found ourselves the happy owners of this old house, Atlin's Old Government Building.

This old house stands fifty feet (18m) square and two-stories high on Second Street where it was actually rolled from its original place on the street behind some eighteen years ago. That is when the provincial government deemed it was too

Dad on Atlin Lake pointing to the Courthouse, 1968.

big and burdensome and ended its public life by abandoning it for squat and unimposing pre-fab. It stood alone for twelve long years looking with the forlorn and vacant stare of all old buildings at the mountains and the passersby.

The Old Government Building has always commanded attention, and after we began repairs prior to moving in, we found tourists wandering in to ask what it was—an old school? An old church? "They don't build 'em like this anymore," was one guy's comment as he pounded on the newel post. "Look, it's real wood." And many times, since that first summer, I have boosted complete strangers up through the trap door in my hallway so they could take a picture from the tower window or just see what it's like up there. One night a handsome young RCMP Constable from Teslin asked hopefully, "Is this where the dance is?"

Downstairs, the ceilings rise fourteen-feet high (4.2m). On the north side of the hallway is the courtroom. Here the judge's platform is framed in dark wood and His Worship looked down at those gathered in the somber gray room and made right the crimes of Atlin.

A small cubicle that served as the judge's chamber (or more often the cloakroom or library) has a faded and worn red carpet, a small luxury to a traveling frontier judge.

In the gold commissioner's office, you think of the men who worked there—J.A. Frasier held the influential post from 1902 until 1922 when Atlin was a thriving gold mining town. In the mining recording office, there is a long handsome wooden counter. Here, all government business was transacted and over this counter poured documents for water rights, homesteads, timber leases, fur royalties and the everlasting torrent of mining claims.

All summer I listen to visitors tell me how they envy me living in such a fascinating old place. I could tell them lots of things about living in an old building, but people steeped in romantic articles about preserving the past and saving historic sites and the current rage of resurrecting decaying barns and calling them home are not interested in the nitty gritty of living in an antique. They'd never believe it, anyway.

Moving into this old house meant first repairing fifty-two panes of glass. It also meant crawling the entire perimeter of the place just under the eaves and stuffing in insulation to ward off icy winds, which those same eaves trap so efficiently. It means to let a puppy out to piddle in the winter you first don parka, boots and gloves, then sprint down twenty-five steps and endless hallway to open the front door, holding puppy at arm's length praying all the way you will make it in time.

We don't heat the downstairs except occasionally. With ceilings six feet (1.8m) higher than normal, we would be heating about 15,000 cubic feet (425m^3) of space we couldn't even enjoy without a high step ladder.

Years ago, a gold commissioner's wife became claustrophobic because there were only three windows in the entire upstairs. Soon four dormer windows were added. This improved the lighting, but the remodelers neglected the fact that they were altering the distribution of the roof load. And in due time the building developed some sags. Now, if you drop a marble on the floor, it can't decide which way to roll. Under each of the four eaves is a huge L-shaped space. Three of these are closets; the closets are the slanting-ceiling, deep, mysterious kind that Grandmother used to have that hint of rare and valuable treasures. The only thing worse than too little closet space, is too much. These things become nightmarish catch-all's that are so darned handy they gobble up tons of miscellaneous items. Until they are someday cleaned out, I have learned to live without countless things that have become hopelessly lost within.

The bathroom facilities we found in this old building were quite unusual. In a very narrow room directly off the kitchen was a long deep tub, standing on four clawed feet, and a tiny washbasin. But where was the john? We discovered it in a strange little room with a low doorway and ceiling that sloped from eight feet (2.4m) high on one side to two feet (0.6m) at the other. The whole room is suspended grandly over the landing of the stairway. To reach it, you must walk through the entire pantry and if a tall man doesn't get brained on the door casing he will surely thump his head on the slanting ceiling.

The bathroom, along with the dormers, electrical wiring, and for that matter, the kitchen were obviously afterthoughts. Originally the building had three staff rooms upstairs. It was probably the evolution of Atlin from mining camp to permanent town and a gold commissioner with a family that brought about the upstairs apartment and the "modern" innovations. One thing we never did find was the water system. Apparently, it was left behind on Third Street when the building was moved.

This old house will be seventy-three years old this year. It served Atlin during its youthful heyday, and then watched sadly as the town declined. Now in a fresh coat of paint, it stands watching Atlin experience a reawakening and a quiet but steady boom quite different from its first gold rush excitement, but probably one of longer duration. If this old house could tell its own life story, what an Atlin history we would have.

————

My mom later sold the Old Government Building/Courthouse, a.k.a. Our Old House, to the newly-formed Historical Society for a modest profit. Formed in 1972, the Society ensured it would forever be protected and properly restored to its former glory.

My Private Nightmare

As a young lad, I had a love/hate relationship with Our Old House, one that corresponded directly with the time of day or night. Although regal and majestic in the daylight hours, Our Old House was spooky and daunting at night. Many kids avoided our street altogether, choosing a more indirect but better-lit path on their way home. Many were convinced it was inhabited by at least one, but more likely many, ghosts. My so-called friends loved to tell me Old Government Building ghost stories every time they got a chance. My mom continued to assure me that it was all jesting and wild imaginations. Of course, as soon as I would bring that up to my buddies, they countered with the well-known fact that ghosts only haunt children and adults can't even see them.

Coming home after dark was an epic and unrelenting battle fought between me and that Old House. You may be asking what a five- or six-year-old was doing out alone after dark in the first place. That was pretty normal for Atlin kids, and besides, in the dead of winter it can be quite dark by 4 pm. There was little to be worried about other than our over-active imaginations and frostbite. Even in the bright daylight, the downstairs of Our Old House was poorly lit and the shadows hid untold horrors.

Imagine I'm six years old, it's already dark out, I'm late and approaching the front steps. There are only street lights at each end of the block and the porch light is out again, as it's hard to keep a bulb working at thirty below. I hustle up the darkened steps and pause at the huge wooden double door. Out here, I'm still fairly safe; I still have the option of jumping off the porch and fleeing down the road. It's what's on the other side of the door that's got me worried. Compelled forward by the threat of another spanking for being late, I slowly open the door and take a quick look inside. There's one light just inside the door and thankfully another on the landing halfway up the stairs. Lone, naked bulbs suspended on long cords, somber beacons of protection that offer some solace, although at times they only expose more frightening details better left cloaked in the gloom.

I quickly shut the door, but only long enough to build some confidence, formulate a strategy and draw a few deep breaths. If I linger too long outside where it's safe, I may lose my nerve and possibly freeze to death. Just inside the front door, on either side of the hallway, are two darkened, ominous portals leading into rooms filled with mummies, vampires and zombies. Now, the trick at this point is to scurry through the front door and close it firmly, making sure it latches, then race toward the stairs. Making sure the door latches is super important because no matter how far away she was, no matter what other sounds and noises there were, my mom could always tell if I closed the door properly. Having to return back down that gauntlet of horror was unimaginable; after all, my only weapon was surprise, and with that taken away, my goose was surely cooked.

Through the door I go, slamming it just right so it latches on the first try. After a couple steps, I'm past the first two obstacles and accelerating down the endless hallway toward the bottom step, snow-laden boots offering little traction on the old linoleum floor. The stairway ascends on the right and the hallway continues on into a murky abyss of death and destruction on the left. Also on my left at the bottom of the stairs, looms another doorway. This, of course, is Frankenstein's monster's chamber and I'm positive I can hear him gnawing at the door and straining to break his chains. Out of the corner of my eye as I sprint by, I can see the door pulse and shake. Now in full flight, completely aware of the werewolves snapping at my heels, their foul breath hot on the back of my neck, I barely feel the steps under my feet.

I know you're thinking, "Okay, he's got it made now." Oh, how far from the truth could you be? Arriving at the landing where the stairs switch back the other way and reaching the second light might seem like a good safe place to be, but that would be the wrong assumption. Remember when I said light, at times, can only serve to expose further abominations? At the back of the landing, there lurks another doorway. This one is small and demure compared to the hulking gateways downstairs. By all appearances, this door is innocent, unless you know for certain the room behind that door is where they keep all of the body parts. My friend Randy Green said he has it on good authority that it's where Bloody Bones lives. I wasn't too sure about that, as Bloody Bones seems to live in a number of scary places around town, but I was sure about the body parts—after all, where else would they keep them?

Flying across the landing—inappropriately named, in my mind, as nary a foot actually lands on it as I speed past—now it's the final push. I pump my legs as fast as I can, convinced I smell the decaying stench of my beastly pursuers. Halfway up the second flight of stairs and above my head on the wall is another small door. This one opens into the eves. There is something about the smaller doors that is almost more horrific than their larger counterparts; it's the fear of the unknown. Who or what uses such a small door? Certainly not children—unless, that is, they are *for* children ... that's where they put the children, never to be seen again. Of course, that small smudge of red paint on the door is most certainly the blood of an innocent child.

At last, crashing to an abrupt halt, I have arrived at the upstairs landing a scant second from safety but still in the maw of danger and now faced with four more doors. The door directly in front leads into the warm, inviting living room, but is not to be used if you have wet, muddy or snowy clothes or boots on, thus it's certainly never used by a six-year-old. The door on the right leads to Mom's workshop. In the day, while occupied, it's a nice, safe, cozy oasis, but at night with the light off, it converts to a lair of monsters and ghouls all fighting to see who will drink the child's blood. The scariest of the four doors is actually a hatch in the ceiling that closes the opening to the tower. At any second, screaming banshees with glowing red eyes and razor-sharp talons are sure to descend upon my head, seize me and drag me into the horrifying recesses of the tower. My salvation is the door on the left—the door that leads to the kitchen, the room with the inviting smells and the comforting arms of my mother; if I'm not late for dinner, that is. If I am, a banshee doesn't sound so bad after all. I was pretty sure banshees did not wield wooden spoons. The last couple seconds as I fumble to turn the knob with my mitten-laden hands is the worst. By now I'm convinced the smallest of missteps, a fraction of a second wasted, will spell my ultimate demise. I'm afraid to look back, but completely convinced all things hideous are queuing up behind, waiting their turn to decapitate me and/or eat my guts. It's a tremendous relief to finally master the complicated doorknob and burst into the kitchen unscathed.

Although often berated for all the slamming, clomping and banging, it is wonderful to have successfully survived another trip through the bowels of Our Old House, and easy to taunt the creatures with a silent *Na, Na, Na.*

That's quite the imagination for a kid who had never seen a horror movie and only knew of such monsters from comic books, the occasional Disney movie and Laurel and Hardy shorts. I was a voracious reader at a very young age, but at five or six, I'm pretty sure I wasn't yet into Shelley or Stoker, although the covers of my mom's *Psychology Today* magazines did provide me with some vivid nightmares.

I was continually grateful for the fleetness and nimbleness of a six-year-old dressed in winter boots, snow pants, parka, and mittens: "Ha, you slow old monsters, foiled again."

Thanks, Mom

One year, my mom thought it would be a good idea to let the older kids from school use the downstairs to put on a haunted house. "Thanks Mom, as though it wasn't already bad enough." On Halloween night, as usual, any self-respecting kid was out pounding on doors by four in the afternoon, me included. Somewhere along the way and after dark, my friends and I built up the courage to go to the haunted house. All I could think was *how much worse could it possibly be?*

With Randy Green whispering in my ear "Watch out for Bloody Bones," a small group of us shuffled amass through the front door, which swiftly and resolutely slammed behind us, and of course it latched firmly. There were some ghostly aberrations there to greet us with high-pitched screams of "Welcome, little children." Unwilling to move or even open our eyes, we stood huddled together, quivering, by the door. I was willing the others to run—didn't they know we had to run to get away from the mummies and vampires and zombies? I opened one eye then the other, wondering why we hadn't yet been torn limb from limb. Suddenly, a bright light illuminated the first landing and on it was a surly looking lunatic, restrained in a white straitjacket. The man had long, matted, dark hair and his expression was a combination of pain, frustration and deranged pleasure. The captive thrashed and giggled and struggled as two hulking, hooded executioners force him down into a guillotine's block. The fact that this maniacal killer, of undoubtedly numerous women and children, looked a lot like our schoolmate Willy Jack didn't sink in.

The psycho's head was clamped firmly in the block as he struggled against his captors. A glint of light shimmered off the honed edge of the enormous blade. The lights went out and for an agonizing few seconds we cowered in the absolute darkness, afraid to move, afraid to breathe. We huddled together like blind penguins waiting for the razor-sharp teeth of a sea lion to tear into our shivering flesh. A scream rang out, a hollow "clunk" echoed down the stairwell, the sound an axe makes as it slices through a round of pine on a cold winter's day, followed quickly by a sound akin to a coconut rolling down stairs. Bumpity, bumpity, bumpity. The lights came up and we saw the decapitated body of the insane killer, inert behind the bloody blade of the guillotine. At the bottom of the slippery stairs sat a wicker basket, tentacle-like wisps of sticky black hair flowed over its sides, and under the basket, a pool of blood grew larger as we stared in frozen horror. Obviously, we were not running that way.

Traumatized and certainly in shock, the rest of the murky tour consisted of touching purported brains and eyeballs and intestines and gore. I do remember James Ennis' head on a platter under a large cloche. When they removed the cloche, his head appeared to be severed, most likely by the guillotine. It sat serenely on the platter, lulling us into a false sense of curiosity. As we timidly approached for a closer look, his eyes sprang open and he screamed a piercing wail of agony and despair. He gnashed his teeth and frantically twisted his head back and forth only to be silenced when the cover was replaced. I remember a madman chained to the wall. He lunged and screamed, scant inches from our faces as we pressed past, dodging his outstretched fingers. His body was covered in scars and blood, his clothes were torn and tattered. Once again, the fact that the madman looked a lot like my friend Keith Carlick's older brother, Harry Paul, registered not one bit.

Thankful to have survived our first official haunted house, we were off to canvas the rest of the town for popcorn balls, fudge, divinity and cookies—oh, and the dreaded orange ... come on, people, that's just cruel. Yes, these were all things we received in our Halloween travels, and neither we nor our parents gave a single thought as to whether they were safe or not—they just were, because Atlin wasn't that kind of place. Don't get me wrong, we received plenty of store candy as well, and it was preferred, mostly for its novelty, as we got baked goods regularly at home.

Later that night I hesitantly returned home. Dreading every minute of it, I slowly made my way up the front steps; of course, the outside light was out as usual. I sat on the front porch for an eternity, a whole new scenario of gruesome horrors running through my mind. Eventually, only after weighing the age-old conflict between goblins, ghosts and a whole new set of nightmares against the most horrific of them all—The Wooden Spoon, I timidly opened that big old door. Much to my delight all the lights were on, the guillotine was gone and the place was filled with the older kids cleaning up the mess. My mom was there and I remember she even let me have a can of coke, which was a first. Willy was there with his head and James with his body, gone were the entrails and eyeballs, in their place bowls of peeled grapes, ground hamburger and link sausages. Harry Paul had normal clothes on and I glimpsed a coconut with a black wig sitting in a basket by the door.

I would like to say that night miraculously cured me from my frightening battle with all things that live in dark corners, but then I would be a big liar.

Boy and the Beasts

Other memories of Our Old House are much less terrifying. Although we moved when I was nine, I cherish my time spent in that creaky old colossus. It's said that some of our most vivid memories are triggered by our olfactory senses. Whenever I smell fresh bread baking, it instantly transports me back to my mom's kitchen in the Old Government Building. Returning home from school, I was often met with the enticing aromas of fresh bread, cranberry muffins or cinnamon buns, their wonderful odors wafting down the stairwell.

I remember the bread rising in a huge bowl on top of a bookcase. Mom always placed a towel over the dough so if it rose too high and flipped out of the bowl it would land on the towel, which it did on occasion.

I'm holding one of our Malamutes in Inuvik, Northwest Territories.

Our house was always filled with huskies and Malamutes, and they all wanted to be in the kitchen where the food was. Sneaking in and hiding under the table might work for a short period, but when five large huskies try at the same time, it usually resulted in stomping and cussing along with the occasional projectile thrown by Mom. Repeatedly banished, they loved to lie just outside the doorway as close as they could get without being in the room. When passing through, Mom or Dad made them move, but I was energetic and impatient, and I thought it was more fun to jump over the pile. I often miss-calculated the distance and landed on top of the heap. One dog in particular strongly objected to my long-jump attempts, probably because he had softened my landing one too many times. Kenai was high-strung to begin with, which made him a great sled dog, but not so great at being my improvised hurdle. I took this on as a challenge and tried to make my approach with enough speed and stealth

Christmas in the Old Courthouse. I'm four, 1970.

to clear Kenai before he shot up in the air. My ego tells me I was mostly successful, but the truth is I failed more often than not, and Kenai sent me flying across the room to crash into the water barrel in the kitchen or pile up under my mom's desk in a cloud of dust and dog hair in the living room. This game often ended up in a huge ruckus that my mom didn't seem to enjoy much. Her yelling and threatening bodily harm sent us all scurrying away to hide.

My dad was adamant about keeping the dogs out of the kitchen/dining room while we ate our meals. His habit was to slide his chair back from the table upon finishing his dinner, while waiting for dessert and coffee. The scraping of his chair became the signal to the pack of drooling hounds outside the doorway that it was okay to come back in. In order to prolong the tranquility of a dog-less dining experience, my dad began to pick up his chair to move it back from the table without making any noise. That seemed a lot like the tail wagging the dog, so to speak.

My Contribution

The furnace was on the first floor behind the stairs. Big square, metal ducts brought the heat to the second floor. Each room had at least one floor grill, decorative cast iron grates twelve inches (30cm) square. I'll get back to that in a minute.

For the uninformed, it's an enormous undertaking peeing outside when you're five years old, it's twenty below (-29°C) and you're wearing underwear, long johns, jeans, snow pants, a parka and mittens. Although I often knew that I needed to go ahead of time, it was always more important to finish my snow fort or dig my tunnel a little deeper. Usually I waited until the very last second and then when I absolutely couldn't hold it any longer, I began my madcap Siberian Striptease. With mitten-clad hands, I frantically fumbled with buttons and zippers in a desperate attempt to shed enough layers to get the job done. I often lost that race. I would like to believe this happened to my friends as well, but it was probably just me. For the briefest moments, the warmth is appreciated. Soon the realization that a rather important area of my anatomy was now wet and starting to freeze necessitated an immediate trip home. With only moments to get inside before something serious happened, off I ran, performing the stiff-leg shuffle as fast as I could go. As important as it was to get inside, there within lay an acute danger. For some strange reason, my mother was under the impression that at the age of five I should not be peeing my pants, and, at times, punctuated her point with a spanking.

Okay, back to the floor grates. The heat during the winter was almost always on in an effort to keep our leaky old house livable. The trick was to get through the door quickly, shed the boots or mukluks, the parka, the scarf and mittens, grab a handful of comics and plop down on a heat grate before Mom knew what was going on. If she commented on my strange reading position or why I was still wearing my snow pants, I just said I was cold and trying to get warm. The extra comics covered up my stain of shame. My devious plot worked quite well even though I'm sure the smell wasn't pleasant. To be honest, our house usually smelled like wet dogs, so it all mixed together and it was hard to decipher one offensive odor from another. It also helped that it was quite drafty and the house had a constant air exchange. Later, when they were dry, I would hide my pants, underwear and long johns in the clothes basket and hope for the best.

Yes, peeing outside was a common practice for most of the kids in Atlin, as well as for a fair amount of the adults. It was always fun to see if you could spell your name in the snow. I envied the Al's and Ed's short names.

As we got older, we made a vague attempt to hide behind a woodpile or a bush or even the outhouse itself. Why take the chance of missing and suffering the wrath of Mother, who didn't seem to appreciate an icy yellow seat.

Subversion

The Old Government Building windows were made up of many small single panes of thin glass. In order to stave off the cold, my parents covered the inside with thick plastic sheeting. Clear plastic was not available, so even though it let in plenty of light, we could not see through it. My mom found this predicament bordering on the criminal. Not only did we have arguably the best view in town of the best scenery in the world, we couldn't see it for eight months out of the year.

For some reason I couldn't resist poking holes in the plastic sheeting at every opportunity, a practice that brought the ire of both parents. When finger-sized holes became too obvious, I took to using a pin or needle. These acts of vandalism were often undetected for long stretches of time until well after I forgot my crime. More than once I was contentedly minding my own business when suddenly, out of the blue, the full fury of one or the other of my parents descended down upon my rear end in a most unsuspecting and unpleasant way. I learned there was no statute of limitations for colluding with the enemy: Old Man Winter.

Not only were our windows cold, but they also didn't offer much of a sound barrier. It was easy to hear conversations taking place on the street below. When it was minus-forty or colder, we could hear the booming, rumbling and cracking of the lake ice as it expanded and contracted. It was an awe-inspiring experience lying in bed at night listening to the thunderous barrage of yet another epic ice cannon duel reverberating off the mountains.

Creating and Caring

The back room that my mom used as her workroom was littered with furs of all sorts, leather of all colors, moose antlers, bolts of material, beads, jade, soapstone, placer gold, polished rocks, ring and pendant blanks, gold chains and wrapping paper of every pattern and color with ribbon to match. At Christmas, my mom wrapped everything she sold for every customer. The aforementioned items and so many more were all used in creating products for The Discovery Shop. I remember sorting buttons and beads and gold nuggets by size and color. I spent hours untangling gold or silver chains and picking flakes of placer gold out of the cracks in the floor boards when a tray was accidentally spilled. Under her work table there was often a box of puppies and their mother. I loved being in that room helping my mom or trying my hand at crafts. During the day that is.

My dad had his own workshop behind the mining recording office on the lower floor where he made buttons and cufflinks and brooches out of

The Discovery Shop

P.O. Box 96   ★   Al Atlin B.C.

DOG SLEDS
<u>Freighters</u> (Shown above)
      Mortised and tied: $250.00
      Bolted $204.00
All freighters are hardwood construction with steel clad runners.
<u>Regulation Racing Sled</u>
      Mortised and tied: $200.00
All hardwood construction. Steel clad runners if desired otherwise teflon.

Advertisement in the Atlin News Miner. *Mom is posing with one of my dad's racing sleds, 1973.*

moose and caribou antler. He had a wood lathe where he literally turned out furniture, lamp bases and ornate walking sticks, among other things. The cutting and polishing of the antlers smelled terrible and often permeated the entire building. He also built racing sleds for dog teams out of white ash and sinew. He made his own steam box to bend the wood and fastened everything with traditional materials, no screws or nails. I remember helping him wrap the wet sinew around the joints to hold them together.

Dad's workshop was also the butcher shop where we dry aged our moose or caribou and where it was cut up and packaged. In the winter when the room was unheated, it was where he stored the animals he trapped before thawing them out upstairs in order to skin them. Dad's shop was at once a place of wonder and horror. There's nothing like dead animals staring at you to get a little kid freaked out. On the other hand, it was where he taught me how to use the lathe and the band saw and showed me how to skin moose, caribou, lynx, otter and beaver.

Their first winter in Atlin, my parents realized there wasn't anything for the teenage kids to do after school and in the evening. Without TV, without a gymnasium or even a place to gather, there was a need. Being of the age where King of the Castle, Kick the Can and snowball fights may have lost their luster, teenagers needed something to do. Mom and Dad decided their newly-acquired monstrosity had enough room to host a handful of teenagers one evening a week. My mom was an expert seamstress from childhood, taught by her mom, who made all of the family clothing. Mom taught the kids sewing and arts and crafts. My dad taught wood shop. He showed them how to use hand and power tools, and they made lamps and moose-horn jewelry.

Over my lifetime, I've been approached by more than a few that expressed their gratitude for those nights they spent in our old house, making dresses and lamps and, more importantly, feeling included and having something that was just for them. I believe they only did this one or two years before the need to completely concentrate on our survival replaced many leisure and social activities. The North can be a harsh mistress, constantly demanding your attention.

Plumbing and Perils

As I mentioned, Our Old House did have a toilet but no water supply. The kitchen had a sink and there was the old clawfoot bathtub under the eaves where my mom kept the cat food and some of our dry goods. There was a septic tank in the backyard, so after my dad repaired the drain system, we were able to send water down to the tank. In my memory, the tub never worked, but the sink and toilet drained for a while. I took my baths in a washtub in the kitchen and I have no idea what my parents did. It seems as though we had some running water for a time, although most likely in the summer only. I believe my dad improvised a holding tank and pump in the backroom on the first floor. I have quite vivid memories of a Porta Potty, a chemical toilet, sitting by the original toilet at the end of a small hallway. When full, it had to be packed down the stairs, along the hallway and out the backdoor to be emptied into the outhouse.

There was a time the whole drain system, as well as the water supply system, if there ever was any, must have failed or frozen, as I remember the slop buckets having to go down and out the back and the water being hauled up. In one particular case, my dad was taking down two buckets of gray water. Not long after he placed the buckets on the top landing and closed the kitchen door, my mom and I heard a tremendous clatter followed by that same "coconut rolling down stairs" sound. This time it sounded like a whole bag of coconuts. That was followed by some sort of bellowed language that I did not yet understand. We rushed out and looked down the stairs to find Dad spread eagle on the landing, dripping wet and covered in potato peels. He was bruised and stinky but otherwise okay. The collective silent consensus was, "Thank God it wasn't the Porta Potty."

Not long after that incident, my dad took work out of town. Coincidence, I think not. Mom and I did our best to live in Our Old House through a bitterly cold winter. The furnace went out regularly, forcing us to rely on the generosity of neighbors to revive the old beast. In cases where it couldn't be fixed in a timely manner, Mom shipped me to the Harvey's across the street and she toughed it out with a small space heater in a huge space, if you can imagine doing that at forty below zero. Thankfully, my parents brought with them a load of U.S. Army surplus cold-weather gear. Included, were two Woods five-star arctic sleeping bags.

Ron Bowden, the town waterman, filled a rubber garbage can inside the main door on the lower floor. Mom and I bailed the water into buckets, lugged them down the hallway and up the stairs where we dumped them into the big barrel in the kitchen. We barely managed a half bucket at a time, so it took many trips. We also had to make sure not to spill because it immediately turned to ice, making the stairs extremely treacherous. With a very short period to work before the water froze, it was quite a task for a woman with asthma and a small boy. I remember leaving the bottom third of the water to freeze in the can before dragging it up, one step at a time, bump, bump, bump, all the way to the kitchen where we let it thaw out before pouring it into the barrel. One time we were half the way up the first flight, both of us straining to get the garbage can with the remaining frozen water up each step. One of us, probably me, lost their grip and the barrel clattered down the stairs, slid across the hallway and slammed into the front door. The plastic garbage can shattered into a dozen pieces, leaving a round, thick slab of ice lying on the floor. As we both stared at the mess, my mom said, "Go get the buckets and the axe. We're not wasting this water."

With Dad mostly away, Our Old House proved to be too much for just the two of us to handle. The cost of heating alone was astronomical, even at 1970s prices.

Mom made sure Our Old House had a new owner, the Atlin Historical Society, and they would protect and respect her. She was an integral part of the Historical Society and would be involved in the life of the Old Government Building/Old Courthouse/Our Old House for many years to come.

The Historical Society, with some help and much hard work, did indeed restore the old building to its original look. Gone are the added-on dormers and improvised paint scheme. With some structural work, a new foundation, new roof, electrical system and water and sewer tanks, back were the original paint colors, and the interior has been completely sanded, painted and polished. The old girl is better than she ever was.

The Old Government Building occasionally holds court when the circuit judge is in town, and the courtroom doubles as an art gallery

Flower beds and sometimes gardens were favorite targets of the free-to-roam bovines. Here they snack on neighbor Jan Harvey's poppies, 1972.
Photo by Terry Milos.

at other times. The mining recording office now houses the library, and the upstairs is used by the community college.

No longer This Old House but still the Old Government Building, and on occasion, The Courthouse, the title matters little. I feel that building is not yet ready to tell her entire history—it's far from concluded as she continues to proudly serve her town.

Years later, as a young man, I was honored to work with the contractor that replaced the roof and restored the original historic look minus the dormers. I spent days removing cedar shingles, letting them fall to the ground under the scaffolding, creating enormous piles of eighty-year-old debris. Inevitably, the next day every last scrap was gone. All through town, the Old Government Building roof continued to provide shelter and comfort. Sheds and small cabins sported newish cedar shingle roofs, and many Atlinite's had their winter's kindling supply. As everywhere in the North, and Atlin especially, nothing went to waste. Like the town, what was once old was new again.

Chapter Five

The *M/V Tarahne*

Named *Tarahne* by Chief Taku Jack in 1917 (his son Leo believed *Tarahne* was the mispronounced Tlingit word for "water runs under it"), the *M/V Tarahne* sits smack dab in the center of Atlin's lakeshore. Featuring double decks and a length of one hundred and nineteen feet (36m), she's a behemoth of a lake boat. She dominates the panorama, commanding your attention from any vantage point.

The *Tarahne* was constructed by the White Pass Company in 1917 to serve Atlin as a freight and passenger hauler from Scotia Bay across the lake to Atlin. She was experimental in the use of gas engines when most of the other vessels owned by White Pass were steam-driven stern wheelers. During the 1920s, the *Tarahne* served Atlin well and, apart from its freight duties, gained popularity as a tour boat. It was lengthened from its original size of seventy-eight feet (24m) to its current length of one hundred and nineteen feet (36m).

Atlin was a popular tourist destination in the late 1920s into the 1930s. Highly publicized by the White Pass Company, wealthy travelers interested in following in the footsteps of the gold rush

The Tarahne during repairs and new paint job in 1969. The Motor Vessel Tarahne was built in 1917 by the White Pass Company for tourism primarily and cargo secondarily.

stampeders, as well as wilderness enthusiasts and adventurers, all wanted to see Atlin and its magnificent scenery.

By the mid-1930s, with the Depression in North America and the economic and political unrest in Europe, tourism died off and the *Tarahne* proved too big and costly to keep running. The smaller *SS Scotia* handled Atlin's freight and passenger needs, and the *Tarahne* was hauled out on rails in front of town and forgotten.

Eventually, White Pass gave the *Tarahne* to the town, but for reasons unknown it fell into private hands. As you may have guessed, my parents ended up owning the massive vessel. One day, my mom was talking to a gentleman who purported to own it. He lived out of town and had little interest in doing anything with her.

Dad painting the wheel house, 1969. The Tarahne was originally seventy-eight feet (23.7m) long but was lengthened to one-hundred and nineteen feet (36.3m) in 1928.

He told my mom that White Pass had sold the *Tarahne* to him for a dollar and he would sell it to her for the same amount. Who could turn that down?

Although most of the boat was permanently dry docked, the stern was normally submerged. The barn and cliff swallows took up residence under the eaves, and she was covered in mud nests and bird crap. The kids couldn't resist throwing rocks at the nests and in doing so most, if not all, the window panes were broken out. In an attempt to keep the swallows away, the town erected a long, narrow, roof-like structure on poles near the boat. The thought was the swallows might like it better and nest there instead. It didn't work and only drew more swallows to the area and the boat.

The gentleman who sold the *Tarahne* to my mom had previously stripped off all the brass fittings, the lighting and the large wooden and brass helm. The lifeboats were gone as well.

The sun setting behind the M/V Tarahne, 1968. The Tarahne was powered by twin gasoline engines, unusual for the White Pass Company's large marine fleet consisting mainly of stern wheel, steam-driven river and lake boats.

With no budget, many volunteers and donations, my parents were able to scrape all the old paint off and apply a new coat in hopes of preserving the wood. The paint was donated by the highway department, so for many years the hull sported a lovely shade of safety orange.

As soon as the Historical Society was formed, my mom sold the *Tarahne* to them for one dollar, thus ensuring it will forever be Atlin's boat. Many years later, while talking to a visitor to Atlin, the subject of the *Tarahne* came up. As it turned out, he, too, was offered the *Tarahne* and paid a dollar for it. It's undetermined how many people actually bought the boat over the years, but it is certain it now belongs to Atlin.

After many years of fundraising and volunteer work, the *Tarahne* has been shored up, painted in its proper colors, and partially renovated. It now has a fire-suppression system, which allows it to be used for public functions that include an annual Gay Nineties Afternoon Tea, a murder mystery dinner and the occasional wedding. Atlinites once again proved that the heritage of the town is important to them, and the effort to save another Atlin landmark was worth the struggle.

The man that sold the *Tarahne* to my mom owned a bar and lodge in a small town on the Alaska Highway south of Atlin. For years my mother, Shirley Connolly and others negotiated with him for the return of the lights, the brass fittings and the helm. As they were prominent decorations in his bar and lodge, he steadfastly refused. Eventually the man grew older and decided to sell his property. He finally relented and agreed to return all the items to Atlin upon the sale of his establishment. Tragically, all were lost in a fire before the property was sold.

Atlin and the *Tarahne* were fortunate benefactors from yet another tragic fire. While being renovated in nearby Carcross, Yukon, the SS *Tutshi* was set ablaze by an arsonist and burned to the ground.

The *Tutshi* was also a lake boat, but a steam-driven sternwheeler, and was for a time an integral part of the early route into Atlin. The *Tutshi* hauled freight and passengers from the White Pass Railway in Carcross up Tagish Lake to Taku Landing. From there it was a two and a quarter mile (3.6km) rail or horse trip to Atlin Lake, where freight and passengers transferred to the *Tarahne*.

The *Tutshi's* lifeboats were not consumed in the fire and neither were rolls of original period floor covering. The kind people of Carcross donated these items to Atlin for use in the *Tarahne* renovations. Although the lifeboats are not identical to the originals, they are a great addition.

Many dreams have been "floated" throughout the years about seeing the *Tarahne* once again ply the tranquil waters of Atlin Lake, but the costs are onerous and, as of this writing, it looks like the *Tarahne* will remain a permanent fixture on Atlin's waterfront.

Chapter Six

What's Happening Here?

When our family moved to Atlin in 1967, it was still a frontier town; most people lived without running water or sewer systems as the town provided neither. A few had water and sewer holding tanks with pumps, but many others had water barrels and outhouses. There wasn't access to TV or radio and the closest station was a hundred miles (160km) away. It was a rare treat when you might pick up a couple minutes of music on a clear night from some faraway A.M. station. We had one RCMP constable and one wildlife conservation officer. They were the sum total of all law enforcement for the town and surrounding hundreds of miles of wilderness. Atlin was to be the last one-man RCMP outpost in Canada.

In the summer of 1971, it was hard to get a cup of coffee in Atlin and hit or miss if you could gas up your car to get back up the road. Since The Kootenay Hotel's demise in the late fall of 1968, Atlin was without accommodations. By 1972, it was a completely different story. After two years of fits and starts, the winter of 1972 saw the opening of the new Kootenay Hotel, soon to be renamed the Atlin Inn. Half of it, at any rate: the ground floor. Atlin's newest business consisted of a large saloon, ten rooms and a windowless kitchen and dining room. By late winter of the same year, Kirkwood Cottages had two of their fine cabins completed, and seven more would be ready by June.

In 1970-71, a two-unit motel was constructed on Second Street with a grand opening the fall of 1971. Adjacent to it, opening the next summer, was a new art gallery housed in the old nurse's quarters from the days of Saint Andrew's Hospital, which served Atlin in its past. Also completed in the fall of 1971, a new grocery store, the Trading Post built by new residents Bev and Harvey Rossiter, was an all-log building with a residence above. With the already-established Edie's Store on Second Street owed by Edie and Gordon Crum, Atlin now had a grocery store open every day of the week.

In the spring of 1972, the long-dormant Sands Store was re-opened by new residents Arthur and Nancy Mitchell under a new name: The General Store. Atlin again had a place to buy hardware, household items, clothes and tools. Atlin now sported three gift and craft shops: The Discovery Shop in the Old Courthouse, The Cache housed in one of Atlin's ancient morgues, and the newly-constructed log building housing The Boofus Shop. These stores all offered unique and unusual gifts as well as necessities for the tourists and locals.

A new garage and gas station, Atlin Esso owned by Norm Bentley and Ron Bowden, was opened in the fall of 1971, offering Esso gas and tire and vehicular repair. Under the same owners, a coffee shop and café were added in the spring of 1972, the Trapper's Cafe.

The Trading Post put in one pump in front of their store providing Gulf gasoline, which gave visitors and locals a choice of gas. Edie's Store began selling propane that same summer to serve camper and trailer travelers. Visitors could now rent boats and fishing gear from Joe Florence or Tom Kirkwood. If they wanted to better their chances at landing the big one, visitors could hire Dennis Odian's fishing guide service, Atlin Fish Camp. If it was sightseeing that interested them, lake tours were available as well as floatplane trips.

John and Gary Thoma opened up a welding and machining service that also offered vehicle towing. Joe Ackerman started up a sawmill providing rough-cut dimensional lumber and three-sided building logs. Atlin's already established big game guiding services were seeing an upswing in business as Americans and Europeans flocked to Atlin in search of bagging a record animal. The price of gold was rising and miners and prospectors were once again fanning out across the land.

The Rec. Centre was being expanded, completing the original idea for an all-inclusive community hall to go with the curling rink and bar. The *M/V Tarahne*, Atlin's centerpiece, received a new coat of paint that summer. A new roof and paint job completed renovations on the old electrical power house that now housed the two trucks used by the Atlin Volunteer Fire Department.

June 1, 1972, saw the launch of Atlin's first and arguably best modern newspaper. Not since 1942, when the first *Atlin News Miner* ceased publication due to lack of circulation, had Atlin been served by a finer rag. When the first *News Miner* closed its doors, the Atlin area held roughly 1,500 people, a number thought too few to support the circulation of a local paper. In 1972, there were approximately 250 people and the new *Atlin News Miner* was born. Tom Kirkwood finagled a deal with the owners of the *Whitehorse Star,* Bob and Rusty Erlum, to do the typesetting and printing. Tom became the editor and dozens of locals contributed to what became a beloved addition to Atlin life.

"How did all this happen in such a short period of time?" was a question asked by visitors and locals alike, and a great question it was, although it was never fully or adequately answered. It just did. Excitement, determination, perseverance, charity, community, love, desperation, vision, pride—these words along with others, or combinations of them, may help, but any theory is probably as valid as the next.

Atlin was a place where you burned wood for heat, water was delivered on Tuesday, you ate moose meat, lake trout or caribou almost every meal, and if you didn't own at least three dogs you must be new in town. No one locked their doors ("How else could the water man get in?") and people always left the keys in the ignition of their vehicle in case someone needed to move it, or borrow it, for that matter.

Atlin was a town where everyone was your parent and you listened and showed respect as if they really were. It was a town where everybody literally knew everyone else. When the community needed something, people volunteered their time and expertise, put

Free-range horses at the Warm Springs, 1970.

on bake sales and plant sales and raffled off cakes and loaves of bread to raise money. Artists and craftsmen donated their wares and creations to be sold or raffled off. Children donated their used toys and books to rummage sales, and everyone, old and young, gave their time willingly to make their community a better place. With a little sweat, elbow grease and Northern ingenuity, the work always got done.

Atlin was the kind of place where you might get in a heated argument with your neighbor at the Board of Trade meeting, but stop to pull them out of the ditch on your way home. The next day, they bought you coffee at the café and you spent a half-hour talking about the weather. At next month's meeting, the argument might resume.

We received mail three times a week and we picked it up at the post office. If you needed to find someone you went to the "coffee shop" at three o'clock and they were there. Our phone book was one page and our numbers were only three digits long. We didn't have a hospital or doctor, but we had a Red Cross outpost and a nurse named Jessie James. As kids, we were proud to proclaim that we had been shot by Jessie James. It was the kind of place where you not only knew everyone's name, you also knew their dog's name.

We didn't have street signs. Even though the streets had names, we didn't know any of them and they weren't posted. If we needed to give directions, it went something like this: "Take a left at The Discovery Shop, go straight past Arnold's corrals, take a right at Nolan's field, keep going past the dump and the old golf course, cross the Baily Bridge at Pine Creek, go past the water spring at the bottom of Monarch Mountain, keep going until you see a big gravel pit on your left, then take the first road immediately past it, stop at the brown house with the big gray husky laying out front, his name's Lobo. Don't worry, he won't bite you."

Places have obvious names like First, Second and Third Island, North and South Lakes or Warm Springs, Black Rocks, Red Bluffs and the Mineral Springs. Horses and cows wandered down Main Street, and you might see a dog team tied up outside the grocery store or a horse outside the bar, or, in one particular instance, in the bar when Stan decided his horse was thirsty.

The gun club shooting range was on the other side of the wall from the library, and no one thought it ironic.

Our water came out of the lake and there wasn't fluoride or chlorine added, and somehow, we survived. The water barrel was in the kitchen, and on Tuesday Ron Bowden brought water. He flung open your front door, dragged his muddy hose across the living room floor and into the kitchen, the hose wearing half-moon grooves in your door casings. With a loud clang, he slammed the nozzle into the barrel, cranked on the valve, and in a matter of minutes you had a supply of clear, cold, Atlin Lake water. On his way out, he might mutter something about a lazy kid sleeping all day. Geez, it was eight in the morning on a summer day. In the spring, you might have to wait for the silt to seep to the bottom, but it was the best water in the world. Ron didn't need to knock and he didn't; everyone knew when the water was coming. Not to say Ron wasn't witness to a few embarrassing encounters with absentminded or forgetful customers over the years. Fortunately for some, Ron took the water-deliveryman-client-privilege privacy pledge very seriously and his lips remained sealed.

Atlin had its own language. When people said they were "up the creek" or "down the lake" everyone understood what that meant. When someone was "in town" or "outside," we knew they were in Whitehorse or somewhere in the lower province or farther. When

A view of town from Brewery Bay, late 1970s. Construction of Atlin's first breakwater is under way, built with logs and rocks and elbow grease. My mom was the construction forewoman for this project.

you were "down river" you were on the Taku or Tulsequah Rivers. If you were "down" or "up the lake" you were out in your boat. "Up the creek" didn't mean what it does to most of the world—in Atlin, it literally meant you were up the creek, usually referring to gold mining. If you were "on the mountain," you were on Monarch Mountain. "Out in the bush" could mean several different places, but all were away from town, isolated and in the bush. Although there were a number of brands, all snow machines were Ski-Doos. If someone was "out on their line," it meant they were trapping. "Out the road" meant you were out the road, and because we knew their habits, we knew where they were. When you said, "I'll see you at coffee," it meant you would see them at 3 pm at the café.

People and a Small Northern Town
Atlin News Miner 1972
Diane S. Smith

Walk along an Atlin street on a soft summer night. Across your way, spears of light from curtained windows make warm, inviting patterns on the gravel. Behind darkened doorways sounds of a town alive and growing trickle into the night. A muffled laugh, a child's sleepy cry, garbled words, the noises of families deep in the business of an evening. They are comfortable and secure sounds.

Two young people representing opposite ends of the continent meet in a small northern town. Something clicks

This buckboard was found at an abandoned farm near Atlin by my parents, 1969. It now resides in the museum yard. At one time, they discovered a complete blacksmith shop abandoned. It was as though the inhabitants just walked away. The entire shop is at the museum.

between them, shreds of loneliness fall away and they decide to join forces. A new life begins for them and adds to the general din of progress.

Atlin is a town experiencing a rebirth. In a few short years it has thrown off the robes of a ghost town, squashed that title with little ceremony. Derelict buildings have been painted and occupied, vacant lots have sprouted handsome log structures, the "city" limits have been pushed back. These things have occurred because of people, and people are what small northern towns are all about. It isn't an easy task bringing a town back. People being what they are, complex and unpredictable creatures, a certain percentage are lost in the effort. Sadness and despair may end a sojourn and partners split to travel separate ways wondering where things went wrong that once seemed so right. Others would never fit in and eventually they drift on.

People thrown together in semi-isolation and hounded by hostile weather are sometimes deprived of the ability to think objectively. Problems loom too close and too large. Irritations fester. All around is wilderness, sometimes friendly, often oppressive and confining, making it impossible to back away and see things for their actual worth. Gossip can run rampant and malignant. Tempers flare and prejudices are cultivated.

The wounds inflicted by a small town can be deep and bitterly painful. But, by the same token, the good times, working together for a common goal, can be gratifying and exhilarating. Honors given are cherished because they are warm and personal.

A tough, tenacious fiber is evident in the makeup of the people willing to put up with the rough climate, cabin fever and small-town discontent to live in the North. Inconveniences and community gripes are endured, not always graciously endured, nevertheless for the compensations on the credit side of the ledger. The feeling of being an individual, one unique human being, is probably the most important prize granted to a Northerner: he counts. Good or bad, his influence is felt and adds an important ingredient to the mixture that comprises his small northern town. In Atlin, the recipe seems a success. The town is alive and thriving in Northern British Columbia. It's the people that made it happen.

————

Chapter Seven

A Move and a New Discovery

We moved into a smaller, easier to manage house in 1974; a much newer Atlin landmark—by four years, that is. My mom purchased The Old Pillman House on the corner of Discovery and Third. With her good friend Peggy Milius, they remodeled and reclaimed another piece of Atlin's heritage. The Pillman House was originally built in 1904 by entrepreneur and businessman Edwin Pillman who owned, among other businesses, a number of grocery stores, the first theater, a courier service and one of Atlin's first mortuaries.

You may have noticed a thread here: every building in Atlin is called "The Old" something or another. Even those buildings that were torn down live on in parts and pieces in homes and businesses throughout Atlin. Nothing goes to waste and nothing is too old to be useful again.

Peggy, an interior designer by trade and artist by choice, was also an accomplished carpenter and upholsterer. With a small budget, some reclaimed material, and a hell of a lot of moxie, they created a fine Atlin home for me, my mom and all our dogs. Wood heat and the quintessential water barrel in the kitchen, our faithful old Porta

The Discovery Shop advertisement 1972 from the Atlin News Miner.

Potty for those cold winter nights, an outhouse, a twenty-foot (6m) Atco trailer attached to the back for a workshop, and we were set.

The workshop was also heated by a small wood stove. When the temperature dropped into the minus thirties or forties, the room between the kitchen and the workshop was blanketed off and left to freeze. The heat from either stove did not quite reach and there were too many cold drafts to adequately heat that room. My mom joked it was the biggest walk-in freezer in town and it was used for that to save electricity on the actual freezer. If you wanted frozen orange juice or a moose roast, you went into that room and there they sat on my mom's desk beside her typewriter or in the top drawer of the filing cabinet. With the middle room effectively uninhabitable most of the winter, it left us less than three hundred square feet (28m³) of living space for two people, five Malamutes, and random litters of puppies, plus my dad on rare occasion. I guess we were ahead of the tiny house trend.

My mom slept in the living room on the fold-out couch. For many years, she endured that thin mattress and the hard metal bar that ran under her back. I slept in a tiny room off the living room separated by a louvered closet door. The Porta Potty was in my room and thankfully I slept like the dead. Our wood stove was in the living room two feet (0.6m) from my mom's fold-out bed. She kept the stove stoked most of the night, but winter mornings were always cold until the first fire of the day took the chill off. The water barrel, only a few feet away in the kitchen, would often have ice on it.

During those years in the poorly-insulated Pillman House, we burned roughly twelve cords of wood a year between the house and the shop. With only a small car for transport, we could not get our own wood, so we purchased it from local cutters. The wood came in four-foot lengths and I sawed it into smaller pieces then split it so it would fit in the stoves. I'm not sure what most kids of the time were getting for their ninth birthdays, but I got a Homelite chainsaw. I was embarrassed because some of my friends had

My first and only modeling gig at The Discovery Shop, 1970. I'm wearing a fur ruff made by Mom.

bigger saws, but that little saw was a trooper and cut our wood for many years.

Once we were able to move into The Pillman House, the ladies shifted their sights to a small residence directly across the street. The long-neglected cabin would be transformed into the new and improved Discovery Shop. My first reaction when Mom told me that the old Walter Sweet cabin would become The Discovery Shop was to recoil in horror. After Walter Sweet moved out, we all knew who moved in: Bloody Bones. The front door had huge smears of blood all over it (a poor paint job). Like I said, Bloody Bones reportedly lived in other abandoned buildings around town, but I was convinced this was his main residence—the proof being the blood, of course. Only after it was gutted, completely refurbished and the door replaced did I believe Bloody Bones had moved on.

While still living at the Old Government Building, my mom had grown and expanded The Discovery Shop into a thriving enterprise. At first reliant on summer tourism, Mom speedily diversified her inventory to better sustain a year-round business. With a seamstress employed full time, The Discovery Shop turned out a myriad of leather garments: everything from the traditional moose-hide bushman's outfits to purple or pink cowhide hot pants. Black leather vests and chaps were sold to bikers, leather gauntlet gloves and mittens were

Mom bought Walter Sweet's old house in the mid-1970s and with her friend, Peggy Milius, remodeled it and turned it into the second Discovery Shop.

The Discovery Shop after renovations were completed in 1975 is a great example of how many of Atlin's old buildings have been refurbished, moved or repurposed in some way. It is now relocated in the museum yard.

After selling the Courthouse, Mom bought The Pillman House, early 1970s. With Peggy Milius as head carpenter, they completely remodeled it and made it livable. Built by Edwin Pillman at the turn of the century, he and his family lived there as early as 1904. Pillman was a businessman who owned a number of grocery stores in the area as well as The Globe Theater, a drugstore and a morgue.

I'm standing in front of the freshly renovated Pillman House, our new home for the next few years.

CASSIAR SAFARI

For a number of years before Christmas, Mom, Dad and helpers packed up the entire Discovery Shop and drove 350 miles (563km) over a dirt road to Cassiar for a weekend sale, late 1970s. Originally published in the Atlin News Miner. Photo by Tom Kirkwood.

a favorite of the dog mushers, and stylish moosehide capes and jackets were a must-have for any Northern lady's wardrobe.

At the height of the, for no better description, "Hippie Movement," handcrafted items were sought after and desired. The Discovery Shop made leather hat bands adorned with grouse feathers and porcupine quills, felt cabin boots of all colors with leather soles and cross fox fur trim, gold nugget jewelry, leather-pants patches, and leather and fur piggy banks called Grubstake Gus and Sluice Box Susie. Moose antler jewelry and cuff links and grouse feather chokers were hot sellers. These were just a scant few items that came from Mom's workshop.

Fur work became a staple. Wolf and wolverine ruffs for parkas were ordered by customers throughout the North. Beaver and muskrat hats sold well, as did wolf and coyote gauntlet mittens.

Many women of the North in those days possessed an out-of-date, out-of-style fur coat, often handed down from their mother or grandmother. Most were full-length behemoths too valuable to get rid of, but out of trend and too cumbersome to wear. My mom decided these old coats could be refurbished and altered into modern, practical and beautiful parkas more suited for the times. A typical coat started as a hulking cloak in the style of a buffalo robe and ended up a sleek modern parka with intricate inlaid leather bands and new ruff and cuffs of wolf or wolverine. Shortened to a traditional parka length and altered to fit the owner, these pieces of art became popular and steady money makers for The Discovery Shop.

My mom took in items on consignment from local artists and crafters near and far, offering them a platform and place to sell their

I'm with Mom at a craft fair in Faro, Yukon, 1973. Craft fairs were popular and The Discovery Shop attended many. It was another way to boost your business and advertise your wears to a wider population. Mom also used them to find artists and crafters that might want to sell their items in her shop.

wares. The Discovery Shop was filled with carvings, beadwork, books and bottles, moose poop, jade and gold nugget jewelry and hand-turned wooden and vintage bottle lamps. Leather was a staple. Moosehide purses and hats, vests, and even the odd bra all saw shelf time. Mom also bought and sold furs and placer gold purchased from local miners and trappers.

Absurd and often bizarre items made their way into the shop. If it was handmade and it sold, my mom found a place for it. Ted Coe's pothole pattern was a big seller with the brave travelers that navigated their way around the thousands of potholes to reach Atlin. The premise was that they could take the pattern home and create their own pothole in their driveway, a lasting memento of their trip. Ted had a great sense of humor. Ice worms were thin strips of fur, usually rabbit, with two plastic eyes glued to one end on either side of a stitched-thread nose. When stroked, they undulated much like how a worm travels. The ice worms sold for twenty-five cents and were a favorite of children. The pet rock even made its way to Mom's store.

Any part of any animal was fair game in those days. Mountain goat hoof ashtrays probably warrant an explanation, but I choose to leave it to the reader's imagination. There was something called a Hootenanny. It was the sliced off rear end of a mountain sheep with two strategically placed glass eyeballs. The end result resembled the face of an enormous white owl.

Pants patches were cut-out designs in leather, in every color, meant to be sewn on jeans. The price was sixty-five cents and they sold like hotcakes. More importantly it was a use for the copious amounts of leather scraps being generated. Nothing was wasted.

Mom spent hours cutting out hands, the peace sign, the smiley face, and the Rolling Stones' lips to mention a few, and I helped punch holes around the edges. After the pants patches and other smaller items, the rest of the scraps were bagged up and sold in bulk. *Nothing was wasted,* Atlin's common refrain.

If there was a need, my mom tried to remedy it. I remember our chest freezer filled with bread pans of ice. For a time, there was nowhere to buy ice in Atlin, so for twenty-five cents one could purchase a block of ice from my mom. When busy, she would send the customer back to grab their own ice. Many came back determined to purchase a loaf of her home-baked bread, generally not for sale, but I know she relented on a few occasions when nostalgic customers lamented on the virtues of their mother's or grandmother's baking. She mentioned this to a friend, Ev Colwell, a great baker in her own right, and suggested she sell bread to tourists. Ev promptly began baking and selling fresh bread out of her home. She was soon to open The Boofus Shop. This was Atlin, where needs were quickly filled, problems rectified with aplomb and gusto.

Prime furs were sold at The Discovery Shop. Beaver, lynx, wolf, wolverine, otter and fox were the most popular. Raw gold nuggets, individually or in bulk, as well as large slabs of polished Northern British Columbia jade were all favorites of the European big-game hunters that flocked to Atlin in the fall of every year.

During any occasion that required costumes or gowns, The Discovery Shop was there to help. Many Halloween costumes came to life in the back room of the shop. Costumes for school plays, gowns for a formal winter ball and, on at least one occasion, a wedding gown were created in that dingy backroom. The Discovery Shop also became a supplier to craftsmen, artists and First Nations' beaders and seamstresses in the area. Mom sent beads, leather, braid, fur and duffle to many of the small towns in Northern British Columbia and the Yukon. I remember reading letters from Mrs. Quock, who lived somewhere along the Stuart Cassiar Highway and was a brilliant beader and seamstress. My mom sent beads and fur and leather, and Mrs. Quock sent back intricately beaded moccasins, mukluks, coin purses and glasses cases for consignment in the shop. Mrs. Quock had little English, and my mom had no Tahltan, so often they glued or taped beads onto their letters as descriptions of what they wanted or were offering.

The height of commerce for The Discovery Shop was the early- to mid-1970s. Although the United States was experiencing economic hardship, people were traveling domestically and into Canada. Because of uncertainty in many areas of the world, traveling the road systems of North America was appealing and nostalgic. The price of gas was low, and the state of Alaska held the allure of the last unexplored frontier. Traveling clubs were popular. It was the time of the Airstream trailer pulled by the big block cars of Detroit, with their wide mirrors and enormous bug screens.

Canadians also traveled, but on a smaller scale. The typical American traveler of the time was middle age or older, successful, had some money to spend and was showing off their expensive trailer and car. The Canadians were usually younger, had their children with them, had less money and were traveling in older truck and camper combinations or tenting.

These visitors held in common the sense of adventure and exploration needed to travel the long one-way dirt road to Atlin. The curiosity of gold rush history, a chance for some excellent fishing, and the promise of beautiful, untamed wilderness brought people. European and American hunters came to have a chance at record moose, mountain goats, sheep or bear.

I remember days when long lines of trailers and campers were parked down the block in front of the shop, all covered in mud from the Atlin Road. My mom worked twelve-hour days or longer in the store and often more in the workshop at night. The old saying that *you have to make hay when the sun shines* definitely applied to the tourism business in Atlin. With barely three months to make

A line of campers in front of The Discovery Shop, mid-1970s.

the bulk of that year's income, it was a mad scramble to succeed. I helped when I could, bringing sandwiches and relieving her for bathroom breaks, but to be honest, I was more interested in playing with my friends.

The Whitehorse people were and always have been great boosters for Atlin, and many visit multiple times a year. Whether it's a day trip or a two-week fishing adventure, Atlin is happy to have them and their commerce. Early spring and late fall, before and after the long-distance travelers, it was nice to see the Whitehorse crowd perusing one's tiny store.

Bad weather, the Alaska Highway washing out, which it did regularly in those days, or high gas prices all drastically affected tourism in the North. At times, it was the fall hunting rush that saved a bad summer. The hunters had money and wanted to spend it on high-end items like gold jewelry and furs.

Mom loved the tourists. She enjoyed the endless stream of questions, and she was well versed on Atlin in general. She spent hours in conversation with curious history buffs and wilderness enthusiasts. More than a few people moved to Atlin after talking to my mom and catching her contagious intensity for the Northern way of life and, in particular, life in Atlin.

Cassiar was an asbestos mining town located in the Cassiar Mountains of Northern British Columbia. The mine is now closed and the town is gone, but for a number of years it was a thriving mine and a town of 1,500 people. It was located north of Dease

Placer gold from the creeks around Atlin. My mom made jewelry with it, mostly gluing it into earing and pendant blanks. My dad dabbled at actual goldsmithing for a brief period. Gold was $32 an ounce when we moved to Atlin in 1967. For years, my mom carried a one-ounce nugget in her pants pocket to show the tourists. A long time later, she weighed it and found over a third had worn away.

Lake, south of Watson Lake on the Stewart Cassiar Highway, and approximately 350 miles (563km) south of Atlin, so it was quite isolated.

Cassiar, being a company town, only had the company store to provide goods to the population. Well stocked in the necessities, it severely lacked anything in the way of gifts. Getting wind of this, and after some inquiries, my mom along with assistants packed up the entire Discovery Shop and moved it to Cassiar for one weekend a year before Christmas. That bold move proved to be an economic boon for us and a much appreciated and needed opportunity to buy Christmas gifts for the families of Cassiar. The long, treacherous drive there and back was worth it, as we often sold out and returned home with handfuls of orders.

The Discovery Shop, like the other tourist-related businesses in Atlin, was hurt by the OPEC oil embargo of 1973-1974. The price of gas shot up and suddenly the long road trip up the Alaska Highway became economically difficult for many. Mom hung on for a few more years, relying on her custom fur and leather work as well as the Whitehorse weekenders and the few intrepid highway travelers.

The Iranian crisis in 1979 spiked gas prices even farther and proved to be the final nail closing The Discovery Shop for good. As The Discovery Shop had supplied most of our annual income, Mom took a job at a local store. She continued to supplement her wages by creating and selling watercolor paintings depicting her favorite subject: Atlin and the surrounding area. She took on the odd drafting job and painted the occasional sign. We raised and sold a litter or two of pups a year, and she also took up carving soapstone, selling over a hundred carvings until arthritis made it too difficult.

Mom was laid off from the store every year during the dead of winter and that made it even harder to make ends meet. After my dad left, big game hunting was impossible without a truck and we had no way to process a large animal in our tiny home. Both my mom and I hunted rabbit and grouse and I continued to supply grayling, but it didn't make up for the lack of a yearly moose or caribou. There wasn't enough room around The Pillman House for much of a garden, although we did grow some carrots, potatoes and onions, and the house was full of tomato plants spring and summer.

I'm standing with Mom, 1969. She's wearing a fur coat she redesigned.

Friends and neighbors never forgot us and most years someone brought us a quarter of moose, and during the summer it wasn't unusual to find a couple large lake trout on the door step. Ollie Green and Kay Mattson, Atlin's premiere green thumbs of the time, were generous with their abundant vegetable harvests.

There were many times when people commissioned paintings or a leather vest or bought a carving at just the right time, when we were down to our last dollar and uncertain what we would do for groceries. Of course, my mom kept our precarious financial situation from me when I was young. I didn't know we were poor because all of us were. We all had holes in our wool socks and patches on our jeans. Those with a little more helped those with a little less. When you were fiercely proud like my mom, people were subtle with their overtures, thus the commissioning of a painting or vest. They knew, she knew, they cared, she appreciated, enough said. That was how it worked in Atlin.

The Question-and-Answer Game
Atlin News Miner 1977
Diane S. Smith

Although the tourists are a little scarce this summer, there are still enough of them here for me to indulge in one of my favorite summer pastimes, the Question-and-Answer Game.

After several years' practice, I should be showing some signs of expertise at the game, but each year someone throws me a curve and I lose points toward my amateur rating.

Most tourists who make it to Atlin already have a good idea of what the town is all about. At least they know Atlin is here because gold was discovered in Pine Creek in 1898. But they are sometimes surprised to find some four hundred hardy souls hacking out an existence in the British Columbia bush. Many expected to find a couple of crotchety old miners and a trapper or two.

Usually travelers have heard of the marvelous scenery, but words can't justly describe it, so at first they may be somewhat speechless and wide-eyed. This soon passes, however, and healthy curiosity takes over. This is the beginning of the Q/A Game.

Since I am mostly in my gift shop on summer days, I am one of the Atlinites who is a handy target for questions. These questions seem to fall into categories. There are the academic ones about Atlin's history, flora and fauna, the town's economics or lack of it, and meteorology. I can usually bungle through history and I know who can fill them in on the plants and animals, but then comes the question that falls under

Mom playing the Question-and-Answer Game in the first Discovery Shop in the judge's chamber in the courthouse, late 1970s.

economics. It is a stumper and it sounds like this: "Aaaa say, just what do people do around here to make a living?" The guys who ask this really want an answer, and do you know I haven't the foggiest idea what to tell them. I can't tell them this, of course, as it is apparent some four hundred Atlin residents are getting along rather well with no visible means of support ... So I mutter a bit about mining and trapping and government jobs and hope this will be satisfactory. If they dig farther, I pretend to have a coughing fit and leave the shop ... Actually though, for ten solid years I have been looking for the answer to this question and haven't yet cracked it. There has to be something going on here that even I don't know about.

Another touchy area is the one listed directly under psychology, and it has to do with the dread affliction called cabin fever. The question comes in hushed tones ... "Do people get cabin fever?" They make it sound like a contagious, unmentionable disease. It is popular presently to call cabin fever 'Arctic Madness' and truthfully I can't say whether we have it or not, all things being relative ... However, I suspect that most outsiders would agree it is running rampant even in the summertime.

Under weather is the inevitable "How cold does it get here in the winter?" It's been a few years since it was 60 below (-51°C) or even 50 below (-45°C), but to make the traveler happy I say casually that it drops to around 60 below in the winter and sort of kick the floor nonchalantly as though I was stuffed with genuine eiderdown.

The fascination for gold never tarnishes, and I explain to people that we use real Atlin gold nuggets on the jewelry in my shop. But one time a guy came in and after several minutes of careful browsing, he sidled up and whispered confidently, "What do you use for gold?" I never did convince him it was the real McCoy.

Another interesting question is one always accompanied by a leer ... "What do you do during the long dark winter nights?" That one is easy. I just leer back sweetly and say, "It's none of your darned business."

The question that requires an immediate, detailed answer always comes from a harassed woman from whose hand dangles a desperate child with crossed legs and eyes afloat. "Where is your bathroom?" she hisses.

"Lady, I haven't had a bathroom since I left civilization ten years ago. In fact, I don't even have a room where I could put a bath if I ever acquired one." Well, I don't really tell her this. Instead, I direct her to the outhouse. "Outhouse?" Do you realize that at least 78 percent of the world's population does not know what an outhouse is? So you can imagine the shock as the woman rounds the woodpile, threads her way through four or five husky dogs and finds—the place which I have had to translate into "bathroom" so she could understand me.

Well, after the initial surprise I have noticed that almost all of our tourists manage our rustic convenience with no major setbacks. In fact, they seem to get a kick out of roughing it with us for a while. And the fact that so many come back makes me think they have discovered something about Atlin while poking around and playing the Q/A Game. Maybe they find out they possess a bit of the pioneer spirit required to exist in an out-of-the-way little town. Something must have made them drive the rather bumpy road to Atlin, and in the end, they fit in nicely with the scheme of things here.

———

Chapter Eight

The Beginning of the End

During the time we were living at the Old Courthouse, my parents became proficient "dog dealers," for lack of a better term. We always had a few huskies in the family and then acquired more when my dad became a trapper. We quickly grew our pack. The trapping never became a profitable operation, but the dog rearing was more successful, and we produced some good sled dogs and a couple of very good lead dogs. The trapping was a sideline, as my dad's real passion at that time was providing Atlin with a hotel. With newly acquired funding, he began construction in 1970. Around the same time, locals began to take notice of our stock of dogs, and people wanted them. The strong traits of our dogs were their disposition and looks. They had the classic husky or Malamute markings and most were good natured and made great pets. They were also perfect dogs for the part-time musher or even the trapper as they were more suited for pulling loads and people and less suited for racing.

In no time we gained a good reputation and were having three to four litters a year. My mom brought in different dogs from other known lots, as well as a few kennel club purebreds. At one time,

Road construction camp in the Ogilvie Mountain Range on the Dempster Highway, 1974.

we had twenty-eight dogs, including puppies. My mom vetted prospective buyers like they were applying for a job at the FBI. More than a few were refused. She took great pride in her dogs and treated them like they were part of the family. Sometimes this went a bit too far, but her heart was in the right place.

My dad continued to build the hotel to the detriment of our savings, Mom's pension, other property we owned and our boat and camper. Since the unfortunate demise of The Kootenay, Atlin had regained a café or two in various guises but was still without a hotel. Around this time, my parents became aware that they had diverging life philosophies. My mom was of the "slow and steady, stop and smell the roses" variety, whereas my dad was more of the "sorry I bulldozed your roses but I have to get this hotel built right now" variety. My mom was happy to run her little shop, go down to the trapline cabin as often as we could, expand her dog business and submerge herself in Atlin's vibrant history. My dad seemed to think life was about getting rich and being the king of Atlin.

My mom drew plans for a magnificent two-story log hotel with twenty rooms, a restaurant with a view of the lake and a large saloon. My dad was able to complete the lower floor that housed ten rooms, a small café with no windows and a decent bar before he went bankrupt.

Caribou crossing the Dempster Highway, 1974. The sun barely rises above the horizon in the winter.

With Atlin's limited economic opportunities, Dad took work on the Dempster Highway project building the road to Inuvik, NWT. The money was good, but the months apart did nothing to repair their relationship.

In 1972, the road camp needed a caretaker for the Christmas holiday and my parents believed this might be a great opportunity to spend some much-needed time together and to work out their differences. So my dad volunteered as long as he could have his family stay as well. Mom and I and three of our huskies flew into a beautiful Arctic valley in the middle of the Ogilvie Mountain Range on a sub-zero, brilliant day. The sun doesn't stay above the horizon long at that time of year. The daylight hours were limited.

Mom was overwhelmed by the pristine beauty of our surroundings, but underwhelmed to discover another fellow would also be spending the holidays in camp. A friend and co-worker of my dad's didn't have any family in the area, so he too decided to stay in camp, a slight omission Dad had forgotten to divulge to my mom.

My mom and I were blown away by the variety and amount of food available. There were freezers full of steaks and chops and turkeys and every other cut and type of meat one could imagine. The pantry was immense and contained more than both of Atlin's grocery stores put together. Mom would later suggest it may have been another reason my dad worked away.

There were stacks of magazines in the break room. I briefly glimpsed them before my mom whisked them away, never to be seen again. I'm pretty sure they were big comic books. She was always so concerned they would rot my brain. What she left were a half-dozen dog-eared *National Geographics*.

The day we arrived, the surrounding mountains were mostly unimpressive flat-topped, snow-covered plateaus. The second day, as we departed on a snowshoe hike to see the sights, we were shocked to find all the mountains were peaked and rugged.

What we had witnessed were mirages, or specifically, Arctic mirages also called *Fata Morgana*. Mirages are formed above land or water when there is a large temperature gradient. Unlike the heat-related fuzzy mirages we have all seen on the highway, those that we experienced in the Arctic were crisp and clear. Throughout the time we spent there, the mountains changed shape daily. I witnessed wind- and water-eroded dessert rock formations, giant columns with enormous boulders perched on top. If watched long enough, the boulder slowly rose into the air and floated away before disappearing on the horizon. I've hesitated to relay this story over the years, but one day I saw military tanks and battleships as plain as day right there on the horizon. My dad saw them too but suggested people would think we were crazy if we told them. John Harvey, a man of sound mind, boldly told of seeing the Toronto skyline on one occasion while working in the area.

We did enjoy the solitude and Arctic wonder, and, of course, the food, but having a stranger present put a damper on my parents' attempted reconciliations. It didn't help that in a veiled excuse to use up the abundance of fruit before it spoiled, my dad and his friend made a garbage can of wine. Yes, thirty gallons. It became quickly apparent that the friend was a raging alcoholic and an obnoxious buffoon while intoxicated, which turned out to be all the time. I'm so glad I got to see that country, especially in the winter, but unfortunately my happy memories are dampened by the constant arguing.

After his Dempster Highway work was completed, my dad got a job in Inuvik, NWT. You guessed it, running a hotel and bar.

Inuvik sits on the high banks of the Mackenzie River approximately a hundred miles (160km) from the Arctic Ocean. Settled in 1954, and becoming a town in 1970, it was founded as a replacement

Polar bear hide drying on rack in front of a home in Tuktoyaktuk, Northwest Territories, 1974.

administrative center for the nearby town of Aklavik that was prone to flooding and had insufficient land for expansion. First called New Aklavik, the name was quickly changed to Inuvik.

By now the "D" word was floating in the air. My mom and I had moved to The Pillman House and my dad's absences were longer and longer and there literally wasn't room for him in our tiny home. By design possibly, I'll never know. When he did come home, they argued incessantly. As The Pillman House was so small and I had a louvered door on my room, I remember listening to the yelling for hours at night and often silently crying myself to sleep. I vividly remember waiting for my dad to come home at least twice. He called and said he was coming, but he never showed up. For days, I would run to the window whenever a car drove by, hoping it was him. Sometimes it would be a month before he called again to offer an embarrassed apology. I was too young to understand my dad was a functional alcoholic and that it contributed to his behavior. As an adult, recollecting particular interactions we had throughout my childhood, it explained a lot. He was never violent and was liked and respected by most people he met. He was incredibly smart and the most capable man I have ever known, but the booze made for poor decision-making at times.

I'm standing in the doorway of Tuktoyuktuk's community deep freeze dug into the side of a pingo, 1974. Pingos are formed when underground pressure pushes up the permafrost. They can rise to heights of two hundred fifty feet (76m). The area around Tuktoyuktuk has the largest concentration in the world.

The last time I let him disappoint me was my eleventh birthday. He was supposed to pick me up in Atlin and take me to Whitehorse for the weekend. He called on a Thursday night; he said he was flying from Inuvik to Whitehorse the next day, renting a car and coming to get me. He should have been there in the early afternoon. By midnight, it was painfully obvious he wasn't coming. He didn't call that time but a month later I got a letter. I don't remember the excuse but the truth he admitted to me twenty years later was that he started drinking on the plane and got so drunk they wouldn't rent him a car so he kept drinking. He took the Monday flight back to Inuvik. I've never cared for my birthday much since and prefer it pass quietly.

My parents made one last try when I was nine. Mom and I joined my dad in Inuvik for the winter. Who knew an isolated, mostly dark, extremely cold, treeless, mountain-less Arctic wasteland might not be conducive to rekindling a shattered marriage? It's not like they hadn't tried that before or anything.

On the other hand, Inuvik was a much larger town and it allowed me to experience things I never would have in Atlin. Like

The Aklavik Road sign in the ice on the Mackenzie River, Northwest Territories, 1974. The sign had to be replaced yearly as the melting river carried it away every spring. In 2017, the land road was completed connecting Inuvik and Tuktoyuktuk.

a schizophrenic squirrel, I wanted to try everything, so in the few months we were there, I joined boxing, karate and hockey. I wasn't very good at any of them, but it sure kept me busy and warded off the loneliness of being the new kid in a new town.

I also took up cross-country skiing in earnest. There was a professional course with long, sweeping, downhill runs and it was lighted at night—a good thing, as it was always night. The experience of swishing across the Arctic tundra at thirty below with a huge moon on the horizon is unforgettable. On one such evening while gliding along the course, a number of caribou burst out of the

Oil rig supply ship frozen in the river near Inuvik, Northwest Territories, 1974. Most of the river craft in the Mackenzie River Delta have relatively flat hulls so they can navigate the often-shallow waterways. In the winter, they are left in a shallow, calm area and allowed to freeze in place. No damage occurs and it is less expensive than hauling out.

The Mackenzie River Ice Road is actually the frozen river surface, Northwest Territories, 1974.

brush and crossed my track not far in front of me. They were closely followed by a pack of Arctic wolves. I struggled to stop before I ended up in the middle of a caribou/wolf fight. Within seconds, the whole lot disappeared into a brushy ravine and none of them seemed to have noticed the gape-mouth human trying his hardest to be insignificant.

I'm not sure who won that night, but it was for certain the wolves were hungry to be taking on healthy adult caribou. That winter a number of dogs were taken from their yards around town and people began keeping their big huskies and Malamutes inside because of it.

Although there was a prolific amount of arguing and screaming on the week nights, we tried to do things as a family on the weekends, often going for day drives on the frozen Mackenzie River.

We drove north to Tuktoyuktuk, on the shore of the Arctic Ocean where, among other things, we visited the famous pingo deep freeze. Pingos in essence are mammoth frost heaves. The permafrost rises up into a small mountain, some as high as two hundred feet (61m). The people of Tuk as the locals refer to it, decided to burrow into a pingo and make a curling rink. They accomplished the task but quickly found even a single light bulb caused melting that left stalactites and stalagmites. Not ideal for a smooth ice surface. As Northerners are known to do, they quickly pivoted and reopened it as the first community deep freeze. What we encountered was like something from Sandro Botticelli's depictions of Dante's Inferno. Upon entering, one is immediately and successively assaulted by visions of copious animal carcasses in various stages of dismemberment. The floor was red with blood and, even in those temperatures, the smell alone could kill. How anyone knew who belonged to which eviscerated seal or caribou carcass, we never knew.

We visited Aklavik, the home of the grave of The Mad Trapper of the Rat River. We drove south on the Dempster Highway to Fort McPherson on the Peel River, the starting point of the tragic Lost Patrol. A mail patrol led by the Northwest Mounted Police headed toward Dawson City in 1911. All four men died of starvation and exposure. Our family friend, Dick North, had recently written the book *The Mad Trapper of Rat River* and only a few years later would write *The Lost Patrol*.

The ice road was wide and smooth and didn't seem to have a speed limit. As you near the Arctic Ocean and along its shore, the road

The Sir Alexander Mackenzie School was named after the great explorer. This building housed every grade and was one of only two high schools in the entire Northwest Territories at the time, 1974.

is plowed multiple lanes wide because of drifting. If it was plowed eight lanes wide and it was windy, you were fortunate enough to be left with one passable lane down the middle. While visiting my dad one Christmas, we drove to Tuk for the day. A blizzard set in and it looked like we would have to spend the night. It was an issue as Tuk did not have accommodations in those days. Dad noticed a man fueling up a grader. Turns out he was plowing the road to Inuvik and said we would be fine if we followed closely. We surmised this to be a common practice as there were five trucks in our caravan. For roughly forty miles (72km) along the coast and further inland, we traveled around fifteen miles (24km) an hour within a couple of yards from each other so we could follow the taillights.

Sometime in January, the sun makes its first appearance of the year, having been a no show since the end of October. No matter what day or what you were doing you made sure not to miss the first sunrise of the year. Like many, we drove south along the Dempster roughly forty miles. The Mackenzie River Delta is flat so finding a land mass of prominence is rare. But there is one slightly elevated wide spot and in those days it became a *mecca* for the vitamin D starved and slightly cabin-fevered residents of Inuvik. A Northern version of tailgating at twenty below (-29°C) ensues. Although I was too young to participate, many libations were consumed by the many attendees. After much anticipation and fanfare, the guest of honor made a grand yet brief entrance: basically a bright pinprick of light flashed on the horizon for a second around 1:30 in the afternoon, then disappeared. Armed with the knowledge that every day after, it would last longer, it is often enough to repair a person's state of mind and help get them through the rest of the winter.

We had running water, and hot running water to boot. I could take a bath for as long as I wanted. When the water got cool, I just added more hot; it was wonderful. There was a real toilet that flushed: wow, paradise realized.

I had TV for the first time in my life; one channel, CBC North. CBC had a mandate to provide a certain amount of French language content even out west, and CBC North also provided a fair amount of Inuit language content. That combination and CBC's penchant for showing fascinating sporting events such as equestrian jumping, the biathlon, water polo, or soccer for an entire weekend left little to be desired. But *Happy Days, All in the Family, Barney Miller* and *Mash* helped make up for the other. They were all good Canadian shows, ha, ha. Well, the *King of Kensington* was boring, what can I say; but I loved *The Beachcombers*.

The school in Inuvik was immense and housed all the students K to Grade 12. I was overwhelmed by the number of students and the size of the building. At that time, Yellowknife had the only other high school in the whole territory. There were kids from as far away as Frobisher Bay (now known as Iqaluit in the recently formed territory of Nunavut), some 1,800 miles (2890km) east and across the entire country.

I was definitely a minority, as I was often one of two or three white kids in a classroom of twenty-five. I was constantly harassed and beat up at recess and after school. I would often look up from where I was playing to find I was circled by local kids. At first, all I felt I could do was curl into a ball to fend off the kicks and punches. My saving grace was my thick winter wear. I quickly found locating the smallest and weakest in the pack, rushing them, punching them in the face, bowling them over and running as fast as I could toward a far-off teacher was a better strategy. This did make my after-school trip home quite a bit more perilous.

The kids from Frobisher Bay fared better but were not immune to the torment; they were Inuit but were not from Inuvik. It was easier to make friends with the out-of-town kids, as we were all in the same predicament. I stop myself here as the comparison is weak. Those kids were away from their family for the greater part of each year, only returning home in the summer and over the Christmas break if they were lucky and their family could afford it. Can you imagine being separated from your family from the early age of nine or ten? It breaks my heart to think about it. It was a failed policy and the ramifications linger today. I will never forget my friends Albert and Leemon from Frobisher Bay. Together we got in all kinds of mischief, especially in Inuit language class.

Inuit class was taught by Mrs. Moses, a grandmotherly figure who treated us all like we were part of her family. A typical class started off with snacks, usually bannock she made the night before, but sometimes peanut butter and jam on pilot bread. Like most grandmas, Mrs. Moses thought it important to feed us. Thinking back, I'm sure she was aware some of the kids didn't receive breakfast at home. Her pockets were filled with hard candy and she handed it out liberally as rewards for correct answers or proper pronunciation.

After snacks, we began the lesson of the day. Mrs. Moses attempted to teach us a few Inuit words every day, but she easily slipped into telling stories of her life instead. These stories were fascinating to all of us and we listened in rapt attention. The latter part of the class was devoted to Inuit games. We learned the knuckle hop, the ear pull, one-foot-high kick, the knee jump, the two-foot-high kick and the airplane to name a few. I have to admit I didn't retain much of the language, but I got a crash course in Inuit culture that continues to intrigue me to this day.

We were given Flintstone vitamins every day, and it was a reward to be chosen to go to the office, retrieve the daily amount for the class and hand them out to each student. Sometime during that winter, a dentist set up shop in one of the unused classrooms and every student was given a checkup and any needed work was performed right there, no charge. I got my teeth cleaned and had two fillings done. I think it may have been a student dentist as both fillings later fell out.

My regular teacher, Mr. Murphy, was an imposing beast of a man. He sported an unruly mane of hair and a long, bushy beard.

He wore Santa glasses perched on the end of his perpetually red nose. He always wore a pair of elaborate polar bear fur and leather mukluks with beautiful beading and tassels. His style of teaching was boisterous, to say the least. I remember once Albert asked him the difference between ferocious and furious. Mr. Murphy rose from his desk with a mean scowl plastered across his prickly face. He ominously stalked up to Albert's desk. Albert visibly shrank in his seat, the rest of us stared in hesitant silence. Suddenly Mr. Murphy jumped in the air and landed on top of Albert's desk. He bellowed down at Albert, "This is ferocious." Then he reached down, grabbed Albert by the shirt with both hands, pulled him out of his seat up to eye level, shook him vigorously, and yelled a string of nonsense words in his face before dropping him back in his seat, calmly saying, "That was furious, any more questions, Son?" Without waiting for an answer, he hopped off the desk, ruffled Albert's hair and stated, "Good question, anybody else?" No one moved. We were pretty sure he was crazy and/or drunk, but every last one of his students loved him. Even Steven loved him, and on more than one occasion Mr. Murphy folded him in half, stuffed him in the garbage can, then encouraged the rest of us to throw crumpled-up balls of paper at him. Steven was pretty annoying. Thinking back, I know Mr. Murphy was neither drunk nor crazy but he was a great teacher and I'll forever appreciate the kindness he showed me at a time when I really needed it.

Having TV, I was exposed to the National Hockey League for the first time in a big way. Every kid in school seemed to be fanatical about hockey and they all wanted to be Bobby Orr, Guy Lafleur or Phil Esposito. My favorite was Darrel Sittler of the Toronto Maple Leafs. Having no hometown bias, I think I was first drawn to the uniforms, then the player. It didn't hurt that Hockey Night in Canada always seemed to feature the Canadians or the Maple Leafs.

If you weren't on an organized team, and even if you were, there were always pickup games and road hockey games played in boots, a constant on most residential streets. Kids in Inuvik had equipment and nets, even for road hockey. When a car came, we quickly moved the nets and let it pass. On the ponds around Atlin, some kids didn't even have skates; we shared sticks and used boots for goal posts.

Hockey-card collecting and trading was popular and most recesses you could find a number of trading circles. Kids, mostly boys, all huddled together on their knees comparing and swapping cards. No matter the temperature, the trading was fierce. The thing to do with duplicates or cards you didn't want was to take your bundle, alert the other kids, then throw the whole lot up in the air. A mad scramble and dog pile ensued while everyone fought over the cards. The freezing cold weather prevented the snow from damaging the card. After I moved back to Atlin, I never collected another card and eventually gave them all away to a nice young friend of the family. As it would be another three years before my mom and I had TV again, my love of the National Hockey League waned for a period.

Lesson learned, Mom and I moved back to Atlin that spring and Dad stayed in Inuvik, where he went on to renovate and run yet another hotel and bar. Finally, after leaving the hotel business forever, he became a highly successful contractor to the oil companies throughout the Northwest Territories and even dabbled in home building in the American Virgin Islands for a time. Oh, and I'm pretty sure he was briefly anointed king of Inuvik right before the oil crash of the early 1980s, which sent him into another bankruptcy.

As we were unable to sustain our huge dog population at the new, much-smaller residence, my dad took a few of the dogs to Inuvik. Some were sold and others given to good homes, but we kept five and still had at least one litter of puppies a year. Five large Malamutes in a space of three hundred square feet (28m^3) was, let's say, cozy and hairy.

For a few years after my parents divorced, I did spend part of my Christmas break and a couple weeks every summer in Inuvik with my dad. When I was eleven, he took me on a trip to Kentucky to see my grandma and then on to Washington, DC, Orlando, Florida, and the American Virgin Islands. I worked for him in the summer in Tuktoyaktuk when I was fourteen and fifteen, but after that I didn't see him again and eventually lost track of him for fifteen years.

Part II — Atlin Kids

The view from the Courthouse tower in 1967. An abandoned car sits in front of a derelict service garage in the foreground. The shuttered Sands Store and the Moose Hall, mid-ground, with the closed Saint Andrew's Hospital in the background. Sands Store would soon reopen as The Atlin General Store and Saint Andrew's would become the Atlin Base for the Foundation of Environmental Research, commonly referred to as the Glacier Institute.

Chapter Nine

Kids Being Kids

Average Kid Atlin Variety
Atlin News Miner 1972
Diane S. Smith

Here he comes down the middle of Second Avenue munching a chocolate bar just purchased at Mr. Craft's little candy and tobacco counter. He wears faded jeans with one ripped knee and a denim jacket with sleeves too short. He hazards a kick at a rock even though his toe sticks out of a hole in his runner. He has an Atlin home haircut easily identified by the rick rack edge at the back and moulting-chicken affect over each ear, the end result of a shearing by Mom who has yet to master the art of barbering. In his pocket, along with a tangled rabbit snare, are two very gray lumps of sugar, necessary supplies in case he should meet a friendly horse with a sweet tooth. Behind follows a large dog of dubious origin traveling a zig zag course that takes him to all the best-smelling places.

This is the Average Atlin Kid and company going about a day's business. Because females of all ages are outnumbered

I'm wearing my Bulldog runners in front the Atlin General Store on First Street, 1969. Our friend's car sported the one and only Atlin license plate.

in Atlin just as in the early days, Atlin's average kid is a boy. He is about nine years old. His way of life differs considerably from that of his counterparts in the southern reaches of British Columbia and beyond. There are a multitude of things he doesn't know about the modern world outside, but he has a special background of knowledge and experience perhaps more boys his age should have.

For an Average Atlin kid, a big city is Whitehorse, Yukon. Beyond his scope are places like Vancouver and Toronto. A shopping trip to Whitehorse may mean snatching a few minutes of TV while mom shops for a new blouse. A rare treat is an overnight trip to town and a whole evening of television in a motel with a real modern bathroom and endless gallons of hot running water in which to shower or have a bath.

He won't be able to tell you much about TV and won't be able to discuss the latest hair- and eyebrow-raising movies. But he could tell you a host of things that concern him more as a boy whose life is closely related to all things outdoors. He could take you along a snowy winter trail and identify each animal track that crossed your path. He could show you how to build a cubby for a lynx set. He could tell you each hide in a Hudson's Bay fur room. He could probably tell you whether or not it was prime. He could identify most mineral-bearing ore samples from around Atlin because he was a pretty good amateur geologist. He could show you how to pan for gold and how to operate a rocker box.

I'm sitting in a handmade chair at an abandoned miner's cabin, 1970.

The Average Atlin Kid has never seen a snake or skunk but he has watched a band of caribou cross the frozen lake in front of town. He has seen moose by the dozens along the roads he travels and has watched a skittish lynx sprint across the trail in front of the dog team. He has never heard the exciting music and raucous barking of a circus or carnival and he couldn't identify the sounds of a busy city street. But he has listened to the ice when pressure cracks form and he knows the faraway howl of a wolf.

Fresh watermelon, strawberries or cherries are infrequent treats for Atlin's Average Kid. Things like artichokes, avocados and eggplant are unknowns. But he suffers not at all from their absence in his diet. He is a sturdy, robust specimen whose winter diet centers on lean, delicious moose and caribou with grouse and lake trout for variety. His mother bakes the family bread and the mouth-watering aroma of fresh buns and cinnamon rolls often greets him at the end of the school day. He helps pick wild raspberries for shortcakes and jams and moss berries for pies and cobblers. There are black currant berries for burgundy-wine flavored jelly. Saskatoon berries, rose hips, wild cranberries and goose berries are made into syrups, sauces and ketchups to whet the appetite of any growing boy.

His life is simple, uncluttered with pressure and problems. He doesn't lack for excitement. It comes in unexpected forms: a forest fire close to town, a moose hunt with Dad, a surprise ride in a bush plane or helicopter. The confidence with which he goes about the tasks of trapping, handling a horse or chopping wood for the kitchen stove often belies his age. He is happy and outgoing, at ease with adults. He is normally full of fun and pranks but causes no serious troubles around town. He is at home in this corner of the Northern wilderness and is missing very little that is important to a well-rounded existence.

———

Mike's Channel

For kids growing up in Atlin in the 1970s, it was a time when our biggest decision might be whether to go swimming at Mike's Channel, or fishing for grayling at Pine Creek, or maybe play Cowboys and Indians, or armies, or simply "guns" as we called it at the Black Rocks out by the dump.

We didn't know who Mike was and it never crossed our mind, but on a sunny day in the middle of summer when the water was warm, Mike's Channel belonged to us. It was our amusement park, water world and adventure land all in one. If you could actually swim, and many of us couldn't, the challenge was to make it out to the old boiler in the middle of the channel, a hulking relic from a ship long since burned to the water line. It was covered with sharp, rusty edges and hidden dangers. If we cut ourselves, we washed it off, stuck a leaf on it and went on with our day. If swimming wasn't in your repertoire, you found a good-size log or an old board and you paddled where you wanted to go. Or you just hung on and kicked.

A small island sits in front of Mike's Channel protecting it from storms. In the fall when the water level is low and the channel shrinks, the separation between the island and the shore is greatly reduced. It is possible to wade out a long way to reach a very deep, but narrow underwater trench. I can remember this being the site of my first swimming lesson/near drowning. After wading to the edge of the abyss and with assurances from my good buddies, Lance Shaw and Randy Green, somehow I convinced myself this was a great place to begin my aquatic training. Lance swam across first, and with Randy behind, I set off using the tried-and-true dog paddle technique.

Somewhere along the way I was sure I had reached the shallow part on the other side, so I stopped paddling and stretched my foot down in search of terra firma. Apparently, I hadn't made as much progress as I thought and immediately sank like a bag of bricks. I only saw the first few seconds of my life flash by when I felt a sharp tug on my scalp. Lance grabbed a fistful of my hair and pulled me from the murky depths, laughing and displaying me like a prize lake trout. I was terrified for the return trip, so we built a raft. It was many years later that I eventually learned how to swim.

A year previously, my mom decided it would be easier for all involved (her) that I should receive a buzz cut for my spring haircut. Lucky for me, I hated it and made such a stink that I was forever after allowed any length I desired—as it turned out, it was a lifesaving choice.

Speaking of hair, the buzz cut was pretty much the norm for most of the boys in town, at least when we were very young. Not because we were a military base or were experiencing outbreaks of lice, but more so because our mothers cut our hair and what's easier than a buzz cut? Hair played a big part with my first girlfriend. When I was five, the Harvey family moved in across the street. They had two kids, Suzanne and Chrissy. Suzanne was much older but Chrissy was my age. Chrissy was cute, had big eyelashes and long luxurious hair. I was immediately smitten. Chrissy and I played together every day. Chrissy was the perfect girl; she loved playing Armies, climbing trees and throwing rocks, and was a good fishing companion. My first relationship met a horrible demise when it was gently conveyed to me that Chrissy was a boy with long hair and he was actually Chris. To my defense, I had never met a boy with long hair or one named Chris, and especially not one called Chrissy; and oh, those eyelashes.

Getting to some of our favorite places was half the fun. Mike's Channel, for instance, could be reached on a nice convenient trail, but that's no fun compared to the death-defying romp we preferred. Between us and our favorite swimming hole stood an intimidating rock outcropping. On the inland side, it rose up out of the willows, a steep, boulder-strewn, moss-covered, slippery colossus unfit for Himalayan pygmy goats (they're a thing, look it up). On the water side, the surface was smooth and worn by wind and water, blemished only by narrow ledges and even narrower cracks. The trail I mentioned skirted around the colossus, but of course we chose the shortcut (twice as far).

As we came to the rock wall, a few footholds and handholds were obvious. Climbing up ten feet (3m) or so we arrived at a narrow, ascending ledge. We could shimmy along the ledge, navigating our

With Dad on the dock at Atlin Lake, 1969. First Island and Tabletop Mountain in the background.

way to the front side of the outcropping, rising higher and higher as we climbed. Everything below the ledge was water so we were relatively safe, unless we couldn't swim (me). At least a couple of us fell (probably on purpose), and at least one pair of glasses hit the drink. Luckily no drowning, and I believe Lance Shaw recovered his glasses with some fine cliff diving.

Below the summit, we reached a smooth, concaved section that held little traction, so speed and inertia were the only things that adhered us to the face. If you weren't fast enough, you could easily slide down the long rock face and end up in the lake with the bottom ripped out of your jeans and a sore ass, not to mention the whole drowning thing. After that last dangerous obstacle, it was a quick, safe hike to the top.

On the very apex of the hill, perched precariously, sits an enormous boulder the size of a house. There is just enough space under the boulder for a couple kids to squeeze in, thus offering shelter from the elements or, at the least, providing a cool hidey-hole to hang out in while contemplating being crushed by a two-ton rock. On the far side of the outcropping closest to the channel, there are a number of descending routes on a scale from easy to "you should have brought a rope, Dummy."

Fishing

On another day, we might ride out to the Pine Creek Bridge on the Warm Bay Road, stash our bikes in the brush and run up the trail along the high bank. If we went all the way to the big rock and the small waterfall, we only needed a willow stick, ten feet (3m) of fishing line and a black fly to haul in as many grayling as we could carry. The pool was deep, the water clear, and we could see thousands of fish milling below our feet, waiting to attempt the leap up the falls. Because the footing was precarious, we clung to the rocks with one hand and fished with the other. The fact that falling in probably wasn't survivable didn't seem to matter. That was where the fish were, so that's where we went, of course. Most of us had fishing licenses, but we all feigned ignorance as to limits and quotas and no one seemed to care too much. If your string was full and you had no way of carrying more fish, then any available pocket worked just fine. We all had dogs to feed and they appreciated grayling stew as much as anyone.

I remember one day, after a fruitful harvest from our favorite hole, a bunch of us were mounting our bikes, preparing for the ride home. Each of us had a string of grayling slung over our shoulder. Who should pull up beside us but the Fish and Wildlife Officer Jamie Stephen? He rolled down his window and asked us how the fishing was.

"Great," we all answered in unison.

I'm ready for a ride down the lake with my dad and Jack McKenzie, 1969.

"Did you get your limit?" he asked.

"We sure did," we replied.

"Did you get over your limit?" was his next query.

"No, Sir," we chanted, having no idea what the limit was. Looking at me, he asked to see my string. I proudly but intrepidly displayed my bounty.

He took a quick glance and muttered, "That's about right, but if you had even one more you might be in violation. Are you sure you don't have any more fish stashed away anywhere, Mr. Smith?"

I quickly replied, holding up my string even higher, "No, Sir, this is everything."

He leaned farther out his window, looking me straight in the eye and asked, "Are you absolutely positive?"

"Yes, Sir, I am." I remember him rolling his eyes, grunting something about Atlin kids and driving off in a cloud of dust. It was shortly after I felt a great pain in my arm where Randy Green had just given me a lamer (what we called it when you punched someone in the arm muscle). He pointed out the three fish hanging out of my jean jacket front pocket and more slimy tails poking out of every pants pocket. So, I wasn't good under interrogation at the age of eight.

In later years, the gold miners got all the blame for the declining grayling stock in lower Pine Creek, but I can't help thinking we may have contributed. Nothing was wasted, though. If we didn't eat them all, they went to family and neighbors and finally to the dogs. Quite often, dogs helped sustain our Northern existence and our family's well-being, so all was fair. Grayling were what we fished the most as they were easily accessible to us. The lake trout resided deeper, and a boat or fishing through the ice in winter was necessary to catch them. Pike were available in North and South Lakes, but it was a six-mile (9.6km) ride and a long walk into the lakes, and the large spoons needed were expensive and easy to lose in the many snags. I have to say, those lakes harbored some gargantuan ancient beasts, though. With no predators other than the occasional human, those pike reached epic proportions.

One day when I was eleven or twelve, a few of us were hiking up out of North Lake toward the road. We each had at least two large pike. I remember them touching and even dragging on the ground when slung over a shoulder (not a fish story). We were being our usual noisy selves when, approaching a sharp bend in the trail, we heard a loud grunt or woofing sound. Instantly recognizing it as a bear, we stood still and pondered our next move.

Grizzlies were rare in the area but they were present, although most encounters were with black bears. We stood and listened for a period of time before cautiously making our way to the corner in the trail. Arriving at the apex and slowly peering around, there was no bear in sight, but strewn across the path was the pungent debris of a rotten stump. Bears eat worms and grubs found in old logs, and we had interrupted someone's appetizers. Believing it to be a black bear, tensions subsided. Still not completely certain it wasn't a grizzly and not wanting to become the main course, we decided to leave an offering of fresh pike. Like bacon-wrapped scallops, we were presenting ourselves as a pike-wrapped morsel of tender goodness that any bear might find hard to refuse. Like hunters do in brushy Southeast Alaska with deer, it may be better to drag your prey rather than have them on your body.

As we only used the pike for dog food purposes (sorry Minnesotans), it wasn't a big deal to share our harvest with a hungry bear. I look at the fish hierarchy like this: to me, lake trout is the lobster, grayling the shrimp, and pike the poop you scrape out of the other two. Sorry, one man's opinion.

I went to North Lake for a day of ice fishing with my mom and our friend, Otto Finney. We knew the lake was well frozen, but it hadn't snowed yet so I took my ice skates. Mom and Otto did most of the fishing while I spent the day skating and trying to herd the fish toward them. The lake is fairly shallow and it's easy to see to the bottom. It was also easy to see the fish. The fish ran from me, whether it was my shadow or the sound or the vibration, I don't know, but whenever I spotted one, it took off in a zig-zag run in an effort to escape. I got to building up speed then gliding after the fish in an attempt to direct them toward the hooks. I have no idea if it worked, but I had a great time tormenting the fish, and Mom and Otto did pretty well.

I have to say, skating on a clear lake can be exhilarating and terrifying at the same time. In the very deep, everything under you is dark, no definition, no reference, and it's not scary. As you get where you can see the bottom, it causes a sense of vertigo. In places where it was twenty- or thirty-feet (6 to 9m) deep, I could see the bottom clearly. Not many of us will walk across a pane of glass four stories above the ground, but it caused the same sensation.

Daniel Connolly and his dad Tom included me on an ice fishing trip to Surprise Lake. We drilled our holes near the mouth of Otter Creek. There might have been four or five of us, all with our own hole. As usual, we brought dogs. After a while, we took notice that one of the male dogs was acting erratically. He rushed from one person to the next, sniffing everything as he went, and frantically raced in circles. We were trying to figure out his strange behavior when someone caught a fish and our attention was diverted. As I watched the fish come out of the hole, I felt something hitting the back of my parka, like someone was tossing handfuls of small pebbles at me. I immediately turned around to investigate, only to be sprayed in the chest and face by a stream of hot dog pee.

As male dogs, and as huskies in particular are wont to do, they love peeing on objects. Snowbanks, bushes, stumps, logs, sign posts, and buildings are all convenient targets. Apparently, in his urgent need to urinate and not finding any of the before-mentioned items, that dog chose me. I frantically wiped off my face and washed it with snow, but the rest quickly froze to my parka. I was not happy to be the butt of the best fish tale of the season, but everyone else thoroughly enjoyed themselves. I also didn't believe it when I was told dog urine was good for the skin. I got even, a little, as on the way home in the truck, the pee ice on my parka melted and stunk up the whole cab. Not sure if that's a win, but I took it as such.

As often as we could, we got rides to Surprise Lake or O'Donnell Lakes for more grayling fishing. I was lucky enough to get to tag along with my friends Craig and Denise Colwell and their mom Ev on many outings to O'Donnell Lakes. While Surprise Lake and Pine Creek could be muddied from gold mining activity, it was rare that O'Donnell Lakes were. With small spoons or a bobber and fly, the fishing was always excellent. All the lakes were great for ice fishing and allowed one to get deeper and go after the lake trout.

The gun club supported a boat trip to Scotia Bay where we fished the Atlintoo River. The grayling in the Atlintoo are three times the size of the grayling in the Atlin area. The few times I got the chance to fish the Atlintoo was a treat, and fighting the bigger grayling on our small rigs was a challenge and a lot of fun.

*Standing on the old dock at Scotia Bay across the lake from Atlin, 1969.
Scotia Bay was the terminus of what was called the Taku Tram, a narrow-
gauge railroad extended only 2¼ miles (3.6kl) between Taku Arm and Atlin
Lake. Pulled by the little train engine that could, the Dutchess passengers
were charged two dollars one way and they had to sit on their luggage. It was
the most expensive rail fare per mile in the world at that time.*

Daniel and Linda's dad, Tom Connolly, prospector, trapper, big-game
guide and long-time wilderness expert, often included stray kids on
his bush outings. I remember puttering along trolling for trout in
their freighter canoe. It was on one of those trips that he showed me
the ancient Tlingit hieroglyphs on the cliffs beside the lake.

Once, we were coming home in his big lake cruiser after a
successful trout-fishing trip to Second Narrows. The waves were so
high I was sure we would swamp and be sent to the depths of the
lake. I was scared, seasick and panicky, but I looked over at Tom and
he had a huge grin on his face as he steered that big boat through
the storm. He radiated confidence and instilled it in others. Soon I

was enjoying our grand adventure. It was as if he was shaking his fist at Mother Nature and saying, "Come on, is that all you've got?"

Because my dad was mostly away and my mom was very busy, I will forever be grateful for Tom; he couldn't help but impart his vast wilderness knowledge. If you were lucky enough to spend time with him, you were a better, smarter person for it.

It was people like Tom and Ev and others that saw a need and filled it without asking. They just did it because it was the right thing to do. I, for one, greatly benefited.

The Black Rocks

Another source of grand adventure and a frequent summer destination lay hidden just off the road and only a quick romp through the trees. Voila, spread out before us was a massive jumble of exposed bedrock protruding from the swampy terrain. It was like a mural from a southwest desert landscape, and we were instantly transported back in time. Right there in front of our eyes was a mystical landscape only seen in John Wayne and Clint Eastwood movies: the "Black Rocks." If you looked hard you could see the campfire smoke from an outlaw's hideaway or a rustler's cabin. You could hear the clopping of horses' hooves echoing through the ravines or the distant gunfire of a cavalry charge. We were at once cowboys and gunslingers, Apache warriors, Mexican bandits and stagecoach robbers. With wooden guns and wild-berry war paint, we galloped and scurried over the rocks and through the mini-canyons yelling, "Vamonos, muchachos," and, "Arriba, ¡Ándele!" We had no idea what any of that meant but we heard it in the movies and it sounded cool to us. We hid in small caves, wedged ourselves into cracks and crevices, leaping out to ambush our friends, screaming, "Bam, bam, bang, bang," and, "You're dead!" "No, I'm not, you missed!" At this point we might throw a rock and proudly proclaim, "Didn't miss that time." Ouch!

The Black Rocks held a magical allure for many of us. Maybe the fact that it was so close to the road but completely screened from anyone passing, or that the landscape was like none other in our realm. A couple rocky overhangs or small caves provided shelter when it rained and were a great place to cook our lunch. We gathered dried wood and lit small fires at the mouth of our hideout.

Often we only brought a can of pork and beans because that's what our heroes ate. We opened it up with a jackknife and set it in the coals to heat. Once it was ready, we shared it around using crudely carved sticks as spoons. On better-planned outings someone might bring Kraft Dinner (Mac and Cheese to the Americans), someone else brought a pot, and with a little water from the swamp, we were set to dine in high style. With our improvised utensils, we squatted around our fire, munched our beans or Kraft Dinner, and contemplated our surroundings, each of us mulling over a different Western scenario. It wasn't hard to imagine The Duke or The Kid or the masked man himself moseying around the corner, reigns in one hand, a six shooter in the other.

We loved to play "Guns," as we called it. Many a summer day found us, a gang of rowdy boys, running through Pete and John's horse corrals and grazing area, bandanas over our mouths, shooting at each other with our finger guns. The campground and hills behind it, the Black Rocks, and the Red Bluffs all provided backdrops for our imaginary battles. It didn't really matter where we were, there was never a reason not to play Guns.

We quickly divided into teams, good guys and bad guys, and we armed ourselves with gun-shaped sticks. I was always confused about what made one team good or bad—it's not like we had white or black hats. Anyway, when we were ready, one team ran off into the woods or rocks to lay in ambush or defend an imaginary fort or bunker. The other team waited an agreed-upon amount of time, usually decided by the oldest or toughest, and then we gave chase.

If you were the first team, you ran as fast as you could to a hastily decided, defensible rocky area, or a jumble of fallen trees and stumps. Once a site was chosen, it was rapidly camouflaged with brush, rocks or whatever we could find. Clumps of dry dirt, sticks and even horse poop were carefully arranged for easy access for ammunition. These were our hand grenades or sticks of dynamite, depending whether it was the Old West or WWII. Of course, with one of these you did not pull the imaginary pin with your teeth. The hiding team knew the searching team would never wait the predetermined time before giving chase, so preparations were done quickly and crudely, and then the wait began. Stick gun in hand, huddled silently behind a rock, listening to any strange noises in the forest, the first team lay abuzz with anticipation and ready for battle.

The searching team had to be cautious and stealthy as they combed the dung-strewn warren of trails that crisscrossed John and Pete's property or the swampy, brushy area behind the campground. The searching team's objective was to find the others' hideout undetected, then reverse ambush them. Just as one's full ninja mode was fine-tuned and you were sure no one else was anywhere near you, Randy Green might drop out of a tree on your head yelling, "Bam, bam, you're dead," or if he, too, was in stealth mode, he might just fake stab you with a fake stick knife and in a hushed tone declare your demise. Once pronounced dead, only when it was completely irrefutable, you were to lie where you dropped until the battle was over. It was always amazing how many horse-turd grenades a dead man could throw.

During any ambush or reverse ambush, determining who successfully ambushed who was always decided by the team that argued the loudest or could physically intimidate the other. Nevertheless, whoever won or lost was soon forgotten in the excitement of rehashing the most recent battle. I'm pretty sure we all won every time, at least in our minds, although it was hard to deny your fake demise when Randy Green fake knifed you in the throat.

The Dump

Every trip to the Black Rocks required a stop at the dump. We never knew what great treasures we might find just lying there. Most people were considerate enough to leave the good stuff at the top, but if you spied something you had to have, you waded in and got it. Of course, a big part of any dump visit was smashing bottles. We had fierce competitions to be the first to hit a particular bottle with a rock. Then there was the ever-popular "throw one bottle up in the air and try to hit it with another."

The dump was often on fire and stuff randomly blew up, and that was cool. If nothing was blowing up right then, we found some aerosol cans and threw them into the fire and ran away as they exploded behind us—and that was cool too. Glass shards, hepatitis and flying-can shrapnel be damned, we knew how to have fun. The dump was always a favorite place for black bears and even an occasional grizzly, but we figured, erroneously, we could hold our own and never gave them much thought.

With Daniel Connolly and Randy Green and our go-cart made from scrounged parts found at the dump and local junk piles, 1977.

The dump also acted as our flea market, rummage sale and Walmart. We often found items that we could re-purpose into other useful things or we found parts for existing items. An old bike tube became a slingshot or tensioner for a catapult. Discarded boards or nails were used in fort building. Rope, string, or chain could help in raft building, a piece of copper pipe might make an excellent blowgun and any wheels could be used for go-carts. By the way, we never saw hand sanitizer in our entire childhood, but we washed our hands in plenty of mud puddles and even drank from the clearer ones.

After the Black Rocks and the dump, we usually took the shortcut (twice as long) back to town. The trail from the dump led through the woods (giving the bears a better opportunity to surprise us), across the Alkali Flats, on to the old Corduroy Road and back to town. With our newfound treasure lashed to our bikes, we set off through the woods and down the trail. I might mention this was before mountain or trail bikes; our simple old bikes went pretty much anywhere we wanted to go and if they didn't, we pushed them or carried them. I remember constantly repairing tires.

Keith Carlick was taking the shortcut from the dump one day, peddling like mad down the trail. Rounding a particularly sharp corner at full speed, he rode straight into a mother black bear and two cubs. His bike went flying; the cubs scurried up one tree and Keith up another. As Keith told it, the momma bear bellowed and snorted and periodically reared up on her hind legs to shake the tree. Knowing full well that black bears are good climbers, he scrambled as far up as he could go, as did the two cubs, scant feet away, perched in their own tree. Luckily, Momma didn't climb up, and after much grunting and huffing, she called her cubs down and they disappeared into the brush. Needless to say, Keith stayed in the tree for a very long time, and when he did come down, he left a cloud of dust behind his bike all the way back to town.

Just beside the Surprise Lake Road on the edge of town is the sight of the old, old dump used in Atlin's early days. I'm not sure when they stopped using it. When I was a child, it was mostly covered with brush, saplings and weeds. The only indication it was a dump was the small seas of rusty cans between the outcroppings of brush. In the pine and spruce forests of the area, bottles and other heavy objects are quickly covered in needles and cones as well as moss and dirt. The cans float above these layers, remaining exposed until the weather completely rusts them away. The condition of the cans is an accurate indicator of the age of the dump.

During the 1960s and 70s, bottle digging and collecting was all the rage. Every shop in town sold old bottles and most households had a few or a lot of bottles displayed on shelves and on window sills. We often went on digging trips to the old dump. Most bottles were not worth much back then, but there were a few that brought in some good money. The kids that went digging got to be experts pretty quick. I remember as a seven- or eight-year-old, educating tourists in my mom's shop. They were amazed that I could tell a hand-blown bottle over one that came out of a mold, or that I knew from the shape whether it was a Worcestershire sauce bottle or lemon bitters. My best find was a gin bottle with embossed labeling from a well-known distillery in England.

Aside from bottles, we found all sorts of things we repurposed into toys and gizmos that kept us busy for days. I'm not sure how many moms of today would let their children dig in an old dump, let alone encourage it.

Water Sports

The water was shallow and warm when it was sunny and the beach was sandy—the only sand we knew of. It was the Riviera to us, as seen in an old James Bond movie. It was called "The Mouth of Pine" and it was where Pine Creek split up into many small channels and poured into the lake. The beach was littered with tiny, sharp sticks and twigs, but we went barefoot to feel the hot sand between our toes. We could get soaking wet with all our clothes on, lie on the beach, cover ourselves with sand and dry out in no time at all. The shallows were warm, but the rapidly flowing tributaries were glacier cold. Some were deep and swift, but we crossed them all, back and forth, many times just to see if we could. It was a challenge, and in our minds, we were Lewis and Clark exploring the West, or Greek partisans fighting the Nazis in the Zygos Mountain Range. We made human chains, and using sticks for stabilization, we slowly fought our way across, struggling to keep our footing as our feet became numb. We emerged on the other side triumphant in our mighty conquest, warmed our frozen feet in the sand and crossed back again.

The Mouth of Pine was awash in dry sticks, poles and logs of various sizes, all great for building lean-tos, forts, bonfires and rafts. Another favorite activity was pole vaulting. We selected long, sturdy poles that hopefully supported our weight, knocked off any branches, checked for cracks, then took a couple trial runs. When we deemed ourselves and our poles up for the challenge, we got a firm grip, ran pell-mell toward a previously selected raging torrent of glacial froth, planted our pole in the sand and flung our bodies toward the far bank. We got pretty good, and most of the time we made it. Our friends lined either bank in the hopes of grabbing us as we tumbled by in case planning and expertise should suddenly fail us. We always had a fire going, even on the hot days, in case someone had hot dogs or marshmallows, but more often it was to dry shoes before our moms found out we were in the water again.

My mom and I had a misunderstanding that went on for years. I would ask if I could go down to the lake or out to the Mouth of Pine or any number of other water-related destinations. She often answered yes but said, "Only wading, no swimming." I never quite understood this as she knew full well I could not swim. But rather than risk a delay or a change of mind, off I went.

In my mind, anything that wasn't swimming was fair play. For example: kicking behind a log back and forth in front of town, making our way around the docks hand over hand, or walking out on the lakebed carrying a large rock until only our eyeballs and nostrils were above water. We often enjoyed riding our bikes down the boat ramp as fast as we could to see how far we could get until we floated. Quite often upon returning home, I was stridently admonished for getting completely wet, and sometimes this angered my mother to the point of reintroducing me to my arch nemesis—The Wooden Spoon. I had no idea why I was allowed to wade but then punished for doing just that. To me, it made perfect sense that anything that wasn't swimming must be wading—there didn't seem to be any other terms that fit.

My mom and I played this complicated game of cat and mouse throughout my childhood. I was constantly calculating whether my clothes would dry on the bike ride back from somewhere or another or if I had time to dry out in the sun before dinner. If you're asking, "Why didn't I swim in my underwear or in nothing at all?" it's obvious you have never been swimming in the frigid waters of Northern Canada. Even on a hot summer day any layer of protection is desired. There were a few spots where cut-offs did suffice, but any swimming in Atlin Lake was usually for the foolish, the young, the inebriated or a combination of all of these.

It wasn't until I was an adult walking around Green Lake Park in Seattle, Washington, with my own kids that I finally figured out the misconception that plagued my childhood. I saw a wading pool, or at least the city version of a wading pool—an ankle-deep concrete box where kiddies run around and splash about like little birdies. Oh, how civilized and boring, in my point of view, but a giant light bulb went on in my mind; at last, the mystery was solved. Upon explaining this to my mom, she looked at me as if I was daft, obviously not believing a word of what I was saying.

I chalked it up to her urban exposure as a child versus my being reared in the bush and let it lie. My sons never had misconceptions about water or mud or anything wet and dirty. If it was there, it was meant to be played in. My sons and I never met a gravel pit, stream, lake or mud bog we didn't love. I'm positive there were times they

Suzie, the little biplane, built by local aviator Herman Peterson in his basement, 1968. Herman often put on stunt-flying exhibitions during Atlin community events.

jumped in only to not disappoint Dad. In my mother's defense, trying to keep up with an adolescent boy's laundry with no running water might just bring a person to anger.

Como Lake, just north of town, was another favorite swimming hole. It held its own unique set of pleasures and perils. Como is a small lake, only a couple miles (3km) in circumference and fairly shallow, so it warms up nicely on a sunny, summer day, especially near the shore.

The north end where we swam had a muddy bottom and was full of leeches, but in some ways these adversities made it better. Hey, it's fun to scare girls (okay, boys too) with a big, fat, juicy leech or squish your toes in the mud. If we skirted around the west shore to the bluff where the water was deeper, the rocks provided a natural diving or jumping platform, as most of us had no idea how to dive. There was a shelf four or five feet (1.5m) off the water. If you were really brave (not I), you could jump from the top, which was ten or more feet (3.25m). I remember jumping off that rock with absolutely no idea how to swim, as did many of my friends. We had confidence we could get back to the rock or that someone who could swim

A derelict fire truck sits beside the Atlin Inn with The Royal Hotel in the background, 1967. Both The Royal and Atlin Inn were torn down for salvage.

would save us, and they did at times. I'm feeling my first disclaimer might be warranted.

As usual, we always had a fire going to dry out by or to cook hot dogs. If we were lucky, someone might have a tire tube to float on or fight over. One single tire tube could provide endless hours of entertainment for many.

Biking

All the previously mentioned destinations were reached by bicycle or on foot. Three miles here, six (5km, 10km) there on bumpy, gravel roads or trails; we never thought twice about it, we just went. If your buddy didn't have a bike, you put him on the handlebars or the seat.

We were kids in the best place at the best time, a place where kids were allowed to be kids and not hampered by rules and schedules. If we did our chores and made it home in time for meals, we were pretty much left to our own devices. If we wanted to play baseball, we grabbed a ball and a bat and we played. We didn't have to reserve time at the field, get our mom to drive us or sign a waiver. We didn't have uniforms or cleats or protective gear. If you had a glove, great; if not, your hands stung. Big deal!

When we rode our bikes, we didn't have helmets—we didn't even know there was such a thing, or maybe there wasn't yet. Our bikes were simple, no gears or fancy hand brakes. If you wanted to go, you

I'm on my bike in front of The Royal Hotel, 1969. Later that year it was salvaged for its lumber. Built and owned by businessman Louis Schulz who also at one time or another owned a butcher shop, two hardware stores and a Chevrolet dealership in Atlin. I remember going into The Royal with my dad when I was very young. I was amazed that the pull-down bins in the kitchen still held beans and rice.

pedaled, if you wanted to stop, you locked up the rear tire and slid to an abrupt halt in a spray of gravel and dust. We all knew how to fix our bikes and it wasn't hard; all you needed was a crescent wrench or a pair of pliers and that qualified you as a bike mechanic. If you were too young to master those tools, then you asked your mom or an older friend to help.

One time in particular my good buddy Randy Green helped me fix my front tire. We were on our way to the lake to try out my new fishing pole. We were both excited to see how it handled the grayling. In our haste, he may have been less than diligent tightening the nuts. We took off down the hill, he on his bike and me on mine with my fishing rod fiercely clenched in my hand. We took a shortcut down a grassy slope to the lake. As was our norm upon coming to any bump or rise in the path, we pulled up on the handle bars hoping to achieve a cool wheelie.

Moving at a pretty good clip, I came to the first bump, pulled up on the handle bars and shockingly witnessed my front tire race off ahead of me toward the lake. I'm sure it was only a second, but that feeling of total helplessness lasted a lifetime. My front forks hit the dirt, dug in, and I went ass over teakettle, tumbling down the hill in a jumble of arms, legs, bike parts, dirt, dust and pieces of new fishing rod. I'm sure my bumps and bruises hurt, but losing that new rod was by far more painful. I know Randy felt badly because after he finally stopped laughing, he went and found my front wheel. I was so mad at him I punished him by not talking to him for a full twenty minutes. I showed him.

I was expecting sympathy from my mom, but instead she seemed angry that I had combined two separate pursuits. "Either you ride your bike or you fish. Why do you have to do both at the same time?" The look on her face made it obvious that any rebuttal by me would not be warmly received. It was back to the old pole with the missing tip and bent eyelets for me.

We fixed our own flats until our tubes were more patch than original tube. If you needed a part, you went to the dump or a friend's junk pile and got one. You didn't take your bike to a shop—what shop? Our streets were gravel in the summer and mud in the spring. We didn't have chain guards and sometimes we had no fenders, so if it was wet, you got dirty. We often had a big, brown streak running from our rear ends to our heads. If you wiped out, or "ratched out" as we liked to say, you got hurt, maybe you bled a little, but you picked the gravel out of your skin, jumped back on your bike and caught up to your friends who had giggled and continued riding. Most of our jeans had one leg chewed up where it regularly got caught in the chain. Bell bottoms were not great for bike riding, but tucking that pant leg into your sock did not look cool so that wasn't going to happen.

We decorated and entered our bikes in the annual First of July Parade. One year, I took first prize and won a helicopter ride around the area and over town. What a unique prize.

We found old, wrecked bikes at the dump and modified them into choppers. A girl's Schwinn painted black with extended forks, banana seat, sissy bar and ape-hanger handle bars minus the basket, bell and streamers made a bad-ass chopper.

I had two bikes growing up. When I outgrew the first one at the age of twelve, my mom bought the neighbors used bike for me. I was initially excited because she told me it had a hand break and three gears. But my euphoria was quickly dashed when I saw it was a girl's bike, missing the cross bar. I was terribly conflicted. On one hand, I had a full-size bike with gears and a cool hand break. On the other hand, I knew I was in for a lot of ribbing especially from John and Pete, as it was their mom's old bike. The basket and bell went immediately. After I spray painted it black and got rid of those bothersome fenders, I felt cool enough.

We all coveted motorbikes as we had seen Steve McQueen in *Bullet* and *The Great Escape*. Randy Green was the first one of my friends to have a motor bike, a Honda 90. The fact that it did not have a working motor bothered us little. I remember constantly pushing that heavy thing uphill three blocks so we could ride it back to the bottom. It was almost more than Randy could push himself, so he was constantly badgering his friends to go with him, and we did. The smooth ride and easy braking was a thing of wonder; even from the back, it was magnificent. I was never allowed to drive, but it instilled in me a lust for riding motorcycles. For a time, he had a Tom Sawyer-esque scam going where he charged a hard-negotiated number of Mojos for a ride, providing you helped push the bike back up the hill. Sounded like a whitewashing to me, but I know I paid and pushed many times.

Sliding

We didn't call it sledding, we called it sliding. We didn't have very many sleds, and a piece of plastic sheeting, cardboard or a garbage bag worked great. If you had a big piece, everyone jumped on in a massive dog pile of mittens and mukluks and you plummeted down the hill laughing and screaming all the way to the bottom. If no one was looking, text books worked the best. Those suckers were slippery, and you could reach amazing speeds, thus explaining the stained and ruffled pages of all the math and social studies texts. The hill behind the school became the hub of our winter amusement. Used so often, it remained a slippery sheet of ice the entire season.

Atlin was strewn with old abandoned vehicles. Clumps of brush often obscured a truck or car or a pile of parts. Once we found a fender from what I would guess to be a 1950s pickup truck. The outside was rounded and smooth and the inside had some sharp edges, but to us it looked sleek and space age. We immediately recruited it for our next sliding adventure. We dragged it to the top

Sliding behind the school, 1971. Originally published in the Atlin News Miner. Photo by Dave Dickinson.

of the hill behind the school and three of us clambered aboard. It turned out to be quite the slider, but lacked any form of guidance system. After a few successful zig-zag trips down the hill, it eventually wandered too far askew and ran smack dab into a poplar tree. A couple bruised knees, a ripped mitten and a bloody lip were enough to convince us to abandon our steely conveyance. That old fender hung around the sliding hill for a few years, and every once in a while, someone dragged it back to the top for another go.

A winding trail to the Alkali Flats ran parallel to the sliding hill behind the school. One year, Mr. Dickinson, one of our teachers, flooded it with a garden hose. In essence, we had a bobsled track right behind our school. Unlike a bobsled track, the corners weren't banked very well, so instant ejections were a norm. Some brave fools even went down on skates. The best method was to form a chain. We each sat on a piece of cardboard or plastic, then wrapped our legs around the person in front of us. A long line of kids all hooked together in this manner helped keep everyone on the track. As we snaked our way down the course, it looked similar to the centipede from the Atari game.

At least a couple times a year, we undertook an impromptu tubing expedition to Thrond Gulch. Parents and some of the older teenagers loaded up kids, toboggans, a few dogs and anyone else who wanted to go. Tire tubes were negotiated from the garage and copious amounts of hot chocolate was poured into thermoses. Our destination lay only a couple miles (3km) north of town and a few hundred yards off the road. The trip was short and if you were riding in the back of a pickup truck and it was twenty below (-29°C), short was a good thing. It always seemed to be a well-below-zero day with the sun on high and the snow surface hard and fast.

Thrond Gulch sports the perfect tubing or tobogganing hill. Treeless and brushless, it's tall, very steep, narrow at the top but widens into a perfect bowl at the bottom. Roughly halfway up is a wide bench, which is a good starting point for the less-radical tuber. It's also a great place for a fire and a quick respite from the long trudge back up the hill. There were always a number of snow machines on site to haul the tubes and toboggans back to the top.

It was exhilarating to be perched on the cornice of that great hill. Two or three of us tightly gripped together anticipating the rush and the fear, willing our bodies to adhere to the tube; will being the only way to stay on that slippery pillow of rubber. Often someone had to push us to start as we were incapable of commencing our final commitment to what could be our final commitment.

We quickly found ourselves plummeting down the face of that snowy monolith, gaining speed with every inch. Out of control, our adrenalin spiked, our hearts exploding with pure innocent joy. For a few seconds, we were the rulers of our universe, masters of our own ship, and gods of our frozen realm. If the first couple dips didn't dislodge you, then surely the bench halfway down would send you and your tube mates sailing through the air end over end as the tube shot off down the hill, rider-less and free. There always seemed to be at least a second while airborne for one to contemplate the less-than-gentle landing immediately in one's future. I know I'm guilty of wishing my fall would be somewhat cushioned by the bodies of my fellow daredevils. The snow was often crusty and rough, so along with the expected bumps and bruises, scrapes and cuts were also prevalent.

Almost never did all the riders make it to the bottom, and it was rare anyone did, but once in a great while someone completed the ride all the way into and out of the bowl at the bottom—only to be thrown high in the air at the lip of the bowl. It's a great hill for toboggans as well as tubes; in fact, your odds at successfully descending were much better on a toboggan, especially if you stayed in the deeper snow and off the hard-packed areas. A slower trip, but the satisfaction of reaching the bottom alive always sweetened the pot. Having something to hang onto greatly increased one's chances of a successful descent.

Toboggans of the day were beautifully crafted, heavy, sturdy and nearly indestructible modes of downhill transportation. They were also fairly expensive. I had long coveted them from afar and used my friends' whenever I could. I was probably eleven or twelve when, on one of my dad's visits home, he showed up with a magnificent toboggan. It was late in the evening and I had to wait all night before I got the chance to use it.

In the morning, my dad had the grand idea we should invite some of my friends and drive out the road to find some virgin snow and try out my new toboggan. We gathered up Randy Green, Lance Shaw and John Wright and took off. For reasons only he understood, Dad chose a place no one had ever tobogganed before. Although it was a pretty great hill with nice fresh powder, the bottom had many large poplar trees evenly spaced with narrow passage between. I'm not sure how much tobogganing my dad had done in his life (none) but he was convinced it would be easy to navigate between the trees. Not wanting to look like wimps in his presence, my buddy John and I took off down the hill. As it turned out, the powder was great and the hill fast, but we ratched out halfway down and decided to return to the top. In the spirit of sharing, I let Randy and Lance go next.

As a packed path was provided halfway, they reached even greater speeds and managed to make it past the first wipeout site. Typically, the rider on the back does the steering by dragging one hand or another. From the top of the hill, we noticed the toboggan and riders were heading straight toward a particularly formidable poplar tree. We all yelled "Steer, steer!" and it appeared Randy on the back was doing his best to avert the looming danger, but to no avail—they smacked dead center into that tree.

In my memory, I was worried little for my friends, but was greatly concerned for the well-being of my new toboggan. As it turned out, it was destroyed, split from one end to the other with a large piece broken off the curl. Oh, and those two dorks were basically okay. I felt sorry for myself and it was hard to understand why my dad seemed to be mad at me, as well as my friends—after all, he picked the hill. It turned out to be a long, awkward ride home and my only tobogganing trip with Dad.

A few things were apparent: one, there was a reason why no one tobogganed on that hill; two, it's hard to steer a toboggan in deep snow; three, Lance and Randy had some pretty hard heads; and finally, I was never going to have a toboggan like that again. After half a ride, it was back to the cardboard and truck fenders for me. Fear not, my mom bought me a shorter plastic version of a toboggan that Christmas and it turned out to be faster and lighter and even had a pad to sit on. Randy and I managed to break it too, but only after much use and enjoyment.

I remember the two pieces of my original toboggan had been lying around beside the house for a time when one day either Randy or I had the grand idea they might make "snow surfboards," as we called them. There was enough curl left to not dig in and off we went to the hill behind the school. We spent the better half of a day snow surfing down that hill. Who knew we were ahead of our time? I still remember the day I cut up that old toboggan into pieces and tossed it into the kindling pile. I used the rope that summer on a go cart. Everything is used. Nothing goes to waste.

"Hooky Bobbing"

I know it has many names, but we called it hooky bobbing. This was the precarious pursuit of hanging onto the back of a car or truck, letting it pull you as you slid on your boots. Not an uncommon occurrence in town, and usually performed at night in the dark. We waited for an unsuspecting driver to start their vehicle before hunkering down out of sight and taking a firm grip on the bumper. Typically, this was a low-speed affair as Atlin had many stop signs and the maximum speed between them was minimal. The bigger risk was being discovered and receiving a smack on the side of the head, or much worse, a call to Mom.

Almost any forward momentum while sliding along on your boots can be exciting. The trick was to let go before the vehicle reached a high rate of speed, preferably on a corner so the driver continued on his way as you slid off in a different direction. To some, this might sound a bit reckless, but in all my memory, I can't think of one serious injury. Atlin boasted around seventy operating vehicles at that time, so it wasn't like traffic was a problem. After six in the evening, it was easy to drive through town more than once and never see another human being.

There was one time hooky bobbing took on a most urgent and dire turn. We were returning from a long day of tubing at Thrond Gulch. A bunch of us were huddled in the back of the last pickup truck to leave. Of course, it was Randy Green that decided this was a great time to try some high-speed hooky bobbing, unbeknownst to the driver, and if not outright encouraged by the rest of us, at least passively condoned. Alright, we outright encouraged him. Anyway, he hunkered down and took hold of the bumper. As we started out, everything went well; Randy had a huge smile on his face and seemed quite proud of his decision. By the time we reached third gear, the smile was gone, replaced by an expression of dogged determination. Upon achieving fourth gear, Randy's expression had turned to terror, his lips were stretched back in a rigor-mortis-like mask, his eyes bulged as he desperately clung to the truck.

After realizing it wasn't all that funny, everyone started yelling at him to climb aboard. The problem being that every time he tried to rise up to get a higher hold, his feet threatened to fly out from under him. A couple of the bigger guys got as far back as they could and leaned out. It was still up to Randy to make the final decision to take a literal leap of faith. Deciding his choices were few, he lunged out of his crouch and sure enough his feet sailed out behind, at the same time the guys grabbed both his arms and hauled him in. For a brief moment his body flapped in the wind like a broken umbrella in a hurricane. Recalling this story makes me ponder the fact that rather than alert the driver and incur his wrath, we all chose, for right or wrong, to handle the situation on our own. Dumb asses!

History and Mystery

As my mom was a historian and instrumental in saving some of Atlin's historic landmarks, I cringe to tell of the following incidents, but in for a penny, in for a pound.

We explored inside some of Atlin's old abandoned buildings. Not break and enter, just enter, as many were not securely closed up. Although it was explained to me later by one of Atlin's stellar RCMP constables that even sticking your hand through an open window is

Hanging out, 1971.

considered breaking and entering. I just want to be clear we weren't destroying anything or stealing anything. It always started off as a dare, and being a boy of a certain age in a certain time, who could refuse a dare and hope to live it down?

The Aurora House on Watson Street once belonged to a madam and housed her girls. In other words, it had been a whorehouse. Long since abandoned and in poor condition, it was considered by all the kids to be the most haunted of all haunted buildings in town.

I don't remember who dared us, but my friend John Craft and I were dared to climb through the broken-out back window and see what was inside. This was a big deal going into the most haunted of all haunted places. So after much consideration as to who would go first, I lost out and went ahead. My biggest fear was that as soon as I got in, John would bolt. To his credit, he followed me in. With no source of light, we waited for our eyes to become accustomed to the dark. Once we could see around, we began to explore. At first we stayed together, but after a while, deciding there wasn't anything waiting to eat us or worse, we separated. There were many small rooms (I wondered why). Anyway, John was in one room and I was in what I think was the woodshed at the back where I found an old hand-crank grinding wheel. Out of curiosity, I began turning the handle. The wheel made a loud, hideous, moaning noise. I heard John yell in panic and knock something over as he scrambled back to the window. Somehow in my mind it had nothing to do with the grinding wheel, and I was sure he had awakened an evil entity that was now trying to kill him. I panicked and crashed my way toward the window, where we met. The next scene was straight out of *The Three Stooges Meet The Monster* as we were both trying to fit through the small window at the same time, kicking, scratching and fighting each other to escape. I don't know how, but we did make it out alive.

I think the next building was in the process of being torn down when we ventured into the basement. I'm not sure who I was with, but there were a number of us. Unknown to us, what we thought was just an old house had a mortuary in the basement. Because it was in the process of demolition or salvage, everything was open.

At first, we found all the glass jars and bottles interesting, and there were some strange tools that I believe ended up in the museum. It wasn't until we found the child's coffin that we realized where we were. Like the Aurora House, it was an instantly chaotic and comedic egress.

For most of my childhood I had resisted the temptation to climb up into the *M/V Tarahne* for a number of reasons. First, it was near and dear to my mom and dad's hearts as former owners. Second, my mom often raved about the hoodlums that were constantly climbing onto the *Tarahne*. Third, it was smack dab in the middle of town and everyone could see it; let's say the odds of getting caught were high. I had been on the boat many times with my parents so it held less mystery for me than my friends.

Needless to say, being one of the few kids that had not been on the *Tarahne* uninvited at night, the pressure was mounting, and eventually I relented. On one particularly black evening, with my friend Randy Green leading the operation, we set off to infiltrate the enemy stronghold. The first deck sits about twelve feet (3.6m) off the ground and is a bit of a challenge to reach. There was a rather clandestine way to enter, but it involved some skill and fortitude. We chose to enter that way, but after nearly falling, I was determined I would not be returning the same way. We explored the entire boat top to bottom, including the food pantries near the kitchen. On one of the pantry shelves we found a complete bedroll: blankets, pillow, and the works. It was recent and meant someone was staying there. At the time I thought it odd, but I later realized it was a kid I knew who stayed there to escape a bad home life. How bad it must have been for a young boy to stay on that scary old boat alone in the dark. It made me sad, and to this day it bothers me when I think of him.

Upon the end of our exploration, I made it known (by deploying my usual tactic of crying and complaining) that I would not egress the way we entered. Randy said it was no problem and we could just slide down the chain that hung off the bow. That sounded good to me. Aside from the fact that the bow was out where everyone could see, we figured if we were fast enough, and aided by the poor lighting, we could escape undetected. Like a spider, Randy effortlessly shimmied to the ground. When it was my turn, I got my legs wrapped around the chain and eased off the deck, but just as my full weight was on the chain, I heard a woman's voice below me. A quick look showed Randy's face illuminated by a flashlight.

It turned out that Sue Morhon, wife of the RCMP Corporal Mike, good friend of my mom's and a fellow historian, had busted us. For some reason, she didn't look up where I was desperately clinging on for dear life. Shaking from lack of arm muscle and fear that my mom would kill me, I tried to remain still. "What are you doing here, Mr. Green?" she asked sternly.

I have to give Randy credit, as he did have a quick comeback, albeit a lame one. "Oh, just swinging on this chain," he replied meekly. Sue didn't buy it and continued to interrogate Randy. She repeatedly asked him who he was with. Around the third time he denied being with anyone, my muscles finally gave out and down I went, landing between the two of them like a bag of sand. I grunted loudly and curled into the fetal position gasping for air. Pretty sure I scared the crap out of both of them as they jumped back.

Somehow, we convinced her we were only in the process of committing the crime and had not yet made it onto the boat. With our begging, groveling, crying and promises to lead an exemplary life thereafter, she agreed to keep it among the three of us. Did I mention Randy's mom was also one of the founding members of the Historical Society? I later wondered if Sue decided the bad press from busting the sons of two prominent Historical Society members in the act of breaking into the town's paramount historic relic might have been too much to bear.

Atlin boasts the world's only log pyramid, a three-story affair with decks and windows on all four sides. During construction and before the dormers and decks were installed, the great structure stood naked with large openings on all sides and every floor. My friend Dan Alexander decided to make a grappling hook and climb the walls of the pyramid. With a makeshift hook, a coil of rope and the cloak of darkness, a number of us set out to scale the great pyramid. With a mighty heave, the hook sailed through a top-floor window opening, and like Batman, we climbed up the inclined wall. I remember Dan climbing up the chimney and standing on it. It was at least fifty feet (15m) up in the air with nothing to hang on to, standing on the rim of a 12-inch (2.5cm) pipe. He was always braver than I. After only a couple ascents, John Harvey snuck up and scared the willies out of us by yelling, "You kids get down from there!" and we did. I waited in fear for my mom to hear about my attempt at Super Hero-dom, but John was a good guy and didn't rat us out. He was probably wishing he had thought of it first. My luck continued.

Swinging and Spelunking

There was a rope swing at the end of town on the side of a hill. There was nothing to cushion the fall at the bottom—only more hill and sharp sticks—but we spent hours swinging out over the void trying to kick a selected distant branch or young sapling. This effort served to top most of the small poplar trees, leaving sharp, punji-like protrusions sticking up under our flight path. I only remember one person slipping off in mid-flight. Miraculously, Kenny Ward missed all the skewers, and even though it was a twenty-five (7.5m) to thirty-foot (9m) fall, he only scraped some skin off his elbows.

A mine shaft dug long ago in the side of a rocky bank above the lake provided us a place to dare each other and to scare our friends and be scared. Someone had previously dynamited the entrance, but it had eroded away, exposing a narrow opening. Once inside, it was much bigger; an adult could stand up without bonking their head. It was carved into bedrock, so there was little chance of a cave-in, but it's hard to convince oneself of that when underground.

My biggest irrational fear was that someone would close us in, leaving us to starve or suffocate to death.

First, we made sure it wasn't occupied by a bear before we slid down the sloping pile of rubble at the entrance. Our bear check was no more than yelling and tossing in a few rocks. The goal was to make it all the way to the end of the shaft. After a hundred feet (30m) or so, the shaft made a bend and continued another couple hundred feet (61m) to the back wall. After the turn, it was complete and total darkness. In a few places, water seeped in and pooled on the floor adding to the eeriness. We tried to make it to the end without freaking out, lighting matches as we went. Later we did it without matches, feeling our way along the slippery walls. Finally, we challenged each other to go all the way to the back alone and without matches. We would leave a can or candy wrapper at the end, so if someone didn't return with the left item, we knew they didn't go all the way.

Skating

Before the town had a skating rink, we skated on the ponds in the Alkali swamp behind town. We were all anxious to skate as soon as the ice formed in the fall, and to test the thickness we hurled large boulders as far as we could onto the surface. Our theory was that if it could hold a huge boulder, it could hold one kid. Somehow, we didn't consider that if we could lift it and throw it, there was no way it weighed as much as we did. Needless to say, our method was imperfect and we broke through every year. It wasn't that deep by the shore. There was only a foot or so of water, but there was also a foot of foul, stinking mud. Not only were you now wet, but your leg or legs were covered in goo and you smelled like a sewer, much to the consternation of our mothers.

Mike Ferrier, Dan Alexander and I were employing our imperfect method of safety testing the ice thickness on one of the ponds at the Alkali one late fall day. The ice held up under a number of big rocks and we decided one of us should venture out. Dan went first. He slowly edged out about ten feet (3m) from the shore. The ice held. Mike went next. He cautiously made his way out about ten feet (3m) to stand beside Dan. Everything seemed fine so they both started jumping up and down. The ice held but began making noise as small cracks spread out in all directions away from the boys.

Both of them, deciding they were in danger of breaking through, began gingerly retreating.

Seeing they were both scared, I thought it a great time to add to their apprehension. I yelled out, "Here I come!" and sprinted toward the edge of the pond. I fully intended to stop near the shore, but I tripped over a hummock of grass and fell on my face. My momentum caused me to slide across the ice toward them. It all seemed slow motion, both of them yelled "Nooooo!" and frantically scrambled for traction on the slippery surface. The next thing I remember is the ice braking and my entire body dropping into the freezing water. Completely panicking, I went berserk, flailing my arms and kicking my legs. Just as I managed to raise my head above the putrid water, both Mike and Dan used my body to clamber to safety. One of them stepped on my head, forcing it under the water and into the goo at the bottom of the pond. Although very cold, wet, and covered in stinking mud, I obviously didn't drown; but I found out a little something about my friends that day. They didn't get wet at all and found my predicament uproariously funny. I did manage to catch Mike in the head with a glob of muck, and that made me feel a little better until I began to contemplate the welcome awaiting me at home where I needed to get to in a hurry before I froze to death.

After our inevitable fall dousing, the skating was great. We shoveled a huge rectangle in the middle of the pond and connected that to a series of meandering paths that snaked around the shore and between the tufts of swamp grass to adjacent ponds. Most of us had old hand-me-down skates with no support, but we were in our glory and didn't notice. Often we shared our skates. If our feet were sore or we needed to warm up for a while, we let a friend use ours. I remember constantly begging Wes Colwell and Daniel Connolly to help me tie my skates. The younger kids had a hard time getting our laces tight and the older guys helped us with it.

We collected dead wood and lit a bonfire to keep ourselves warm. Someone always had a thermos of hot chocolate. Skating at night by the light of the bonfire and the aurora borealis was something I will never forget. After sluffing along on hand-me-down, broken-down skates for years, I got my first new pair of brand-new Eddie Bauer skates. Turns out I wasn't a bad skater with the right equipment.

Alkali Obsession

Alkali is a basic, ionic salt of an alkali metal or alkaline earth metal chemical element, but to us it was a place. There was other alkali around the area, but when we referenced alkali or "The Alkali" we meant the area behind town—more specifically behind the school. The Alkali held some sort of magnetic allure and we were drawn to it like moths to light. Covering a couple dozen acres, it consisted of sloughs, small creeks, mud bogs and flats of drying white muck. On a sunny day while standing in the middle of the flats, it felt like we were on top of a glacier. It was so bright it made you squint and it hurt the eyes.

The original road to Discovery and the gold creeks beyond ran straight through The Alkali. It was called the Corduroy Road. The corduroy method of road building consists of logs laid side by side. Historically, it was used for covering unstable ground. The road had long since been abandoned and was in complete disarray. Many logs were missing, having succumbed to rot. We made a game of crossing that old road. In the spring during run off, it was the only way of getting to the high ground in the middle of the two bogs. We jumped from one slimy, rotten log to another, often slipping and landing in the pungent ooze. At least once a week, we found an excuse to play in The Alkali and were covered in noxious goo.

Getting wet was enough to send my mom into a tirade, but coming home covered in alkali was a real pain in the ass—mine. More than once while covered in white goop, I weighed my options and decided it was better to head to the lake and wash off; the lesser of two evils, so to speak. One day I realized there wasn't time to get to the lake and then home for dinner. As I walked through the woods behind the house, I visualized the welcome I was sure to receive. Upon reaching our yard, I noticed laundry hanging on the line. An idea quickly formulated in my desperate mind. Only my bottom half was soiled, so I grabbed socks, jeans and underwear and ducked into the outhouse. Like Superman, I speedily changed out of my soggy garb, wadded it all up and hid it behind the outhouse. I ran across the yard in my socks and onto the porch. As we normally left our shoes on the porch during the summer, I walked in as though nothing was amiss.

I'm on snowshoes with Kulane and Tutshi on Atlin Lake, 1972.

During dinner, I noticed my mom sniffing the air and even looking under the table a couple times. Once again, I was saved by the dogs. I'm pretty sure she thought the sulphur odor was one of our flatulent mutts. After dinner, I changed back into my soiled pants and shoes, took my socks and underwear and headed off to the lake. It wasn't pleasant putting on my soggy, stinky pants, but it was far better than it could have been.

Another quick clothesline story comes to mind: hanging wet laundry on the line when it's below freezing works quite well. The water in the clothes freezes to ice then sublimates into water vapor, drying the clothes.

For years we had a portable wash machine but not a dryer. My mom bailed water into the machine where the clothes washed and spun and then she drained the water into a bucket. The bucket had to be hauled outside and dumped, which was usually my job. Eventually our friend Dave Dickinson rigged up a detachable hose and we could drain the water all the way outside. I was also in charge of retrieving the laundry from the line. Some material dried just fine and reverted to its normal state, but other material stayed stiff and frozen until I brought it inside where it quickly thawed and was just slightly moist.

One particularly cold day, I gingerly removed a number of my very stiff long johns. I carefully stacked them in my arms like a load of wood and proceeded toward the back door. Somehow, I tripped over a chunk of ice and the whole load went flying. I was horrified to see one leg on several pairs snap cleanly off. Sure I was in trouble, I hesitantly brought my damaged wares in to show my mom. I was pleasantly relieved, yet bewildered, when she burst into laughter. I joined in the hilarity and soon we were rolling.

Between fits of giggles, a suggestion was floated that I should hurriedly return them to the cold where we could snap off the other leg and call them short johns. Mom eventually sewed the legs back on. For some reason, she used black thread instead of white. I suspect that was so every time they turned up in the wash it reminded her of that hilarious episode and helped her endure an unpleasant drudgery.

Frostbite Folly

In the winter, we played outside no matter how cold. We all got frostbite at one time or another, and for most of us it was a regular occurrence; it was just part of our lives. We tried to watch each other for signs, like noses, ears and cheeks turning white. We played hard and breathed hard, drawing ice crystals into our lungs—it's a wonder we didn't cause real damage. I'm convinced I got frostbit on my tongue on more than one occasion just by breathing.

The huge piles of snow pushed up by the highway department were our playgrounds. King of the Castle was a brutal game that was not for the faint of heart. We violently shoved each other off the top of those icy ramparts, frantically fighting to retain supremacy of our frozen redoubt, yelling, "I'm the king of the castle, you're a dirty rascal." Or we pretended to be Geronimo and dove off the top, landing on one of our friends, fake stabbing them with an icicle as we drove them into the street.

Our snowball fights were often ice-ball fights because it's impossible to make a snowball at thirty below. Sometimes you got hit in the head and it hurt and you cried, but the next day you did it all again. We dug intricate tunnel systems and forts and slides, and we played hard and got snow down our boots and down our pants. Sometimes we did swan dives and somersaults and belly flops into the deep snow and got yelled at and told, "You kids get the hell off of my roof!"

As I matured, I realized I had psoriasis. Psoriasis often attacks where skin has already been damaged. My psoriasis showed up on my ears, my knees, elbows, hands and my stomach, all places I'd been frostbitten repeatedly as a child. Ears are common targets of frostbite as they are often exposed. I remember at least a couple of times realizing mine were hard and having to thaw them with my hands. Afterward they burned for a few days and then peeled. The knees and elbows were victims of warmer weather and wet snow. We kneeled for hours digging tunnels and snow forts until our knees were completely numb. When I got it on my wrists and calves, it was caused by getting snow in my boots and mittens and not removing it. The stomach area was from icy cold wind penetrating my zippers.

Spring Soaker

Spring was a time of excitement and relief. The streets were thick with soupy mud. Enormous puddles formed at intersections, the ditches rushed with wild torrents of mocha-colored water, and the swamps overflowed. It was a perfect environment for adventure and exploration. With the weather warming, off came the clunky winter boots or mukluks and the long johns, and on went the gumboots.

It wasn't possible to make it to and from school without getting a "soaker." A "soaker" was what we called it when you waded into water deeper than your boots. I believe if our boots had reached our armpits, we would still have experienced at least one soaker a day. Many a spring day was spent in class with squishy wet socks. We spent hours diverting streams and racing little wooden boats carved from cottonwood bark. To this day, I harbor an affinity toward irrigation activities. When I see a puddle that could be drained into another puddle by simply breaking down a small section of land or ice, I find myself kicking or digging away until the water flows. I derive great pleasure in creating unrestricted flows of ground water.

Hot Mess

If you were born in Atlin or raised there from an early age, there were many things you didn't know about that other kids of the time found commonplace, like going to a mall or a theater. On the other

An autumn view of Atlin facing northwest, 2017. The white areas in the foreground are Alkali Flats. Table Top Mountain is in the background. Photo by Caroline Moore.

hand, we did things all the time southern kids might consider a once in a lifetime adventure. I remember kids eight, nine years old who hadn't even been to Whitehorse yet, a little over a hundred miles (160km) away by road.

Our grocery stores carried the basics in fruits and vegetables. The fruits we were exposed to were oranges, apples, bananas and grapes, and that was pretty much it. The first time I saw cherries I was six or seven, and of course I ate the whole bag and regretted it later. Pineapple was so rare someone brought one for show and tell at school. Pears were an occasional treat in the summer only. We never saw kiwi, plums or apricots. The first time I saw an artichoke I thought it was from another planet and could not believe my mom intended to feed it to me.

I was twelve or thirteen the first time I saw a jalapeño pepper. Previously I had only seen green peppers. My friend Dan brought one to school, intending on slipping it into someone's sandwich as a joke. A number of us curiously sliced it up and passed it around, daring each other to try it, and as far as I can recall, no one did. Right before our class began, I visited the restroom. Upon my return to class and as I slid into my seat, I began to feel a warm sensation on my guy parts. Pretty soon it was getting damn hot down there and I started squirming and sweating.

Having just started sex education classes that month, I was completely convinced I had somehow contracted a venereal disease from the toilet. I had to ask to use the bathroom, go through the inevitable chastising, as in, "Why didn't you use the bathroom on your break, Mr. Smith?" Of course, this drew attention to me, and the whole class wondered why my face was beet red and I was sweating and fidgeting profusely. By now I suspected the jalapeño as I could feel it on my hands as well.

Our bathroom consisted of a toilet stall and a sink. The door did not have a lock. I was trying to wash my you-know-what in the sink, and it was difficult because I was too short. I was on my tiptoes splashing water over the area and soaking it with wet paper towels when, of course, Mr. Dickinson walked in. To his credit, he quickly stepped out, closing the door, and never mentioned the incident again. I was able to get the burning to subside, but by this time the front of my pants were soaking wet. My choices appeared to be return to class and explain that I was a complete dumb ass and got jalapeño on my bleep or return to class and have everyone think I peed myself. As I began the trudge back to my room, trying to walk straight with my crotch pointing sideways, I passed the coat closet and had the bright idea to grab my jean jacket and tie it in front of me effectively hiding the wet area. Now they could speculate all they wanted, but they never knew for sure what happened until now.

The "wrap the coat around the waist" trick was not new to me. This next story continues to show me in a less than stellar light, but, oh well, here goes. I was very young and apparently bored, as was a friend of mine, John Craft (yup, same one as the Aurora House). We noticed the congregation of the St. Mathew's Church congregating in front of the church as congregations are apt to do. One of us had the bright idea that we should join them. I was new to this church, or any for that matter, so I was unprepared for what I was about to experience.

We thought it a good idea to sit right up front and we were the only ones on our pew. Unfamiliar with the proceedings, for some reason we found everything quite funny. If you have ever gotten the giggles, you will understand. Unfortunately, church, aside from a funeral in a church, is probably one of the worse places for this to occur. So, there we were, two little heathens giggling uncontrollably at everything Pastor Dave was saying. To make it worse, we were on full display in front of everyone.

At some point a hand descended from the heavens and ripped John from his seat, dragged him back a few rows and plopped him down. Winnie Atcheson was an elderly lady of high esteem in town and also a lady that didn't take crap from anyone, especially a snot-nosed brat. She had taken offense at our obvious ignorant display of disrespect and decided John would be better off sitting with her for the rest of the service. One quick glance back to see John, his eyes wide and face red, was all it took for me. I was instantly converted, so to speak.

Very afraid the same fate might befall me, I sat rigid with my eyes front and tried hard to understand what was going on. Of course, I immediately and intensely needed to pee. I was not going to walk back out of that church, facing all the people who by now must have thought I was a complete punk. So I sat and squirmed and pinched myself and squirmed some more, until finally I couldn't hold out any longer and I peed my pants. I'm sure most would have chosen the aforementioned humiliation over what I went with, but that was not how I rolled when I was five. Hey, I didn't mean to pee ... I thought I could hold out, but it was a long service.

So there I sat in my own pee for another hour. The pews were hard wood and there was nowhere for the pee to go, so I just sat there in my little puddle, trying to be a paragon of virtue and not draw attention to myself. I casually placed my jacket over my lap so Pastor Dave couldn't see what I had done, and I silently hoped I hadn't put the *pew* back in pews. Finally, it was over and I could make my exit, but everyone was just standing around talking, and no one was leaving. I desperately needed to get out of there, but I had a huge pee stain on my pants. That was when I got the "tie my jacket around my waist" idea. To my horror, when I got up, I could see a puddle where I was sitting, thus adding more motivation to flee. The jacket only covered the front, and I remember walking by people normally but after passing them I turned and walked backwards, repeating this until I got out the front door.

Even then I knew I had not fooled anyone, and I spent the next year avoiding everyone who was there that day, especially Pastor Dave and Winnie.

I'm thinking at this point the moral of the story may be that my mom was taking the "kids need their freedom" thing a smidge too far. I was, like, five—didn't she wonder where I was? Notice my use of deflection here? By the way, I never made it into the Catholic Church as I was afraid the same or worse might happen.

Respect

Like I said, Winnie did not take crap from anyone and she demanded respect. For both of these reasons, a lot of the kids in town were afraid of her. One day Pete Wright and I were walking around town and we passed Winnie. For some idiotic, six-year-old reason we decided not to acknowledge her. As we passed, Winnie said, "Hello," but we stayed mum.

An hour or so later we were in the Trading Post and once again we ran into Winnie. As we approached her in an aisle, she again greeted us and again we did not respond. I'm guessing that Winnie had had enough of our insolence. Before we could blink, she had us each by an ear and was loudly dressing us down in front of a store full of friends and neighbors. She pulled us both close to her face and told us our behavior was not acceptable and that she knew both our parents and knew they did not raise us to be disrespectful twerps.

She went on to describe what she might do to our bottoms in front of everyone if it happened again. We quickly sputtered our apologies and promises to be much better humans in the future. She let go of our ears and we made a hasty retreat from the store. From then on, neither Pete nor myself missed greeting anyone we saw, especially the elderly and definitely Winnie. It takes a village. I can still smell her perfume.

You Can Take the Boy Out of the Bush

Our lack of urban knowledge manifested itself in amusing ways. My first time on an elevator I was with my mom in Whitehorse. I believe there was only one elevator in the whole town at that time. I don't think I fully understood why we were going into the little room with the buttons, and when we arrived at another floor, I freaked out. In the blink of an eye, everything had changed. Pretty sure I thought I had arrived in a parallel universe.

I was four when my grandpa got sick, so my mom and I went to see him. I don't remember the flight much, but I vividly remember two things: one, we were in a department store and I saw an escalator. As my mom told it, I began yanking at her shirt and yelling loudly. "The stairs are moving; the stairs are moving." I'm sure I was way cooler than that, but if you have ever seen the movie *Elf* with Will Ferrell, then you will understand my first ride on an escalator. Needless to say, glad I was flexible.

The second memorable event from that trip was our meal at McDonalds. Not the food so much, but I was fascinated by the Ronald McDonald statue. That turned out to be somewhat portent, as a year later we went to Kentucky to see my dad's family. His first cousin married Michael Polakovs AKA Coco the Clown, the man who invented Ronald McDonald's clothes and makeup and played him in the first eight TV commercials—sorry, Willard Scott, you're full of it. Oh yeah, and I loved the fries—it was my first time having skinny fries.

On our trip to Kentucky, we had dinner at a steak house. I always emulated my dad, so I wanted a steak like he did. I think they ordered a filet mignon for me. Halfway through the meal, the waiter approached and asked us how everything was. I immediately answered that it was the best moose I ever tasted. My grandma almost lost her false teeth. The waiter wasn't sure what to make of that, so he stared at me for a minute, smiled and quickly moved on. I think he thought I was challenged. If I had said possum or coon, he wouldn't have blinked an eye.

Speaking of false teeth, I almost pooped when I saw my grandma's teeth in a glass by her bed. All kinds of things ran through my mind, none of them rational.

Around the same time, my parents and I were having dinner in Whitehorse. I'm guessing not in one of the classier establishments. Like all kids, waiting for your food was excruciating. To distract from the hunger pangs and boredom, my strategy was to go to the bathroom as many times as I could get away with.

I have to admit I also had a fascination with modern bathrooms, most likely stemming from the fact that our facilities at home were anything but modern. The flush toilets were mesmerizing, but the urinals held a special allure for me. Although I could not reach most of them, I was very intrigued by the look and function. The silver handle was cool, the fact they were mounted on the wall interesting, but what I loved the most was the wonderfully scented white hockey puck at the bottom of each urinal.

The writing on the walls was mostly incomprehensible at that time, but the drawings were much easier to decipher. I really did not understand the obsession with depicting the human anatomy, especially the covered-up parts, but even at that age I could appreciate good drawing.

This particular bathroom had a new attraction, something I had never seen before. There were toy machines on the wall. Apparently, one could put a quarter in the machine, turn the knob and receive a toy. I thought the price rather high, but I could not resist trying something new. I dropped in my quarter, twisted the knob and out dropped a tiny, colorful box.

From the picture on the box, it looked as if I had purchased a large, elongated balloon. I was incensed. I just wasted a whole quarter on a balloon. Even a little kid knows when he's been ripped off. I could buy a whole pack of balloons for half that price and this one wouldn't even work for a water balloon.

I marched out of the bathroom straight to our table and began loudly protesting my fleecing. I waved the balloon pack in the air to make my point. I had never seen my dad move so fast. In the blink of an eye, my new purchase was snatched from my hand and had disappeared into a pocket. At the same time, my mother quickly put her hand over my mouth to stop my clamor.

I remember my parents' faces turning a crimson shade, and people at the neighboring tables began snickering and staring. I had no idea why the big fuss over a balloon. All I could think of was I had embarrassed them by being gullible and wasting a quarter.

My dad never did explain it all to me as he repeatedly promised he would throughout our meal.

Years later, my "aha" moment was pretty funny.

Chapter Ten

The Campground

"Hey, what do you want to do?"

"Let's go to The Campground."

We simply called it The Campground, and everything worth happening, happened there. Originally it was Queen's Ranch, a nine-hectare vegetable garden owned by Elsworth P. Queen, a successful farmer who supplied early Atlinites with fresh and/or frozen vegetables year-round. Queen's Ranch operated from 1903 to 1907. As many of the miners moved on to richer ground, so did Mr. Queen. Left fallow, many years later it eventually became what we called The Campground. It was actually a big field at the north end of town with an old wooden backstop at one end and a huge sawdust pile where a sawmill once sat at the other end. It was humble in appearance but an integral part of our lives.

It was our recreation area, sporting complex, gathering place and hangout. It was where we played softball, had track meets, made forts in the sawdust and threw a Frisbee or a football. It was a good place to fly a kite or ride a horse. Our First of July parade ended there, it was the terminus of the walkathon, and it was where

Sack race at The Campground, 1971.

Foot race at The Campground, 1971.

I'm in a gambler costume Mom made at The Campground after a parade, 1971.

Gary Thoma and Gordon Crum pillow fighting at The Campground while Lucille Jack looks on, 1971.

we gathered after the town cleanup. The gun club had an outdoor shooting range at the back of the field, and, oh yeah, the tourists camped there because we didn't have a real campground yet. There were a couple of outhouses and a few scattered fire pits, and if the campers needed water, they went to the lake and got it.

An occasional herd of horses followed closely by a pack of barking huskies might stampede through in the middle of the night, pulling tent pegs and kicking over coolers in their wake. It really was camping at your own risk. A tourist commented at the café one day that he was awakened by his camper violently rocking back and forth. Thinking he was experiencing a great earthquake, and wearing nothing but his undershorts, he flung open the door and leapt to the ground only to find a local nag contentedly scratching her ass on the corner of his camper. *Camp at your own risk.*

At one point a few crude signs were erected asking tourists not to camp on our obscure ball diamond. Although Wrigley Field to us, it was barely recognizable to some. At night we played hide and seek or red rover or just tried to scare each other. It was where we flirted and chased girls and the site of many a first kiss. After they built the picnic pavilion, we spent hours swinging from the rafters

With Dad at The Campground after a parade, 1970.

and jumping from picnic table to picnic table or just sitting up in the rafters or on the roof talking.

On Sunday evenings, we played fast-pitch softball. Our backstop was plywood and chicken wire, our bases were smooth patches of dirt in the grass and we didn't have a mound. We had a worn area with a board stuck in the dirt for a toe hold. The outfield fence was the street, but every ball that wasn't foul was in play, even if it went across the street, through the puddles and into the woods. If the outfielders couldn't find the ball, we all helped them look until we found it. Our field had dips and divots and the occasional boulder peeking above the grass. You might be all set up on a ground ball and at the last second, it could careen over your head or straight into your face. How many times did we lay out for a fly ball and land in a pile of fresh horse crap?

We took all comers: if you could walk, you could play. Not entirely true, as I remember Terry Jack playing on crutches and at least one determined player batting from a wheelchair, so even if you couldn't walk you could play—men, women, boys and girls, young and old. The first few to arrive played "500 Up" until there were enough for a game of Scrub, and then when we had enough for two teams, we chose sides and played nine innings. It wasn't unusual to have a dozen players on a team all on the field at one time. *Everyone got to play.*

If you had a glove, you shared it with someone on the other team who didn't. If you were the pitcher and Don Shaw, Sly Jack or Cheryl Stephens was up to bat, you brought the heat and tried to strike them out. If you were staring down a younger player like Suzan Carlick or Tim Frasher, you might lay in a lazy changeup and hope your fielders could bail you out. The strike zone was ambiguous and the close calls at the plate were sometimes arbitrary, but the final say went to Uncle Dave Goodwin, our resident ump extraordinaire. When Uncle Dave passed judgment, that was the end of it: "Play ball, move on."

At the opposite end of the field from the ball diamond and behind the mounds of sawdust were huge jumbles of slabs and cut-off corners of logs. With the sawmill long gone, the slabs were tinder dry and perfect for bonfires. We placed two long, sturdy poles side by side like a stretcher, then piled shorter pieces across and lugged our load back to the fire pit. One or two loads could feed a big fire most of the night.

The sawdust pit was a great place for horse races and later, a small dirt-bike track. The mounds of sawdust looked to us like sand dunes straight out of the Sahara Desert. We had great fun pretending we were Lawrence of Arabia and his band of Bedouins battling the Turks at Aqaba. We dug pits and covered them with thin sticks and a dusting of sawdust, then tried to lure our unsuspecting frenemies into the pit of doom. Since we had seen John Wayne in *Green Berets*, we even tried our hand at punji sticks, although ours were a less lethal offering. I mentioned we played guns in the willows behind the field, but it was also a great place to explore and wade during the spring flooding. In the winter, we snowshoed the trails and set rabbit snares.

My favorite time of the year was autumn because it got dark early and the weather was still warm. We had so much fun sneaking around in the dark pretending we were commandos or spies. Hide and seek and kick the can were a lot more fun in the dark. If we weren't playing, we were talking.

We were adept communicators, possibly because we had fewer distractions and more time to relate to each other. Everything

I have written so far speaks to the fact that we found distraction in everything, so that may not be true. But no matter the reason, we spent a lot of time just talking. It was common for friends to converse under a street light for a couple of hours in the evening.

My friend Mike Frasher and I had a favorite game we played on our moms. He was allowed out a half-hour longer than I was, so we went to my house first. I brought Mike in so it was harder for my mom to say no. I would ask if I could walk him home. Inevitably, she relented. Although he only lived three short blocks away, we could stretch our journey to at least fifteen minutes, maybe more. When we arrived at Mike's, we did the same thing there. He asked if he could walk me home. This little ruse extended my curfew and allowed us to continue the evening's conversation.

Chapter Eleven

The Movies

We didn't have TV, radio, social media or video games. We had a movie every two weeks at the Rec. Centre. It cost a dollar and we didn't know the movies were out of date. We could buy popcorn for a dime a bag, and it was delicious. If we wanted anything else, we brought it ourselves. The ticket cost and popcorn money paid for the next movie. The out-of-date movies were the ones we could afford, so that's what we got, and we loved them. Most were 1950s and 60s westerns and WWII flicks, with a healthy smattering of Disney, and even old slapstick Laurel and Hardy and The Three Stooges films thrown in for good measure.

I remember in grade one or two asking a girl I liked to a movie. We held hands and neither wanted to be the one to let go. After a time, our hands were cramped and wet with sweat. Thank goodness for intermission. As it turned out, she ditched me for John Craft because I ran out of Mojos and he still had some. That scenario played out the same way more than once. Damn that John—him and his chiseled good looks and endless supply of Mojos. Adolescent love can be a cruel master. I just wanted to be liked for me, not my Mojos.

Going to the movie was anticipated and cherished; we got excited and went a little crazy in the days leading up to the big event. The stackable chairs were placed in rows, benches in the front for us kids, and the projector was set up in the aisle between the chairs. Every movie had a couple of cartoons at the beginning. It was the only time we got to see Bugs Bunny, Wile E. Coyote, Yosemite Sam and Woody Woodpecker. Even the MGM lion was exciting. We had intermission because we had to. The reels needed to be changed and rewound and it took a while, so there was plenty of time to get some fresh air or visit with a friend.

Before the Rec. Centre, the movies were shown in the old one-room schoolhouse. For a period of time, from when it was Atlin's only schoolhouse until it became the museum, the building was used in conjunction with the Moose Hall as a community center. It was serviced by two outhouses—a men's and a women's; both two seaters, for efficiency, I presume.

Often, just as John Wayne was facing down the "no good yeller-belly sapsucker" in the middle of the street and we were all on the edge of our seats tingling with anticipation, a loud bang and some urgent muttering could be heard as the image on the screen flickered madly and suddenly went black. Someone has tripped over the projector cord, AGAIN!

We always dreaded the inevitable ending; it made sense to us that the movie should go on forever. It didn't matter how neat a package it was wrapped in: the good guy riding into the sunset, the bad guy lying boots up in the street. There had to be one more outlaw to kill or bunker to take or damsel to rescue ... "ewww." Eventually reality set in that it was over, the lights were on, people were rising and putting on their coats. We immediately turned to our closest friend and began speculating on the next film. "I hope it's a John Wayne again." "Yeah, but a war movie this time."

We didn't just leave; we helped stack chairs and sweep up the mess. If you did try to sneak out, somehow Mrs. Colwell always managed to catch you. She didn't even have to say anything, just gave you that look and you quickly found a chair to stack, nonchalantly pretending it was your original intention all along. When everything was done to Mrs. C.'s approval, we burst out the door in an insane posse of prepubescent exuberance. "Bam, bam, bang, bang, you're dead!" "No, I'm not, you missed." "Ouch!" Off into the night we ran shooting each other with our finger guns and throwing imaginary hand grenades, first pulling the imaginary pin with our teeth, stopping periodically to dramatically fake die an excruciating, slow-motion death in the middle of the street. The movies we saw were jet fuel for our already fertile imaginations.

We mimicked what we saw, thus the Cowboy and Indian and war games we played. Pirates and Zorro and Roman gladiators were all in our repertoire. We made swords and daggers from sticks and pieces of wood we found lying about. With a bandana or improvised eye patch we became Black Beard or Long John Silver. We made the Zorro Z in the dirt or snowbank. We yelled, "All for one and one for all!" as we ran through the neighborhood brandishing our wooden swords, fighting back the evil bad guys.

I personally had some confusion when it came to movies. Without TV, we had no way of knowing about various actors or movies. Typically, we knew nothing about the movies we were about to see aside from maybe the genre and sometimes who the star was.

They showed a fair amount of black and white movies because they were old and affordable. I had no idea they made black and white movies for aesthetic or artistic reasons. To my reasoning, black and white movies were all old and color all new. I thought *Young Frankenstein* was an old movie from the 1940s. Upon seeing Gene Wilder in *Blazing Saddles* a few years later, I could not believe he hadn't aged one iota.

The reverse was true for John Wayne. I saw him in *Donovan's Reef*, a Technicolor film, and next saw him in *True Grit*. I had no idea thirteen years had elapsed between the two and I could not believe he had aged so much so fast.

I was so sheltered that the first time I saw a man get shot and bleed in a movie, I completely lost it, jumping from my front-row seat, screaming my head off in front of the whole town and running crying all the way home. "There goes that Smith kid again ..."

Chapter Twelve

School Days

Our school was two back-to-back, double-wide trailers—the evolution of the one-room schoolhouse from just a few years earlier. Later another and finally one more was added, making a large T with four rooms in all and three bathrooms. In the spring, the roof leaked and buckets were strategically placed around the classrooms, and our desks were moved away from the drips. When the snow got too high on the roof, the older kids shoveled it off.

Our school yard was a patch of gravel and at times was covered with muddy water. At first, we only had a teeter-totter, a double swing set and a tetherball. Oh yeah, and a strange u-shaped pipe sticking out of the ground that the girls twirled around on. Only the girls, as it was anatomically impossible for the boys from what I can painfully remember. Our swing set was sturdy, the chains were thick and the seats were hard slabs of oak that could lay you out cold if you got hit in the head with one. Later we got a slide and a merry-go-round, a new teeter-totter, monkey bars and even later some half-buried loader tires ... "Huh." When the slide, the merry-go-round and teeter-totter arrived, the grade-school kids all helped

School was originally two back-to-back double-wide trailers; later two more were added, 1974. Originally published in the Atlin News Miner. Photo by Dave Dickinson.

assemble them, and we dug the holes and mixed and poured the cement to anchor them. Eventually the old deadly swing set was replaced with a much safer version.

We didn't have a gymnasium, so we used the Rec. Centre, which was three blocks away. It was fine for floor hockey and most P.E. activities and it did have two basketball hoops, although there were large log beams running across the ceiling ten feet (3m) off the floor, thus making it hard to shoot baskets. Needless to say, we were all very good at passing and layups, but a lot of us couldn't shoot to save our lives. In the spring after the thaw and in the fall, we had P.E. at The Campground four blocks from the school. The ground was mushy in the spring, and we slipped and slid our way through our various activities, returning to class with wet feet and bottoms and muddy knees. I'm certain it was quite a chore herding a gaggle of doddering, puddle-hopping children down the street to The Campground and back.

On any given day, the schoolyard could have more dogs than kids. And it was always an exciting disruption to math class when a dog fight broke out in front of the window. The rules stated no dogs in the schoolyard, but no one in town tied them up, and dogs do have a mind of their own. If they didn't go home when you yelled at them, what were you to do? Of course, those same dogs insisted on following us to the Rec. Centre or The Campground. Down the street we went, our little caravan of bundled-up kids with a long train of dogs trailing behind, barking and fighting with all the other dogs along the way. Passing my house was always an event.

Our school was small and intimate and often smelled like armpits and stinky socks. There were usually two or three grades in the same classroom with sometimes less than fifteen kids per room. The teachers had to be diverse and flexible. They might teach math and science in the morning, then P.E. and typing in the afternoon, often at the same time. They had to cover for each other as well. The junior high teacher could suddenly find themselves teaching the grade one and two class for a few days and vice versa. Anyone in town with a degree in anything was a qualified substitute teacher, experience not necessary; they just had to keep us from killing each other until the full-time teacher returned.

It was mandatory to take French, and it was often a challenge to find a qualified French teacher. We had a lady that was actually from France and we had a French-Canadian man for a while. We had a gentleman who learned his French at university in the United States, a lady who learned French in high school and university in Canada, and a fellow who admitted learning the next day's lesson the night before from his French-Canadian wife. We came to learn that there were many pronunciations of the same word; it was all a bit confusing, or a lot confusing, depending on your aptitude or lack thereof.

We also combined correspondence courses with our regular curriculum. I remember taking mechanical drawing and art through the mail. A particular art assignment may have been sketching a nature scene from a photo or painting a still life of selected objects from around the room. A few rudimentary examples were provided and we were then left on our own to prepare our masterpieces.

Some class time was set aside for the correspondence courses but usually at the same time as another class was being taught. So, as we were refining our charcoal smudging techniques or mastering our feathery brush strokes, the loud repetitive droning of French class or math class resonated through our minds and destroyed any hope of concentration.

Upon completion of our great works of art, they went in envelopes and were mailed off to the giant head—it may as well have been a giant head for all the connection we had to whoever eventually looked at, or maybe didn't even look at, our work—we were then assigned an arbitrary grade for our effort. Many might refute the fact that art can be graded at all, especially at the grade-school level, because of the whole "beauty is in the eye of the beholder" thing. I

Class photo grades 3 and 4, 1974. I'm second from the left, standing. Originally published in the Atlin News Miner. Photo by Dave Dickinson.

quickly figured out that if you followed the letter of the assignment you could do no wrong and achieve at least a B average with little or no effort. For example, if you were instructed to paint three apples, as long as there were three objects in the painting and they were red, you passed. If you threw in a splash of green, then a B-plus might be in your future.

Home economics was taught by the principal's wife in their house down the street. She was also a full-time classroom teacher. Imagine your small, home kitchen hosting six or eight rowdy pre-teens, armed with flour and mixing devices. The straw that broke the proverbial camel's back was when the teacher found that her Lazy Susan had been cleared of pots and pans and was being used as an amusement ride by some of the boys.

Soon after, another trailer was brought in to act as teacher housing, and later it ended up as a spillover classroom for home economics, typing and special education.

My friend Mitch Alexander and I were the only boys in our home economics class. We were to take what was explained to us as a more useful, practical course. We were separated from the girls and given completely different assignments. At first, I bought into their reasoning, but later I came to suspect sexism had a hand to play. I'm guessing we were supposed to find us a good little woman to do our cooking, or forever eat out, as we barely set foot in the kitchen. While the girls learned how to make soufflés and rues and bake pies and cakes, Mitch and I learned how to sew on buttons and darn socks. We might as well have learned typewriter repair, although the button thing proved handy. I did enjoy knitting, but apparently, I bit off more than I could chew when deciding I would knit a blanket—I ended up with the longest, thinnest scarf ever made.

The only kitchen time we saw was when the gravy needed stirring or the frosting needed to be whipped or the dishes needed to be washed. I guess we were okay to do the manual labor part of cooking. I do remember eating all the wonderful delights the girls learned how to make, and I was thankful for the sharing. My feeble attempt at reciprocation was continually turned down as no one wanted a scarf built for two. To be completely honest, Mitch and my ostracizing may have had something to do with our lack of maturity, as I've found boys are often a few years behind the girls in that department, and maybe the teacher wanted to avoid another Lazy Susan event or worse.

Our principal did double duty as a full-time teacher as well as ringmaster of the entire circus. Countless unpaid hours were spent making sure everything was humming along seamlessly and the students, staff, and facilities were taken care of. On top of all that and so much more, he needed to produce a full curriculum for the three grades he taught in his classroom.

Despite whether or not one got along with any or all of the teachers, it is undeniable that they were a huge part of our community. In many Northern towns, the school is the hub of the community and Atlin was no different. The teachers and staff were so much more. They were examples of what altruism and sacrifice mean. They were a continual positive presence in and out of the school. In a small community, teaching is more than a full-time job. Thousands of unpaid hours are put in on weekends and evenings. Teachers act as social workers, psychologists, pseudo-parents, friends and good examples to their students and their families.

Field trips were to places like the highway department and the police station, or if we were lucky, the museum. Local expertise was called upon regularly; a watercolorist might give a class at the lakeshore with Atlin Mountain as the subject. The local botanist might take the class out to identify edible plants. The rescue and climbing expert showed us how to fight hypothermia and belay a rope. Our education was a community effort before "it takes a village" was a catchphrase.

Atlin's school only went up to junior high, and after that we went to Whitehorse, 120 miles (193km) away in the Yukon, where we boarded in dorms or private homes. On Friday after school, we scoured town looking for someone from Atlin who could hopefully offer a ride home. If we couldn't find anyone, we hitchhiked, weather permitting, or stayed in town. Sometimes it was two or three weeks between home visits.

At times, our schooling was a communal effort. Older kids often helped out with the younger students in the classroom, during track meets and Christmas concerts, or even helped with the herculean task of getting a couple dozen excited six-or-seven-year-olds properly dressed for recess when it was twenty below (-29 °C) outside. We helped with the mundane tasks that kept everything rolling. We washed the blackboards, shoveled snow, and many of us acted as projectionist for films and filmstrips. We ran the old hand-crank mimeograph machine, cranking out hundreds of pages and punching holes with the three-hole punch. The paper cutter was a wicked device. With its long sharp blade and lack of guard, it's hard to fathom schools these days allowing students to use such a device.

There was a collection of cross-country skis and boots at our school. They were primarily for P.E., but we were allowed to check them out before and after school. Mitch Alexander and I immediately found a hill to ski down that was "real skiing" in our minds—the fun kind. We got pretty good at downhill on those skinny skis. Gliding across a field or down the lake was boring and seemed like nothing more than exercise. Of course, during P.E. we had to do the flat skiing, thus the physical part of P.E., I guess. Back then I never thought twice about it, but for a lot of us who could not afford skis and boots, this was a unique and generous gesture that allowed many of us to experience skiing in both forms. I loved the thrill of the downhill skiing but could appreciate the beauty and grace of an experienced cross-country skier.

Although technically inside, but nevertheless cold, we also curled. Most of us curled at least once a week on community teams as well as our school team. Atlin produced some excellent curlers over the years. I enjoyed the challenge of reading the ice. In the days before artificial ice, it wasn't so easy. Dave Goodwin, Ron Bowden and Jack Green, as well as countless others, did a great job with limited

I'm at the bottom of the crude ski hill built by the community, 1968. This ski hill came to be like many things did in those days. A group of friends thought it would be fun to have a ski hill. My mom and dad were key players as Mom skied throughout her life. A little planning culminated in a weekend work-bee to slash brush and set up a tow rope. The rope was an old one they borrowed from the ski hill in Whitehorse. My dad and others set an old truck on blocks and stripped the wheels. Using a rim for a drive pulley, all you had to do was fire up the truck and put it in gear. You could change gears for different speeds.

resources and hundreds of unpaid hours, but there was a limit, even for those guys. If we had an unusually warm stretch and the frosty ceiling began to melt, small stalagmites could appear overnight. These had to be scraped down and the area resurfaced. Both sheets often had a pronounced fall at either end. Once you figured this out, it may have been an advantage over visiting teams until they became wise to it and often showed up early to throw a few rocks. I think our sometimes-less-than-perfect ice made us better curlers.

An ice-skating rink was erected behind the Rec. Centre and eventually teachers, students and parents built one behind the school. We spent endless hours, nights and days playing hockey, tag,

A group of student curlers enjoying Atlin's fine curling rink, 1978. Originally published in the Atlin News Miner. Photo by Tom Kirkland.

red rover, broom ball and other games we made up. If we wanted to skate, we shoveled off the snow. If we didn't have a puck, a frozen horse turd worked surprisingly well, although it was often hard to find a goalie.

The lights were left on in one of the classrooms at night so we could see to skate, although this only lit one end adequately; once again, it was hard to find a goalie for the dark end. We didn't have a Zamboni, but Mr. Dickinson kept a nice surface on it with his garden hose. The best sliding hill in town was behind the school, and most recesses were spent sliding down it or skating on the rink. We went out for recess in all temperatures and conditions; we needed the break from school and the teachers needed the break from us.

Once or twice a year, we went to Carcross or Teslin, both roughly a hundred miles (160km) away, for track meets or floor hockey or curling competitions. We didn't have a school bus, so the parents drove us in their old beaters. We never wore seatbelts because we didn't know we should and there probably weren't any anyway. We slept on the gym floor if they had a gym, or we billeted out to people in the community, at times quite intoxicated people. "What's a background check?"

Cassiar, another sporting-event destination, was over three hundred miles (160km) away, a long six-to-eight-hour trip on a gravel road jammed in the back of someone's station wagon. Our parents and teachers were very dedicated and patient. At one point, students and teachers erected a wilderness commando course in the trees below the school, complete with rope-ladder bridges and even a zip line that meandered through the tops of the trees. Meant to instill confidence and help conquer fears, it was a big hit with the kids, but it proved hard to keep us off during unsupervised times.

One year, a number of grades all camped out at the Mouth of Pine. We walked from town along trails and crossed Pine Creek upstream on a rope bridge at a place where the creek shoots between two rocky outcroppings. The water was deep and violent, and the bridge consisted of three ropes: one to walk on and two for hand rails. It was suspended about fifteen feet (4.5m) above the raging torrent. It was a shaky affair and high enough to scare the bravest. Eventually we all made it across with a combination of coaxing, encouragement and peer pressure. I've noticed during my time in both countries that what Canadians call a creek, Americans would consider a raging river.

That day we set up our tents, made fire pits and played in the shallow warm water. The next morning after breakfast we prepared chickens, wrapped them in tin foil and buried them in the coals of our fires. We heaped sand over the coals and left camp. We spent the day climbing Monarch Mountain and returned late that afternoon to unearth our nicely-baked chickens just in time for our dinner. That evening our RCMP Constable came out to discuss firearm safety and allowed us to shoot his revolver.

On other outings, we canoed around Pike Lake. Kendall Merry's dad, Wayne, taught us how to rappel down a cliff face. Craig and Denise's dad, Harold Colwell, taught us how to build a proper raft. My mom held watercolor classes by the shore of Warm Bay. We were taught how to build a sauna out of willows and plastic sheeting and shown gourmet cooking with local ingredients cooked over a fire. We attended wilderness first-aid classes and orienteering as well as basic wilderness survival. A gentleman brought out his black powder musket and showed us how to load and shoot it.

One year, we all piled into various boats and headed down the lake for a week of fishing, camping and exploring. We walked to the Llewellyn Glacier, climbed the south side of Spruce Mountain, explored Copper Island and went lake trout fishing every evening.

The next spring, we all took a helicopter to the top of Spruce Mountain on Teresa Island, where we followed the caribou herds and slid down the long snowy bowls. We marveled at the view as we ate our sandwiches and drank our Kool-Aid. As Atlin kids, we were exposed to things kids anywhere else couldn't possibly dream of.

Mr. Dickinson started school dances in his classroom. Once a month or so, we decorated the room with paper chains, balloons and crepe-paper streamers, and someone even produced a disco ball. It was the height of the disco movement, so the guys zipped up their platform boots; in my case, my dad's cast offs from one of my visits to see him. We donned our best velour or satin shirts. Mine were also Dad's hand-me-downs, always way too big but much better than my worn western shirts with the pearl snaps. We threw on our favorite bell bottoms and grabbed our Members Only jackets and out the door we ran. Quite often it was minus twenty or more so we froze in our skimpy clothes and leather shoes. We didn't care; we were way too cool to care. I will say the leather-soled shoes were excellent for sliding down hills and perfect for Hooky Bobbing. I won't pretend to know what the women's fashions of the day were, but I do remember liking the jeans without back pockets a lot. We were always a few years behind the trends, so I'm not sure if we were cool, but it didn't matter to us.

It was always an eclectic playlist, with everything from Abba to Zeppelin. As a rhythmically-challenged person, I just want to say I have not been able to dance since disco went out. We were so sheltered back then it caused a huge scandal when Keith Carlick snuck on Elton John's *"The Bitch is Back."* Oh, the horror.

Thanks goes out to Mr. Dickinson and all the other teachers and parents that chaperoned those memorable dances. We may have been out of style, un-hip and even square, but we knew how to have fun and shake our groove thing.

This might be a good time to apologize to all of my past teachers for wasting their time. Some come late to wisdom.

Chapter Thirteen

The Road to Town

Whitehorse was the big city in our eyes. In 1970, it boasted a population of just over five thousand people. Everyone in Atlin called it "town," as in, "We're going to town" or "I just got back from town." To the kids it was a wondrous and amazing place, and going to town was a treat ... but getting there was not. The trip was long and arduous—one hundred and twenty miles (161km) from Atlin to Whitehorse. In the early days, only twenty miles (32km) were paved. It is sixty miles (100km) from Atlin to the Alaska Highway, thirty (50km) of those in British Columbia and the other thirty in the Yukon, and from there, another sixty (100km) to Whitehorse. The Alaska Highway was wider, smoother and straighter and it was always a relief to reach it.

The Atlin Road was built by the Canadian Army Corps of Engineers from 1950 to 1951. Before that, Atlin was serviced by boat or plane. It was a winding, twisting track that meandered through the boreal forest and over steep mountain foothills. Little thought was given to safety or convenience; expediency and cost were paramount.

Most creeks were spanned by single-lane wooden bridges, usually at the bottom of a steep-sided valley. Crossing these bridges, in the winter especially, oftentimes required a game of vehicular Russian roulette. Road maintenance on the Yukon side was sporadic at best. As the road did not service a Yukon community, it was on the bottom of their priority list. Plowing was usually late, if done at all, and sanding was a rare occurrence. When approaching one of the bridges, it was a fine balance between caution and chaos. Drivers descended into the valley cautiously because black ice was a constant concern and most approaches harbored at least one blind corner. Meeting an oncoming vehicle on the bridge was a real concern. Once determining that the way was clear, the driver then stomped on the gas pedal, rocketed through the narrow opening and hopefully gained enough speed to make it up the other side. Many a weary traveler spent hours stuck down in these valleys, backing and surging, slipping and sliding, trying desperately to free themselves from those hellish hollows.

In the summer, the road was so dusty that when passing an oncoming car, a driver could lose sight of the road completely. It was often wise to pull over and let the dust settle before continuing. The fine granules infiltrated through every crevice. When you did arrive in Whitehorse, you were covered in a film of grit. If you hadn't used the ventilation for a time, it was prudent to open all the car doors and windows, stealthily crank the fan to the highest setting, and run away as fast as you could while the tornado of debris chased you across the yard. My mom came from a time when you dressed up to travel, and she fought a never-ending battle to keep her clothes clean.

In the spring or after a good downpour, the road was slick with a greasy mud and strewn with bone-jarring potholes and washboard. Washboard, a threat on many stretches, is a series of small ridges caused by water erosion and traffic. Hitting an area of washboard unexpectedly was a real danger and could quickly send a car out of control, vibrating across the roadway and into the ditch or toward another car.

Vehicles were indistinguishable underneath a two-inch (5cm) layer of slimy muck. Entering and exiting was not achievable without transferring at least some of the mire to your clothing. Atlin folk were easily identifiable by the citizens of Whitehorse because of the brown pallor or streaks of grime on their clothes.

The severe winter temperatures caused a myriad of issues with vehicles and there was always the chance you might get stuck in a blizzard or a whiteout. People didn't travel much after dark on the Atlin Road in those days. If you broke down or hit the ditch after six or seven pm on a winter's eve, chances were good you would be on your own till someone came by in the morning. At forty below, you had better be prepared. People carried sleeping bags and survival kits, food, kindling, an axe and fire starter on every trip. Extra gas and a spare spare could never hurt.

Glaciers formed in the same places every year. Without proper drainage, water seeped over the roadway then froze, building up, over and over until it was completely impassible. Heavy equipment had to be brought in to scrape it away and the process started over. At times, these areas mounded up a couple feet high (0.65m) and were as long as football fields. Scattered with wheel-swallowing potholes and slippery hillocks, these sites were the locale of many a winter mishap, in some cases life-threatening.

There are many stories of the less prepared burning spare tires, seat covers and, in one case, all the linens from The Kootenay Hotel in order to stay alive while stuck on the Atlin Road at night in the dead of winter. There was an unspoken code of conduct while traveling the Atlin Road: *You always rendered assistance to anyone who needed help.* My dad went into the ditch one thirty-below evening around twenty miles (32.6km) from Atlin. Shortly after assessing his peril, a truck sped past without even slowing. Luckily, he was picked up shortly after by a passing friend. He was so incensed, he tracked down the driver of the truck and ripped him up one side and down the other.

The British Columbia side of the road, thirty (48km) of the sixty miles (96km), had survival cabins spaced roughly ten miles (16km) apart. These were small 10'x 10' (3m x 3m) structures with a wood stove and a bunk. They were stocked with firewood and kindling, fire starter and wooden matches. Each one had an axe and sometimes people left a few canned food items. If you had to use the cabin, you restocked the wood and kindling and left it as you found it, ready for the next person. Those cabins saved lives. There are a number of cases where, in the nick of time, a person reached one and was able to light a fire to save themselves.

In the late 1970s, a man in Atlin raised chickens. He flew into a fit of rage one winter night, setting fire to his home, his coops and all the chickens. He was forever after referred to as Colonel Sanders.

The Colonel turned himself in and for a time was the guest of Atlin's one RCMP Corporal. The accommodations in Atlin's small jail are not ideal and stays are usually short. Atlin was served by a traveling circuit court judge, so nothing could be done immediately. Normally crimes committed in Atlin were of a petty nature and the offenders were issued a summons to appear before the judge, and sent home to wait for the next court session. Because of the severity of the crime, it was determined the Colonel should be arraigned before being released on his own recognizance.

The judge happened to be very busy and didn't have time to travel all the way to Atlin. The RCMP explained the urgency to the judge and asked if something could be done. As the judge was traveling to Tagish that day, a unique plan was agreed upon to save time. They decided to meet at the last survival cabin on the British Columbia side of the Atlin Road.

Corporal Mike Morhon and the jail guard, Joe Florence, loaded up the prisoner, grabbed a picture of the Queen and headed up the road. The judge was waiting at the cabin with the crown lawyer and a court reporter. A fire was lit and the small cabin was warming nicely. The corporal hung the picture of the Queen. The judge quickly arraigned the Colonel and made a hasty retreat back up the road, Northern justice served.

As well as the survival cabins, sand boxes were provided at some of the longer, steeper hills along the route. If travelers were having a hard time ascending a particularly slippery stretch, they could always shovel some sand onto the road for traction. Kept in a wooden box to stay dry and strategically placed beside the road on the hill, these simple conveniences saved many a driver.

As time went on, the road was improved and more frequently traveled, and the winters became milder. Squatting and vandalism became an issue and the cabins were eliminated.

For a time, Mom owned a small two-door Mazda car. Perpetually muddy on the outside and chewed and hairy on the inside, it was reliable and good on gas. With its short wheel base and winter tires, that little car never let us down. On one trip home from "town," we approached the base of the longest, most notorious of hills: Twelve

Mile Hill on the Yukon side of the road. As there was a severe right-angle turn at the bottom, it was hard to get up enough speed to make it to the top. When we rounded the turn at the bottom, we noticed a crew-cab pickup truck stranded just below the crest. From the many sets of skid marks, it was apparent the driver had made numerous attempts to reach the top but had failed at every try. We saw two men sitting in the cab of the pickup; they had either given up or decided to take a break and think things over. Locals knew of the sand boxes, which at times were snow-covered mounds indistinguishable to those unfamiliar.

As it happened, the men were parked beside one of the covered boxes. Mom pulled our little "car that could" up beside the pickup, and I rolled down my window as did the driver of the truck. A mixed expression of relief, frustration and incredulity spread across his face. I guess he was a man of little words as all he could manage was a grunted "huh" as he glanced behind our car, possibly expecting that we were being pushed by a bulldozer. My mom quickly pointed out the close proximity of the sand box and asked if they needed any other help. A shake of the head, another glance behind our car and a muffled thanks was all we got. We effortlessly pulled away from the stricken truck and its disbelieving occupants. As we continued on, a slow grin spread across my mom's face and, with a twinkle in her eye, she said, "Guess I should have offered them a tow."

I remember one cold trip to Whitehorse in Mom's car. The temperature the morning we left Atlin was around forty below (-40°C) and in the river valleys it was ten degrees colder. We were on the Yukon side of the road and approaching one of the small bridges at the bottom of a steep valley. At one point, Mom tried to shift and could not get it into any gear; we were stuck in neutral. Trying to stay warm in the much-colder back seat was our friend Lucille Jack. Knowing we were in trouble and concerned about the car quitting altogether, we decided we'd better get a fire going as soon as possible. We quickly pushed the car to the side of the road and began gathering wood. Mom tried one more time and the transmission shifted into gear. We slowly drove up the hill in first gear, happy to be moving but afraid to shift. Mom waited until we got to the top of a long downhill section before she attempted to shift again; luckily, the transmission worked and behaved the rest of the trip. It was a reminder of how fast one can be in a dangerous predicament in the North Country.

Places on the road were named for people who had bad accidents in one particular spot or another. For example, Bentley's Corner, the site of a particularly severe wreck that the Bentley family barely survived.

Wild and domestic animals also posed a real threat to drivers. When the snow was particularly deep, moose, horses and cows alike preferred the easygoing travel of the roadway. Moose and horses were the most commonly struck animals in those days. Many a split-second decision saved drivers and animals but sent vehicles careening into a snowbank or worse. More than a few trucks and cars were destroyed, animals killed and people injured.

My mom and Ev Colwell were on the way to "town" one fine spring day when a rabbit bounded in front of the car. My mom quickly braked and it was believed the rabbit was spared. The ladies arrived safely in "town" and decided to gas up the car. They pulled into a full-service station and the attendant started the fill-up. As was the custom, he proceeded to wash the windows. Starting in the rear, he moved around to the front, reaching from one side then the other. As he crossed in front of the car, he abruptly recoiled, dropping his squeegee. Seemingly horrified and angry, he yelled out, "That's not funny!" Perplexed, the ladies got out to see what all the fuss was about. Unfortunately, the rabbit did not escape its encounter with the car—its sheared-off head was stuck in the grille. As if carefully placed, it faced forward, unseeing eyes wide open, a grisly hood ornament and superfluous souvenir of their trip.

Chapter Fourteen

In Town

The first thing we did when arriving in Whitehorse was find something to eat, especially important for those of us who left their breakfast back at Davey Hall Lake or on Bentley's Corner. I remember the milkshakes at the Edgewater Inn. They filled your glass and gave you what was left in the mixing cup. They also had the best tuna salad sandwiches and great cheeseburgers. There was a glass case with what seemed like a hundred different kinds of pie and cake. There was also the cafeteria at the Hudson's Bay department store. A cafeteria was a wondrous thing to an Atlin kid; so many choices, all of them ready instantly. No excruciating wait while your stomach growled and gurgled. They had seven colors of Jell-O (seven!) with whipped cream. It didn't come with that at home.

After the Jell-O, it was on to the big wall of televisions; a kid could spend the rest of the day right there. I remember that even the test pattern was cool to me—all those bright colors. Of course, before long your mom would drag you away and subject you to the excruciating and embarrassing ordeal that was "trying on clothes." We only put up with it because we hoped we could go to the toy aisle next.

Main Street, Whitehorse, Yukon, is the territorial capital and Canada's largest northern city, 1964. First Nations people hunted and fished in the area for thousands of years before the first Europeans arrived in the late 1800s. Whitehorse, originally known as Canyon City, rose to prominence during the Klondike Gold Rush. It cemented its permanence when copper was discovered early in 1898 by Jack McIntire and Sam McGee.

The toy aisle was indescribable. It turned most of us into deaf and mute zombies. All sounds faded into the background and at best we could only mumble and nod as we slowly floated past the many wonders. There were Tonka trucks posed magnificently on the shelf, their brilliant yellow paint jobs gleaming in the florescent lights; crimson Flexible Flyer Planet Junior racing sleds, so sleek and beautiful, seemed to call your name. They had toboggans and race car sets and train sets and Hot Wheels, pogo sticks and Daisy BB guns, Wrist Rocket slingshots, cap guns and army men. When your mother yelled you back to reality, you felt exhausted and a little sad. You reluctantly followed her out of the store lost in thought, dreaming about all the great times you could have with those toys.

The next part of the day was often filled with endless stops at building supply stores and auto parts shops, the drugstore or post office or—the worst ever—the bank. These were all places no kid wanted to go. We found them tedious and boring, and it didn't help that we couldn't see over the counters. Many hours were spent looking at a wall and a parent's leg.

The only thing that kept us going was the promise of Hougen's Department Store. Oh, glorious Hougen's. It was the greatest place on earth. There were large display windows in the front, adorned with colorful lights, fake snow or lawn and life-like mannequins dressed in the latest fashions. One display might hold a downhill skiing scene from the Swiss Alps, another a beach scene or Santa and his elves. Those displays transported us to another place and time, places we only read about or saw in movies. Walking through the big double doors, you were overwhelmed with sights and sounds and smells. To the right were sporting goods, guns, fishing tackle, lures, reels, boxing gloves and heavy bags, skis and snowshoes. To the left were more TVs and also furniture, record players and appliances. Although the TVs were hard to resist, the "pièce de résistance" and the paramount reason to go to town lay just ahead.

There he stood, surrounded by washers and dryers, resplendent in his entire majestic wonder. With his ebony mane flowing down his muscular neck, silver bit clamped fiercely in his teeth, he rose proudly above the household appliances. In front of you stood the most magnificent of all beasts—the mechanical horse. Excitement mounted as you shuffled along the line, and there was always a line, giddy with anticipation, attention riveted. Lost were the surrounding sights and sounds as you neared your prize. When it was finally your turn, you carefully placed your foot in the stirrup, got a firm grip on the saddle horn and you leaped atop.

With the reigns in one hand, one sweaty dime in the other, you slowly placed the coin in the slot and hesitantly released it. Suddenly you were galloping across the Badlands, chasing outlaws or being chased by a posse. You threw your head back and laughed as the powerful beast surged forward. You wanted to ride and ride and ride forever, but sadly a dime only got you a couple minutes of exhilaration and fantasy. If you had another dime and your mom was still shopping, you just might get a second spin, but first it was back to the end of the line. There was nothing quite like the mechanical horse at Hougan's. Kids for hundreds of miles around loved that old horse in all its faded, chipped-paint glory.

The old mustang's allure only slightly diminished after he was ingloriously moved upstairs to women's lingerie. Undoubtedly it was the idea of some salesman to convince women to buy more bras if their kids were busy riding a mechanical horse—like that

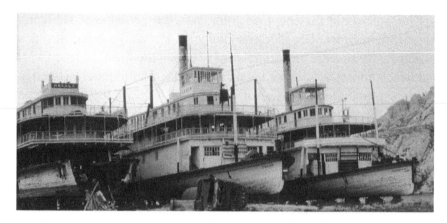

Vessels beached along the Yukon River near Whitehorse, 1969. On the right is the SS Whitehorse, built in 1901. It was a 167-foot (50m) long stern wheeler that navigated the Yukon River for fifty-four years before being hauled ashore. In the middle is the SS Casca, a 180-foot (55m) stern wheeler that was put into service in 1937. Sadly, both ships were lost to fire in 1974 before they could be preserved. The third ship was torn down before the fire.

makes sense. Although no longer surrounded by guns, bullets, bows and arrows and washing machines as he had been downstairs, somehow even surrounded by panties and stockings, he was able to retain his maverick enchantment.

A stop at Kentucky Fried Chicken was exciting because, weather permitting, we usually took our food to Rotary Park to eat at the picnic tables. The park's playground featured items Atlin kids didn't have. The circular slide was my favorite; it seemed futuristic to me. Its polished metal winked in the sunlight as if summoning me. It was all I could do to choke down my snack pack so I could go play. There was a merry-go-round and more slides, one with a hump in the middle and one that was twice as long as the one we had in Atlin. I was very impressed with the park's manicured lawns—something never seen at home.

We happened to be in town the day Kentucky Fried Chicken opened, and I got to meet Colonel Sanders. He made personal appearances at every new store opening anywhere across the globe. I wasn't all that impressed because I had never been exposed to the advertising campaign. I thought it was a local store and the strange-looking man who had his likeness on the buckets owned the place. Many years later, while pretending to attend high school, I worked at that same store and was the only employee that had ever met the Colonel.

Chapter Fifteen

We Worked

Even at a very young age we had summer and after-school jobs. It was a time when kids worked, and not just the chores we all had at home. We stacked wood for the old-timers, cleaned up yards and sheds, washed the trucks at Atlin Trucking, vacuumed the floor and scrubbed the grill at the Atlin Inn, cleared brush, painted houses or sorted gold for the miners. Then there was babysitting—we all did that, boys as well as girls. There were no TVs or video game systems, VCRs weren't out yet, or if they were, we didn't know anyone who had one, and there were no radio stations to listen to, so we read comics or books and listened to records or eight tracks if they had them. If they were country music fans, we listened to Conway Twitty and Patsy Cline, or Willie and Waylon. If the parents liked contemporary music, we listened to Nana Mouskouri or Neil Diamond or Engelbert Humperdinck, and, if you were lucky, maybe the Beatles or The Beach Boys or the Rolling Stones.

We didn't know much about bands or singers so we tried it all, especially the ones with cool album covers. Any music was better than none and we were exposed to all genres. We listened to everything

The Adams brothers had the entrepreneurial spirit. Here they are selling old bottles to the tourists, early 1970s. Originally published in the Atlin News Miner. Photo by Tom Kirkwood.

from Pavarotti to the Irish Rovers, Herb Albert and the Tijuana Brass to Marty Robbins. I remember being continually sucked into listening to Ray Conniff because his album covers often featured scantily clad vixens. I wonder if I thought by playing those records, somehow the beautiful women would come alive before my eyes. I particularly enjoyed Judy Brasseau's collection of crying songs as I called them, featuring Johnny Mathis, Freddy Fender and the like. To this day, my favorite music makes me cry. Thank you, Judy, for trusting a ten-year-old with those prized albums.

If one of our friends was also babysitting, then we talked on the phone, something we didn't do in the evening at home. Our parents had strict phone rules back then. No calling in the evening and never during meals and no idle chit chat—get to the point and get off. You never knew when you might miss an important call—after all, there wasn't call waiting, voicemail or call display back then.

A dollar an hour was normal for babysitting and was a lot of money for a ten-year-old. This was back when a dollar could buy you five comic books at old man Craft's store, or you could get a hundred Double Bubble chewing gum or Mojo's at Edie Crum's grocery. A dollar got you ten Pep Chews or Fun Dips or five candy bars at the Atlin Trading Post.

At the age of nine, I got Atlin's only ever paper route and delivered the Whitehorse paper, the *Whitehorse Star*. Three times a week I picked up my bundle of papers at the post office where the mail, as well as small freight items, were dropped off. I had roughly fifteen customers and was paid fifteen cents of the twenty-five-cent cost. Not a bad deal for a nine-year-old. Six-something a week was a fortune. The problem was that my customers were spread out all over the dang place. I might have a couple people up the hill at one end of town, then three at the opposite end, a few in the middle, then a couple more a mile (1.6km) out the Atlin Road and up the hill. They were miles apart and always at the top of a hill, or so it seemed to a nine-year-old. When I could ride my bike it wasn't too bad, but walking seemed to take forever. Don't

Atlin's Whitehorse Star paperboy Brad Smith.

My mom staged this photo with my friend Lance Shaw, 1974. Originally published in the Atlin News Miner. Photo by Tom Kirkwood.

tell, but my mom helped when it was really cold out. I was proud to hold that job for a year and a half. Of the paper deliverers to follow in my footsteps, the longest tenure was three months by my buddy Randy Green, who resigned his position, declaring he could no longer work for The Man. Preferring his independence and poverty, I'm assuming.

Before the paper delivery job, I had a brief stint with my friend Pete Wright. We were hired to clean the dining room and kitchen at the Atlin Inn every evening, approximately an hour and a half a night. The job included vacuuming, sweeping and mopping as well as taking out the garbage and cleaning the grill. I remember being too short to reach the grill so I stood on a chair. The grill was often still hot. We used a pumice stone to clean it and I remember burning my wrists on a number of occasions. We weren't employed long as for some strange reason, pie slices and cans of ice tea mysteriously disappeared during our shift and we were blamed. Who knew they inventoried pie slices? I say that's what you get for hiring unsupervised child labor.

Forest Fires and Missed Fortunes

When forest fires were raging in the area, Atlin was often a staging ground and local pilots were busy supplying the firefighters with everything they needed. Planes and choppers were flying in and out twenty-four hours a day. The thirteen- to sixteen-year-old kids got jobs loading floatplanes at the docks in front of town. It was exciting to be part of something so important.

In those days, Northern Canada had a program that, for lack of a better term, we called conscription—but instead of the military, one could be pressed into service fighting a fire. Conscription was enacted when towns or park land, or at times hunting and trapping areas, were in danger. If you were sixteen and up, you could be conscripted. If you refused, you could be fined and even jailed. To a northern kid, it was a rite of passage and we all longed to go. Pretty much every one of us went at least once.

When I was five or six, my uncle and his family came to visit from Bremerton, Washington. They weren't in town a day when a fire broke out just a couple of miles (3km) north of town. My uncle, being an able-bodied man, was conscripted. It mattered little that he wasn't from Atlin or the North or even the country. Off he went with my dad in borrowed work clothes and boots. He found it all a grand adventure, but my aunt, who could see the glow of the fire from town, was a nervous wreck. The fire was quickly doused and my dad and uncle returned safely. Aside from falling face first into a swamp with a heavy pack on his back and nearly drowning, my uncle was no worse for wear and returned home with a great story. Interestingly enough, none of the family ever visited the North again.

I must say the entrepreneurial spirit was alive and well in Atlin's youth. Randy Green and I tried many "get rich quick" endeavors. We picked Labrador tea for my mom to sell in her shop. I think that lasted one, maybe two days at the most. Do you know how many distractions there are in the woods and how easy it is to become bored with squatting in a bog pulling tiny leaves off a bush? "Hey, did you see that squirrel?" "Yeah, let's go see where it went." "Okay."

The most exciting and easiest job, with assuredly the highest earning potential of them all had to be when, I believe it was Sweden, offered ten dollars a gunny sack for pine cones. Ten whole dollars. "Holy crap, Batman, we're gonna be rich this time for sure."

I'm posing with my new snowshoes made the traditional Tlingit way by craftsman from Teslin, Yukon, 1970.

Okay, so first, a gunny sack is huge when you're ten. Second, as it turned out, they were not talking about the dry, light pine cones conveniently lying on the ground, but rather the new, hard, prickly and sticky ones that tear your hands apart while trying to pry them off the tree as you precariously hang from a branch. From what I can remember, a few people may have filled a couple of bags; but as far as Randy and my feeble career as arborists, it ended in lacerations, bruises and a good scolding from my mother for using her butter to remove the pitch from various places on our bodies.

Strike two, but we persevered and moved on to the next grand plan: diamond willow jewelry. Some of you are saying, "Huh?" right now, but yes, it was a thing then. When a branch is removed from a diamond willow, it leaves a diamond pattern. If you cut small pieces, peel the bark, sand them, shellac them and glue a pin to the back, they make nice brooches. At times, a gold nugget was glued to the middle of the diamond. My mom offered to sell all we could make on consignment. She offered as well her workshop and supplies, including the gold at no cost. One would think that a good deal and a no-fail money maker. As it turned out, the diamond willow was a long bike ride out the road, and Como Lake was along the way, and it was a hot summer ... you can guess the rest.

My mom even gave us a ride to the diamond willow once where we harvested enough to make some big bucks. But alas, somehow, we just never found the time to sit still long enough to complete very many. I have to say, we finally did finish a couple and they sold, but by then we were on to the more lucrative field that was "rock ducks." After all, we considered ourselves rock experts. What's a rock duck, you may be asking? Try to remember this was the 1970s—anything with a flower painted on it sold. A typical rock duck consisted of a flat oval stone, the body, with a smaller, rounder stone glued on top, the head. A little leather bill and two plastic eyes were glued to the head, and with a colorful floral pattern painted on the body, a rock duck was born.

The part we excelled at was collecting the appropriate rocks—after all, we were throwing rocks daily and we knew where to find the right ones. Where production slowed was the actual assembly. Production ground to an agonizing and shuddering halt with the painting of the body. Randy was much more artistic than I, and I believe he completed some on his own after it was obvious his business partner was in no way holding up his end of the deal. Eventually my mom bought my rocks for a root beer float and my rock duck business was officially over.

A couple of us started a snow shoveling company, but after only one substantial snowfall that winter and only a few customers, we quickly forgot about it.

Of course, we did the proverbial lemonade stand; in our case, Kool-Aid, but all in all, the same concept. If recollection serves me correctly, building the stand and making the sign was more fun than waiting for some unsuspecting victim to fall prey to our lukewarm semi-sweet concoction served in a wax paper cup with the minimum of dirt and bugs. One great business lesson was learned: Do not give credit. Do you know how hard it is to get a nickel out of a seven-year-old if they don't want to pay you? After first pondering whether or not to hire Lance Shaw as our collection agent, we quickly gave up that idea and the Kool-Aid business altogether. The stress of high-pressure retail sales did us in—that and counting all that money.

Like the stampeders of old, we were continually looking forward toward the next strike.

I believe the Kool-Aid stand was resurrected as an old bottle stand beside my mom's shop for a few days one summer, but as always, patience and perseverance were both lacking and it, too, went by the wayside. Parts of it were later used in building a catapult.

Fortunately, not all Atlin kids were as inept or lazy as Randy and I were. The most obvious example was L&J Industries, started by Linda and Janice at ages thirteen and eleven. L&J Industries was a real business with real profits. Most Northerners are familiar with the Moosequitoe, consisting of a varnished moose poop with

Linda Connolly and Janice Green proudly display jewelry made from local "products!"

Moose nugget art, mid-1970s. Published originally in the Atlin News Miner. *Photograph by Tom Kirkwood.*

a porcupine quill for a stinger, pipe cleaners for legs and grouse feathers for wings. Well, the girls took that one or two steps farther and began to produce jewelry from moose poop and porcupine quills. The moose nugget necklace contained roughly fifteen prime moose turds, and at one time, with over three hundred necklaces sold, the girls had harvested and processed over forty-five hundred turds. L&J's jewelry has traveled all over the world and caused many a customs officer consternation. In fact, it's told that one officer, convinced the turds held some diabolical drug, dissected a nugget and tasted _ _it.

Take what you will from all of this. Boys against girls, attention spans of boys and girls, and so on. All I know is those girls worked hard, stuck to it and made some money. "Oh hey, Randy, I just figured it out. There is no such thing as get rich quick—apparently to make money you have to work hard and be patient. They could have told us that at the beginning." Janice is Randy's sister after all. You would think something might have rubbed off.

Beer bottle collecting was a constant income source for many kids in those days. Ten cents a bottle was a lot. In a way, the bottles became micro commerce. They were sometimes payment for odd jobs, used as trade for comics, or even payment for allowances on occasion. We scoured the camping areas and the dump. We often found old beer bottles buried in the dirt around abandoned cabins. There may have even been a few unsubstantiated cases of "borrowing" from a back porch or two. The liquor store only took new bottles, so we often washed them and made feeble excuses to Glen McKenzie, the liquor vendor, that they somehow got wet and the labels came off. I'm sure we didn't fool Glen, but I think he admired our spirit and tenacity. He bent the rules a little here and there to accommodate our dubious wares and to encourage our continual entrepreneurial spirit. Many a summer day, you could find a gaggle of seven-year-old kids with a wagon full of beer bottles, banging on the back door of the liquor store.

Years later my family and I lived in Seattle, Washington. My boys were young and we were trying to keep them busy. Remembering how young I was when I first started work, I immediately suggested a job. We quickly discovered the lawn mowing was being done by companies that descended on neighborhoods en masse. Half a dozen trucks showed up, a couple-dozen workers jumped out and within a matter of hours, all the lawns in the area were done. The newspaper routes were now worked by adults in cars covering many neighborhoods in a day. Where was the work for kids? Babysitting was mostly out of the question if you didn't know the client intimately. My kids were left with chores and thankfully, somehow, we were able to instill a great work ethic in them.

I have to tell the story of how I came about having the paper delivery job, even at the detriment of my good boy image ... ha, ha. Anyway, I offer no excuses aside from boredom and stupidity, but I got caught shoplifting at the Trading Post.

Crimes and Misdemeanors

Here's how it went down: I was at school doing my usual grade four stuff, when out teacher Terry Milos announced that Brad,

Pete Wright and Ken Ward were needed in the hallway. Pete and Ken are not pseudonyms to protect the guilty. With trepidation, we all rose—a summons to the hallway was never a good thing. Who should we see waiting for us but our local RCMP Corporal Mike. He proceeded to tell us we had been seen stealing from the store and he wanted us to meet him at his office/jail after school.

I have to say, the rest of that day was the longest and scariest of my young life, and hindsight says it was designed to be so. Anyway, after school the three of us dragged our sorry carcasses down to face our executioner. After we entered the small office, Corporal Mike immediately put us in the jail cell and locked the door. The cell consisted of two bunks one above the other, a small sink and a toilet.

Ken acted like an old hand as he jumped up on the top bunk, stretched out with his arms behind his head and feigned sleep. Nerves of steel, that kid. Pete and I huddled close together on the bottom bunk and I fought back tears.

As it was explained, David Sniegocki's mother, owner of the Trading Post, witnessed us stealing from her store. Pete and I had been together on our crime spree, but we had no idea about Ken's criminal enterprise. Corporal Mike let us stew in our fear for forty-five minutes or so as he did paperwork or ran our mugs through Interpol, I'm not sure which. I was the first removed from the cell and brought to the counter three feet (0.9m) away. He asked me what I had stolen. I should have lawyered up right there, as it appeared there may have been no actual eyewitness, as it wasn't known what I had stolen. I wasn't a very slick criminal or, as I have already established, any good under interrogation, so I copped to a bag of caramels and a can of Coke.

The Corporal seemed satisfied that I was being truthful and asked me to take a seat in his office on the other side of the counter, five feet (1.5m) from the cell. I was pretty happy I didn't have to go back in the cell, but what he said next put ice in my veins and I burst out bawling. He spoke the dreaded words I never wanted to hear: "Okay, Mr. Smith, I just need to call your mom." My life as I knew it was over. My long run of criminality and blatant disregard of the rules was finally catching up to me.

He picked up the phone. "Mrs. Smith, this is Corporal Mike, and I want to let you know I have your son down here for shoplifting."

"WHAT?" Her voice reverberated throughout the room, bounced off the walls and pierced my soul. We lived two blocks away and my mom didn't have a muffler on her car at the time, so all I heard was her Mazda screaming toward the police station, getting louder and louder until she skidded to a stop in a spray of rocks and dust. I was basically a puddle of sobbing mush by then.

Kudos to Corporal Mike, for he must have realized he'd awoken a momma grizzly bear and she was bent on a little filicide. He quickly rushed outside to head off the attack. He spent over half an hour talking her down. In retrospect, I should have used that time to escape and go on the lam. Thinking back, I'm sure he explained that after his tactics of making us sweat it out at school and throwing us in the cell, we may have already learned our lesson and further punishment was not necessary.

The same was repeated for Pete and Ken. I have to say in my case I remained shoplifting-free for the rest of my life and I'm sure it was the same for both of them. "It takes a village."

The short ride home and for many hours after were very tense at the Smith house, but The Wooden Spoon stayed in the drawer. Determining I stole because I didn't have money, it was decided I needed a job. My mom wrote for the local paper at the time and knew the *Whitehorse Star* was looking to set up a route for their paper in Atlin. That's the long version of how I came to be Atlin's first paperboy. Along with our time served in lock up (one hour), the Trading Post asked us to stay out for two months. I was very embarrassed and decided I would never go back in that store.

After a few months, Pete started revisiting the scene of the crime and was welcomed. I, on the other hand, could not face David's mom, and it had been almost a year when one day I was casually leaning/ hiding against the side of a building beside the store, waiting for my friends who were inside, when suddenly David's mom rounded the corner. I figuratively, and almost literally, crapped my pants. She obviously knew of my lurking and hesitancy to come back in the store. She was exceedingly gracious and warmly invited me back in. She made me feel welcome and I got over my embarrassment.

Chapter Sixteen

Active Imaginations

Comic Caper

My mom read to me even before I entered the world and then every night before bed. Starting with children's books, but quickly exhausting the local supply, she took to reading me more mature content—often the books she herself read and loved. I, too, became enamored with the adventures of the early explorers, prospectors, miners, trappers and First Nations peoples. Constantly encouraged to stretch my boundaries and genres, I quickly became a voracious reader, and at an early age was reading at a college level.

My mother was a consummate storyteller as well. She often made up stories in the spur of the moment; detailed tales about Inuits and explorers, intrepid youngsters and their faithful dogs, or hidden gold mines or pirate treasure. I don't know how she kept it all straight, but some of these stories went on for months, night after night. Unlike a book, they only ended when she decided they should.

All of the boys collected and traded comic books and couldn't wait for the latest shipment to come in at the General Store or Mr.

Craft's. If we could scrape up twenty cents, we bought one. If broke, we surreptitiously thumbed through them as fast as we could while hiding behind the magazine rack, perusing frantically until shooed out of the store. If we couldn't afford one of our own, then we hoped our friend could, as it basically meant the same thing and taught us patience as we waited our turn.

For a while, I suffered from tonsillitis and that usually manifested itself into bronchitis. This happened a couple times a winter during most of my early childhood. Of course, I hated it but there was a silver lining, as it was the only time my mom bought me comics. I was bored, suffering and stuck at home for long periods of time, so it was her way of picking up my spirits.

I remember getting word that Bob Fassel, a forty-something fellow, was interested in trading comic books. We were blown away and excited to know there was at least one adult out there that shared our love for comics. A few of us loaded up some of our Archie, Richie Rich, Casper the Friendly Ghost, Superman, Spiderman and Batman and headed over to see what Bob had. Although Bob had a daughter in school our age, we didn't know him well and definitely had never been in his house. Bob's place was another of Atlin's charming (meaning scary) old homes. My friends and I were at ease around most adults, but Bob hadn't been in town long and was somewhat of an enigma to us. He dressed like a biker, had a long black beard and a handlebar mustache and wore an earring in one ear. None of these things were completely unusual, but altogether it made him different than most of the men we knew. His demeanor was inhibiting to eight- and nine-year-olds as he mostly grunted his salutations and uttered one-word commands.

One of us built up the courage to knock on the door and it immediately flew open. Bob loomed large in the doorway. Without saying anything, he stared at us for what seemed an eternity. "W-w-we'r-re here to t-t-trade," I managed to stutter. Eventually he grunted and gestured with his head, turned and started up a nearby stairway. We all stumbled to follow as we passed the second floor and approached a lone doorway at the top of the second stairway.

Bob produced an old skeleton key from a large ball of keys that hung down beside his leg. I know what I was thinking, and the others later confirmed they were on the same page. First of all, who locks doors, especially doors inside your house? Second, what is he hiding in there? And third, oh my God, we're all dead. Bob fiddled with the key and finally got the door open while we stood cloistered in a group waiting for someone to break from the herd and flee back down the stairs. Bob stood in the doorway, turned to look at us and once again just gestured "come on" with his head.

Possibly sensing our hesitation, he flipped on the light and gruffly said, "Come on, Chickens, I don't bite." That didn't help much, as we were already fearing cannibalism—what was up with the biting reference and what the heck did this have to do with chickens? Does he like to butcher chickens up here? Has he been practicing on chickens and now is finally going to try out the real thing?

Somehow, we all managed to shuffle into that small room under the eaves of another scary old Atlin house. Once in, our fears were somewhat alleviated as the room was completely empty except for one large wooden trunk sitting in the middle of the floor. Now, I for one was quite relieved to not find knives, meat hooks, rubber aprons or chicken bones, for that matter, but what was up with this guy and this trunk locked behind a door in the attic? I know he could have stuffed a couple of us in that thing, but assuredly not all. This left only the nightmares of what might be in it. I was pretty sure it was the last kid who had come to trade comics, or at the least, it was full of dead chickens.

We all cowered close to the door that had thankfully stayed open as Bob knelt down in front of the trunk and produced yet another key. He unlocked the lock and opened the lid. From where we were standing, we could not see any bodies, and no chicken feathers flew out, but none of us rushed to look. In his gravelly voice, Bob said, "Well, get over here, you chickens, you can't see nothing from there." I was in the back, so I pushed a couple guys forward until we could see that the trunk was full of beautifully preserved comics. Our guard completely dropped as we rushed forward to behold the wonderful bounty.

That trunk must have held a thousand comic books, but just as someone reached out to pick one up, Bob quickly closed the lid. We all quietly panicked a little, thinking, "Great, the comic books were a trap." But Bob sat back on his haunches and said, "Before you get to see what I have, let's check out what you chickens brought." What was up with the chicken references?

Okay, now he was talking our game. Most of us thought ourselves pretty adept at the old comic book trading ritual. I was first to set my stack in front of Bob. Within seconds he had shuffled through, grunting with disdain at any of my Archie, Richie Rich and Casper the Friendly Ghost comics. Anytime he came across a book with a torn or missing cover, he glanced up at me with a mixed look of disappointment and sadness, and then cast aside the offensive rag as if it might burn his fingers.

In a matter of moments Bob had shuffled my stack into two piles: in one sat a Spiderman and a Sergeant Rock comic, in the other pile were the rest of my offerings. Bob looked at me and said, "I might be interested in these two," pointing to the small stack. Then, gesturing to the large pile he said, "I got no use for any of this crap." He'd just crushed me ... had he referred to some of my most prized comics as crap? Had he said crap? Who says crap to kids? I remember mumbling something unintelligible as I humbly picked up my crap and shuffled back.

Now the others were hesitant to approach, upon witnessing my embarrassment, but they eventually placed their stacks in front of Bob as if they were an offering to the God of Comics. Some did slightly better than I did, but none fared well. In the total of roughly 150 comics, Bob chose a dozen at most. Gruff and scary at first, Bob turned out to be a big kid at heart, although a very serious collector and comic aficionado. We did end up making a few insignificant trades and I suspect it was Bob's way of encouraging our enthusiasm for collecting comics. He exposed us to a few things that day. One, collecting comics was a passion shared by all types and ages of people. Two, if we wanted to be serious collectors, we needed to be selective in our genres. Three, us chickens needed to learn how to take better care of our comics so they didn't end up in the crap pile.

Our trading over in a matter of minutes, Bob let us spend most of an afternoon perusing his collection. At that age, we were exposed to the genre of comics I've previously mentioned, but looking through Bob's amazing collection opened up a whole new world of characters and adventures. We were unaware of the darker horror comics of the time—for example, DC's *House of Mystery* or *House of Secrets* and Marvel's *Chamber of Darkness* and *Where Monsters Dwell*. I'm not saying I didn't have copious nightmares for months to come, but I was glad for the experience, even though apparently most of my comics were crap. I did end up with a couple pretty cool *Jonah Hex* comics that only scared me a little.

We spent hundreds of hours with our noses in comics, and we made complicated and strategic trades with our friends. We also read books, and lots of them. Our little library was stocked by donations from Atlinites and regional libraries throughout British Columbia and the Yukon.

If you bought a book or got one as a gift, you passed it along to a friend when you were finished. Books passed from hand to hand for years. It was a little discouraging finding all your old books in the library ... "Thanks, Mom." Aside from Hardy Boys and Nancy Drew, there wasn't a huge selection of books for young people. Of course, as boys we never let on to our friends that we might read our sister's Nancy Drew books, but we read those, too. At an early age, we were into Agatha Christie, Alistair McLean, Robert Heinlein, Farley Mowat, Louis L'Amour and Wilber Smith, to name a few. It was not unusual to find a handful of twelve-year-old boys sprawled around a living room all completely absorbed in paperbacks or magazines.

Magazines were prevalent in most households, as they were one of the few connections to current world events; current as in a month ago current. Any magazine was fair game. *National Geographic* was read from cover to cover and often many times. Even the *Sears Catalog* could captivate one's attention for hours, especially the Christmas edition, which was thumbed through many times until it was well worn and torn. It was continually amazing to most of us that the world possessed so many toys, which were all jammed into that wonderful catalog, so tantalizingly close yet mostly unattainable. Just the thought that our moms had that catalog gave us hope that we might receive something from it. I remember trying to make sense of my mom's *Psychology Today* magazine but failing to understand much, and then having nightmares about brains and people with split personalities, thinking it meant they had two heads.

Monkeys and Marshmallows

Let's go back to *National Geographic* for a minute. I remember one particular edition that had a long article about primates' use of tools. Randy Green found this particularly interesting and decided to emulate some of the primate behavior displayed in the article;

irony not yet fully understood, I presume. I have a vague recollection of him trying out a couple of the behaviors, but there was one that is still vivid in my memory. The article showed monkeys wetting a long blade of grass in their mouth, poking it into an ant hill, slowly pulling it out covered in ants and as quick as a whip pulling the blade through their mouths, sucking in the ants and contentedly munching down dinner.

Randy Green took a long blade of grass, wet it in his mouth and stuck it in an ant hill. Fortunately for him, only a couple of ants were on the grass when he sucked them into his mouth. Almost immediately, he yelled out and frantically pawed at his mouth. Who knew but ants don't like being eaten and have the capability of fighting back? Professor Green suffered from a number of painful bites and a swollen lip. That test marked the last of his primate assimilation experimentation and put an end to his brief, yet informative, career as a primatologist.

A big deal to any Atlin kid was a trip to the Warm Springs, and an overnight camp out was even better. The Warm Springs are twelve miles (19km) south of town down a windy, dusty, rutty road. To us it was like a tropical oasis, a Jurassic adventureland. The Warm Springs is a small, glimmering pool in the middle of a picturesque pasture. The water that bubbles out of the ground isn't hot, only warm, thus the name—it's approximately 70°F (21°C). A small stream spills out of one end and meanders through the pasture toward the Atlin Lake, splitting into even smaller tributaries as it progresses. The stream's banks are a couple of feet (0.6m) high and we had competitions to see who could jump across without getting wet. The vegetation is like none other in the region. Watercress and skunk cabbage, fiddlehead ferns and salmon berries are abundant, and everything grows bigger than anywhere else around. The little streams were full of tadpoles and frogs and minnows.

We roasted hot dogs and marshmallows over a fire in between dips in the pool. At the deepest point, it was approximately three feet (0.9m) deep and the whole pool could fit in a small backyard. For kids who only read about swimming pools, the Warm Springs was as close as we got to one. It was always a competition to see who could find the biggest frog or capture the most tadpoles.

When we tired of swimming or chasing critters, we played softball in the field or threw a Frisbee. We pitched our tents around

Pioneer and farmer John Fink used the warm thermal waters in the area to grow vegetables. The warmth of the water lengthened a short growing season.

The Warm Springs was once a tourist destination serviced by Louis Schulz's touring car company. Tourists traveled 12.5 miles (20km) over bumpy, muddy dirt tracks in open cars. When they arrived, they were received by the Mortons who opened their lovely two-story home and gardens to them. Mrs. Morton provided meals and refreshments. The water temperature is 70°F (21°C).

the pasture, built huge bonfires, and told scary stories. We stuffed ourselves with marshmallows and pretended we were exploring the Amazon jungle. It was light most of the night and we stayed up late chasing each other around, emulating characters from the *Lord of the Flies,* screaming like primates and having the time of our lives.

Just up the road is the Grotto, which is fed by an underground creek that boils out of the base of Sentinel Mountain. I was mystified by the fact that there were creeks that ran underground, and I always wondered what was past the mouth of the cave from which the water rushed. I imagined an underground world of vast caverns and canals where fantastical creatures lived. The Grotto was also where we harvested watercress for use in salads.

At Atlin Lake, into which the Warm Springs drain, is Warm Bay. It offers another good camping spot or place to launch a small boat and a great place to fish for grayling and even trout as they come in to feed on the smaller fish.

Forts and Fist Fights

We were creative kids and we had great imaginations—everything wasn't laid out or done for us. Summers were short, and being the prime money-making period, our parents were busy. We were mostly left to entertain ourselves. We made go-carts, modified our bicycles, built forts and rafts. We made slingshots, bows and arrows and catapults. We carved spears and made wooden swords, we built swings and teeter-totters.

I remember that my friend Keith Carlick—yes, the "bear up a tree" guy—at a very early age was able to build a snow machine from old derelict wrecks found around his own and other people's yards. If I remember correctly, it never had an engine cover or windshield and he had to stop every so often and bang on the clutch pulley with a rock he kept handy. What an amazing feat for a twelve- or thirteen-year-old. He also maintained and operated a small skiff and outboard. While in his early teens, with quick thinking, quicker actions and expert boatmanship, Keith single handedly saved a drowning man.

Fort building was an art and we built many, some even reaching epic notoriety in the community. The three-story monstrosity erected in Daniel Connolly's backyard was by far the most famous, not only for its size and intricacy, but because it had the dubious reputation as the only fort the adults forced us to dismantle, claiming safety reasons or some such nonsense. We figured it was pure jealousy.

Some forts were as simple as building a hidey hole behind the wood pile or digging a hole in the side of a dirt bank and pulling brush in front. Others were sophisticated tree forts with escape routes and rope ladders. In the winter, we honeycombed the large piles of snow pushed up beside the road. We made multi-level chambers with connecting tunnels and passageways. If we were forced inside by the severe cold, we pushed some furniture together, threw a couple blankets over them and, ta da, a fort we had.

We didn't often find ourselves inside, but when we did due to brutal weather conditions, sickness or broken bones, board games were king. Anything we could get our hands on, we played. Our constant favorites were Monopoly and Risk. Battleship, Chess, Sorry and Klondike, the Dawson City version of Monopoly, all amused us for hours, but they came second to our love of Risk and Monopoly.

Long winter days were filled with strategic and often violent games of world dominance or the dogged pursuit of real-estate moguldom. Often, games ended with the board being tossed and one or more players storming out the door, yelling, "It's your game, you pick it up." I did that once and halfway home realized it was, in fact, my game. Of course, upon my return I found it lying where I left it, scattered around the room encircled by lounging, giggling hyenas.

I remember receiving a new Risk game for Christmas, and friends Pete and John Wright had an older version with real wood pieces, but they were the only two we knew of. They, for years, had the only Monopoly game amongst the group. Pete and John's mom, Pam, was English, so we grew up coveting Mayfair and Park Lane, not Boardwalk and Park Place. Old Kent Road, Whitehall and Piccadilly were all to be avoided if hotels were present. I remember being quite confused the first time I sat down to the American version of the game.

We were quite passionate and fiercely competitive while doing anything, but board games seemed to bring it out in spades, Monopoly and Risk in particular. I didn't realize how serious we took these games until many years later when I sat down to play Monopoly with my then in-laws, all females. It wasn't long before they were forgiving each other taxes and fees and making nonsensical trades because they liked one color better than another, or someone felt bad for someone else so they gave them a wad of money. "What was happening here?" Everything I knew about competition and gaming was being trod on and disrespected. I was incensed, and apparently in no uncertain terms I vocalized my concerns. It was an affront to my sense of fair play. It wasn't until after I was gently talked down off my high horse, asked to leave the room and vows were muttered never to play board games with Brad again, that I realized that in all our board game playing, we rarely played with girls. Another life lesson learned: boys and girls do pretty much everything differently.

Plastic army men offered endless hours of entertainment. While most were your standard army men, I ended up with a set depicting the German army all in gray, as well as the green Americans. We always flipped for first pick because no one wanted to be the German army, but having an evil opposition made it more fun. We meticulously set up our defenses in preparation for a violent thirty-second battle. My set even had howitzers and mortars that shot little projectiles. One of us might take the high ground, the couch, the other the floor or coffee table. We made bunkers and fortifications from normal household items. There we were, our armies poised for battle, entrenched behind socks, books and Rice Krispies boxes. With a dramatic countdown, firing commenced. In a matter of seconds, our carefully positioned men lay strewn across the smoky battlefield. Nothing was left standing, even if it meant jumping on our opponent, putting him in a headlock and giving him a "noogie" just to get to the last of his men.

Of course, the inevitable argument would ensue as to who had won or lost, and as with the board games, the army men may have ended up thrown around the room and you were left to pick up the mess by yourself as your friend stormed out, slamming the door behind him.

Setting up Hot Wheels tracks could also occupy a full winter day. Some of my friends had electric race car and train sets. They could be completely exhilarating one minute and totally frustrating the next. One Christmas I got a table hockey game, the kind that has rods you push and pull and twist. My two teams were the Toronto Maple Leafs and the Montreal Canadians. We had some intense contests over the years, and like real hockey, it sometimes ended in a fight.

As would be the course of my life, my big mouth got me into my first fist fight. I don't recall the insignificant details of what brought me to be standing at the bottom of the sliding hill behind the school that fateful spring afternoon. The tension was palatable and had hung heavy around me the entire day. Like Charlie Brown's Cloud it followed me about wherever I went. Note to self: Don't agree to disagree until closer to the end of the day.

Like I said, I have no recollection how it started, but I'm sure I was responsible because Mike Frasher was a nice guy. I was filled with dread. Peer pressure was the only thing anchoring me to the spot and preventing me from fleeing. I had a modicum of courage and an even smaller amount of confidence, until I saw Mike casually and confidently stride down the hill as if he hadn't a care in the world. As he approached, I fixated on his hands. I had never noticed before, but they were enormous. Another note to self: don't pick fights with a brick layer's son. Mike and his brothers worked with their father who built foundations for homes in town. I had seen

Mike carry three cinder blocks on each arm on occasion, where I struggled with one. What was I thinking? I wasn't, obviously. He was a twelve-year-old with the strength of a full-grown man and fists the size of hams.

The rest is foggy, but I remember begging, crying and slobbering a lot. It was a self-defense technique I worked hard at perfecting from an early age. As I said, Mike was a decent fellow and I believe he only hit me once, knocking me down, but overall, he took pity on me and probably realized that I had defeated myself before it even started. He may have also known that my mom might do worse, as I ended up covered in alkali.

The physical part of my first fist fight was minimal, but the psychological aspect stuck with me for the rest of my life. The dread, fear and regret were powerful lessons. It didn't keep me out of future fights, but it helped me be more selective when I mouthed off.

Canoes and Canines

In the summer, we built rafts. On a sunny day in July, the top couple feet (0.6m) of water on the lake was relatively warm, and anything below that was ice cold. There was always an abundance of driftwood along the lakeshore. With some rope, a few nails and a lot of effort, we constructed serviceable rafts. They weren't fancy, but they worked. Like I said before, most of us couldn't swim, but it didn't stop us from paddling around First Island, dodging floatplanes and pissed-off seagulls, as we rowed along on our half-submerged collection of logs and twine.

We made sure each raft had at least one log large enough that we could all hang onto it and kick our way to shore if our vessel fell apart. We weren't shipwrights and our rafts weren't the Kon Tiki, but we did okay with what we could find and our imaginations. I might add that our mothers would have killed us had they known the extent of our intrepid voyages.

One day Randy Green, Lance Shaw and I "borrowed" a canoe from where we found it on the shore of the lake. Any adventure with Lance included his adolescent St. Bernard named Sam. So, the three of us and the hundred-pound shaggy beast all boarded our temporarily-acquired vessel.

I'm out for a ride in the boat with Dad, 1969.

At first everything went well. It was a beautiful calm day as we paddled along, very contentedly enjoying our impromptu adventure. At some point, I felt we were drifting too far from shore for my comfort. I loudly voiced my concerns, whining, crying and sniveling. Considering we didn't have life vests and I couldn't swim, I felt it was a merited request. After a few minutes of boat rocking and torturing me with threats of heading for deeper water, they turned the canoe toward shore.

For some reason, this was a signal for Sam to jump out and start swimming. In the process of dragging his immenseness over the side of the boat, he managed to flip the whole kit and caboodle and send us all into the drink. My survival instinct immediately kicked in and I put my now much-improved dog paddling skills to work and frantically struck out for shore.

There I was in a race for my life, neck and neck with a St. Bernard named Sam. I did not see it as a competition and only wanted to reach shore alive. Sam, on the other hand, was of a competitive bent, so when I began to pull ahead, beating him at his own game, so to speak, he took exception and tried to slow me down by climbing on my back. I was in a struggle for my very existence with a hundred-pound drooling monster riding on my back. I made one last valiant lunge and thankfully I felt bottom.

Slobbering and splashing, gasping and crying, I pulled myself out of the water and flopped down on the rocks. Sam thought we were in the middle of some grand game and pounced on me, knocking the breath out of my lungs. As I lay on the rocks gagging, he licked me with his huge, slobbery tongue. I finally drew my first ragged breath just as Sam shook himself violently, spraying stinky, hair-laden dog water in my mouth.

After a brief period of self-pity and an adrenalin dump, I suddenly realized it wasn't all about me and Sam. Looking out at the water I saw Lance swimming after a wayward paddle, the other clutched in his hand. No sight of Randy anywhere—only the overturned canoe, Lance, and two paddles. I immediately started screaming at Lance to save Randy, not the stupid paddle.

Unbeknownst to me, Randy was trying out a canoe-flipping survival technique he had recently read about in an out-of-print issue of *Nudist Canoeist* magazine. Long story, but remember I said we read anything we could get our hands on? The technique involves staying under the capsized canoe, hanging onto a thwart and enjoying the safety and protection of a giant air bubble. You can then assess the situation, check your direction and kick your way to shore, saving yourself and retaining your mode of transportation. Randy had already communicated this to Lance, so he was going after the paddles.

It was double heart attacks for me, an adventurous romp for Sam, a brisk swim for Lance and an opportunity to test some knowledge for Randy. Yes, we returned Bill Boyko's canoe—sshhhhh—nice and clean and no worse for wear. Our buddy Sam was nonplussed, to say the least, when I forcibly denied his boarding for the return trip. He ran back along the shore and, at first, he seemed to be casting me some scathing side eye, but he soon lost himself chasing seagulls and forgot all about me. I'm pretty sure he resented losing the hundred-foot (33m) dog paddle to a human. Come on, it's called the dog paddle after all. He should have been embarrassed, the cheater.

We were a tight-knit group. Extreme proximity demands a heightened familiarity, mostly for the better, but at times it's a detriment. We knew each other as brothers and sisters. Not to say there weren't small cliques, but they were often fluid. For a summer you might find most of your interests closer aligned with so and so, but that fall you hung out more with what's his name and who's it. I think an Atlin kid would have always defended another against anyone, no matter if you liked each other that day or not.

Chapter Seventeen

Christmas

In those days, Christmas in Atlin was virtually Rockwellian, a quaint and charming affair with the Christmas concert as the jewel in the crown of events. Technically, it was the school Christmas concert, but it wasn't just for students and parents—it was truly a community event in every sense. We practiced our plays and songs for weeks; we made costumes and decorations and sets and props and tried in vain to contain our excitement. Every kid was in the concert, whether in the choir, a play or skit, or a soloist ... no one missed out.

Before they built the Rec. Centre, the concert was held in the Moose Hall. Cramped and stuffy, somehow the whole town jammed into that antiquated hall. The floor was uneven and rolling, the kitchen dilapidated and rustic. Any cooking was done on a wood-fired cook stove and there was no running water. His and hers outhouses were right out the back door, only single-seaters this time. The hall was heated with a large barrel wood furnace situated in the back of the main room. When it was thirty below, as it often

With Dad and Joe Ackerman on Christmas Eve Day in 1971 before caroling. Joe was a friend of the family and worked for my dad in Juneau on a couple of projects. After we moved to Atlin, he came for a visit. The next year he moved to Atlin and started farming near Surprise Lake.

was, the people in the back stripped down to their undershirts and the people in the front left their parkas and boots on.

The stage was minute and the back stage so small it took a Christmas miracle to squeeze in all the performers. On the night of the concert the atmosphere in the hall was electric. Kids and adults alike vibrated with anticipation. Any Christmas concert wouldn't be complete without a visit from Santa. After the songs, the carols, skits and recitals were over and the Polaroid pictures taken, the lights went up and everyone helped themselves to coffee, tea and cocoa. An array of home-baked pastries was offered, and kids and adults mingled and visited with friends and neighbors.

Suddenly, clanging bells were heard and a loud clatter erupted outside the back door. No matter how anticipated, it always caught us by surprise. Every head turned, every small face alight, little eyes sparkling, mouths agape. The door crashed open and a chorus of *"Ho! Ho! Ho!"* echoed through a billowing cloud of steam. Through the mist bounded the jolly old elf himself. Over his shoulder was a huge red sack and in that sack was a present and stocking for every single child in town.

Santa sat in a big chair on the small stage. When your name was called, you went up and got your present and talked to Santa. Little did we know at that time that some wonderful friend or neighbor was inside that hot, itchy suit, patiently and lovingly enduring the frenzied attention of a mob of excited and hyper children.

On Christmas Eve, we went caroling. Joe Ackerman hitched up his old horse to a sleigh and we piled aboard. I don't remember the horse's name, so let's call her Nelly. Nelly did fine on the flat ground, but we were too heavy for her to pull us uphill. When we neared an incline, we all bailed out and walked beside the sleigh. We made sure we went to all the old-timers' houses as we meandered through town.

Mac White's place was always an interesting stop. Old Mac was hard of hearing and it usually went something like this: We assembled in front of his house and began singing. After a couple carols someone had to knock on Mac's door. A few carols later, Mac

Santa at the annual Christmas concert, 1972. It was a volunteer job that was difficult to fill. After many years, it became impossible to convince another man to do it, so like many things, the women took it over. Not sure how many female Santas there have been, but gender doesn't matter much to a four-year-old. Originally published in the Atlin News Miner. Photo by Tom Kirkwood.

Caroling by horse and sleigh, Christmas Eve, 1970. I'm center, no hat.

would throw open the door. Dressed in his robe and PJs, he'd stare at us for a moment as if wondering why we were all standing in his yard, and then he'd slam the door. A carol later, Mac would reappear with Mrs. White on his arm. The two of them bundled up and huddled in the doorway to stay warm and would sing along until Mac, cupping his ear, would yell, "I can't hear you!" We immediately sang as loud as we could. After a couple more carols, he'd again yell, "I can't hear you!" and dismissively wave us away, hustle Mrs. White inside and slam the door a final time. We all knew Mac and especially Mrs. White loved the carols, and we suspected his abrupt dismissal had more to do with him worrying about Mrs. White getting cold rather than his inability to hear us.

Don't get me wrong, Mac was far from being a Scrooge. The White's place was always an enticing Christmas spectacle. With their house and fence carefully adorned with bright lights, it often looked like it was straight out of the game Candy Land.

I think Nelly only made it a year or two, then Gary Thoma hooked up a big flatbed trailer behind his truck, filled it with hay and there was no more walking up hills. To be honest, most of us kids were there for the hot chocolate and the ride, not the singing.

People did things in Atlin during Christmas that are forgotten or considered outdated today. We came together and enjoyed each other's company as neighbors, friends and community. The Recreation Committee, set up to promote community spirit, started the Seventy Club. The Seventy Club made sure that all seniors over seventy received a basket with cakes, candies, fried chicken, fruit and even tobacco for those that smoked. These baskets were delivered around to doorsteps before Christmas, and were given and received with pride and appreciation.

On Christmas Day, neighbors had "open houses," opening their homes to everyone. People dropped in and visited all day and into the evening. The host provided an array of baked treats and beverages, and visitors brought gifts, libations and the ever-popular fruitcake. Yes, people made and ate fruitcake; of course, being soaked in a half bottle of Lambs Navy Rum increased the enticement.

While the parents visited in the other room or upstairs, we ran amuck with our friends, playing with all their new toys. Sometimes we went to three or four open houses in one day. No one in town was ever left out. The old-timers were invited for dinner and people dropped off baked goods and casseroles on their doorsteps.

If someone had no family in town, they were adopted by a neighbor or friend and sometimes spent the whole Christmas season with their new family. If people were having a hard time making ends meet, those that had a little more that year helped out. Game was shared with those who didn't have the means to hunt or fish. A hind quarter of moose or caribou was a welcomed gift; a large lake trout, string of grayling or bag of moss berries, an appreciated treat.

On Boxing Day, Dennis Odian fired up his double-track Ski-Doo and cruised through town, picking up kids as he went. If you had a sled or toboggan, you tied it on to the back of the Ski-Doo until there was a long train of laughing, screaming kids snaking their way around town and out on the lake, over the islands and back through town again. If you didn't own a sled, you piled on top of someone else's, or even on top of someone else.

Ghosts of Christmas Concert Past
Atlin News Miner 1973
Diane S. Smith

I remember our first Atlin Christmas concert. We joined the crowd at the aging Moose Hall that somehow looked beautifully festive that night. A sparkling tree stood near a shaky portable stage and loud whispers and titters came from behind homemade curtains. Mary Reid was the principal then and she and another girl attended twenty-nine students at a very old Atlin Elementary School. It was 1967.

A fate which often falls to the man of a new family had befallen my husband that particular year. He was given the dubious honor of playing Santa Claus. His stage career was nil and his temperature was three degrees over normal. He was positive he had the flu, but it was probably opening-night jitters.

During his performance, a persistent little blonde kid kept tugging at his trouser leg while Santa muttered tersely, "Beat it, scram, and go find your mom," and tried to shake loose. Finally, the little kid said, "Daddy," in a loud and insistent voice and Santa's identity was known to all.

I can't remember much about the program that night but I do recall wondering how those teachers managed all the excited kids in the tiny room backstage.

After the program, the ladies of the Community Club served cookies and sandwiches, and tea and coffee flowed like Pine Creek. The big Yukon wood stove crackled so efficiently everyone nearly roasted. Somehow this small discomfort was forgotten in lieu of the shining eyes of the smallest children as they received presents and candy from Santa-Daddy.

How different that magical night from the last Christmas program I attended when my older boy was a tiny blue spot on a distant stage in a huge new auditorium. Hollywood lighting effects accompanied a nearly professional production. No cookies or coffee followed the program, only a tense drive home through crowded wet streets.

The next two years, while Bob Grenhil was principal, the Christmas concert was held in the brand-new Atlin Elementary School (Two double-wide trailers back-to-back). I remember Greg and Kevin Neufeld singing together at one of the concerts, Kevin the picture of sober concentration while Greg grinned toothlessly from ear to ear. The next year when Betty Thoma was co-teacher and producer with Bob, Greg Kirkwood and Mels Melberg cracked us up with a dazzling bit of stomach-muscle virtuosity done to the tune of 'alley cat.'

In 1970 and 1971, a live wire Australian couple, Wayne and Sandy Barwick, were our teachers. The town had grown and so had the school enrollment, so the concert was held again at the Moose Hall. Wayne had taught the kids some flashy tumbling routines that were a grand finale to his first concert. John Harvey was new here, so he played Santa. He discovered a full black beard is quite a hindrance in the role of the famous white-haired elf.

The Christmas concert of 1971 was laced with certain nostalgia. We knew it would be the last time the Old Moose Hall would resound with the sound of familiar carols and ring with the high excitement of a Christmas concert. The curling club had just received a grant to build a new recreation centre. The Old Moose Hall, which started life in Discovery during the gold rush as the Arctic Brotherhood Hall, would no longer be used for this all-important event.

At that last Moose Hall concert, a mixture of Australian and Northern humor turned "Tie Me Kangaroo Down, Boys" into "Tie Me Moose to a Spruce, Bruce." Sterling performances were abundant, but one I remember best was the lament of a "forty or so year old waitress" for the loss of her logger sweetheart. The lesson learned was that loggers and gentlemen were synonymous and you can easily spot a logger because he "stirs his coffee with his thumb." The poignant accompaniment to this act was a harmonica solo recorded by Harold Colwell.

Later, when the older children recited the haunting lines from Robert Service's "The Spell of the Yukon," a tear slid down the cheek of an old miner in the audience as memories of a lifetime in the North flooded back.

The curtains closed on a page in Atlin's history that night. After traditional coffee and cookies and presents given by Santa Clive Aspinall, new in town, who betrayed his own identity with his English accent, nearly two hundred people left the last Christmas concert in the old Moose Hall.

———

PART III — A Dogged Determination

I'm with Mom in Pine City, commonly referred to as Discovery. This is the site of the first gold strike that would forever put Atlin and its gold fields on the map. From a town that once housed thousands, only one building was left standing in the 2020s.

Chapter Eighteen

Dogs

Propensity for the Preposterous

As I mentioned earlier, dogs were a big part of the Atlin fabric. We were not far removed from the time dogs hauled the town's water, brought the mail in across the lake system, pulled the big hand pumps for the firefighters, brought supplies to the creeks and were used as general transportation. Although snow machines and vehicles quickly replaced them, in some cases, dogs were still being used by trappers and prospectors as well as for recreation for many. More and more, the teams were being used for competitive racing.

Claudia Lombardi utilized Malamute hair for winter wear ... I said hair, not hide, calm down. We actually saved the combings from some of our shaggiest beasts, which she then spun into yarn and knitted into hats, mittens and scarves. In my opinion, there is nothing softer or warmer. Of course, when you get them wet, they tend to smell like a wet dog. Who knew?

At that time in Atlin's evolution, it appeared as though every yard housed at least two or three doghouses and a fair amount had a dozen or more. Whether they were beasts of burden, or more likely pets, it seemed we all had dogs. It was hotly debated whether one could proudly claim the moniker of Atlinite if one did not own at least three dogs. At one time, I believe an effort was afoot to adopt local artist Dixon Pagnella's sketch "Three Dog Night" as our official emblem. The sketch depicts a rugged pioneer spending a winter's night in his cozy cabin, snuggled up with three huskies to ward off the penetrating cold.

My dad took pride in the duplex log structures with sod roofs he erected for our gang of huskies. They were well-insulated, sides, top and bottom, fresh hay for bedding and a burlap bag to cover the doorway. Even a short hair Pekingese could survive a forty-below night in one of those doggie penthouses.

At one point on a nice summer day, a friend and I decided one of these snug abodes would make a fine fort. I'm a little foggy as to who was with me on that most memorable day, but I'm going to go with Randy Green because he was usually getting me in trouble. Okay, I may have been a tad gullible and easily led astray, but that's beside the point. I will say on this particular occasion I can only blame myself ... and my dad a little.

So, there we were hanging out in the left house of the duplex just chatting away, pretending we were cavemen or something akin. We had the burlap bag down, making it dark and more cave-like, I assume. Every so often the rightful owner and recently evicted shaggy husky nosed the bag aside trying to enter, at which point I yelled and pushed him away.

Sometime during our Stone Age interlude my dad happened along and heard us in the doghouse. Upon witnessing my pushing and yelling, he thought it might be good fun to take a stick and poke the burlap door. Apparently by that time I had reached a heightened level of frustration with our canine friend. The next time I saw the bag move I unwisely yelled, "Get the hell out of here!"

I understand in this day and age the word "hell" is probably a long way down the swear-word lexicon of most five- or six-year-olds, but in that time and in that place, it was not something you yelled at your father without expecting recourse.

Much to my surprise, a real caveman hand and arm reached in and grabbed me by the shirt. I was immediately outside, suspended in the air, pants pulled down and a stick falling upon my naked buttocks. Fortunately for me, the stick was small and soon broke. The broken stick and the obvious terror on my face spared me any more physical punishment.

The reason I mentioned some of the blame belonged to my dad was that, at that time, I'm sure the only reason I knew the word hell was from listening to him and his friends. I had not even heard the f-word yet.

By the way, nary a peep was heard from Randy Green. Even when the husky entered, he didn't emerge. I'm sure my dad realized that the uncertainty of his continued safety was as fitting a punishment as any. As I was hustled away to my room, I am not sure how long Randy cowered in our cave/dog house. My dad was an intimidating fellow when he was angry, and some of my friends were quite afraid of him.

I was with my friends one winter day and everyone was jumping off an old roof into the snow. I was four or five and smaller and younger than my friends, so I couldn't jump as far. Long story short, I landed on ice, not snow, and sprained my ankle. My good friends were nice enough to tow me home on a sled but were so intimidated by my dad that they just rolled me off the sled at the bottom of the front steps and ran away. I was left to yell for my mom.

Our dogs out for a spin in our Mazda. Kluane in the passenger seat with Attu driving, late 1970s.

Most dogs of that time were huskies, Malamutes, Siberian huskies, or a combination of all three, affectionately referred to as mutts or mongrels. Although there were a few bowlegged labs and at least one Afghan-poodle-looking thing around town, most were a northern breed. No Shit-poos, Labradoodles or St. Burwawaws back then.

Not only was Atlin a free-range zone for all livestock, leash and tie-up laws were non-existent. Most people had some control over their dogs, be it a whistle or hardy yell. Canines, being territorial creatures, mostly stayed in their yard or close to where they were fed. It was not uncommon to take your thirteen mutts for a run behind the pickup truck, snaking through town past every other dog, on your way out the road. This led to multiple fights and squabbles along the way, although brief, because none wanted to be left behind. Since everyone knew everyone else, if you saw my mom's car weaving

Some of our pack waiting in front of Our Old House/The Courthouse, 1970s.

down the road toward you, you knew to slow down and be wary of the obligatory train of slobbering canines strung out behind.

We definitely did our part to sustain the dog population of Atlin. At one time, our household numbered close to thirty dogs. Although

Kluane cleaning one of her pups, 1970s.

we had doghouses for most, it was not unusual to find a half-dozen Malamutes lazing around the living room on any particular frosty evening. My mom had a complicated winter, revolving dog schedule so none felt left out and they all got a night in the house at least once a week. The schedule was open to immediate change depending on what they had been eating at the time. Of course, pups and mothers were inside, usually in a big box under the desk or work table or both.

If it weren't for my dad's protestation as well as vague adherences to societal norms, I'm quite confident my mom would have had all the dogs in the house all the time. In some circles (the whole town) she may have been referred to as "The Dog Lady" and her car held the bona fide distinction as the North's most expensive and only mobile dog house.

She happily told the story of the day I arrived home from an afternoon of play. When she asked whom I had been playing with, I answered quite seriously, "Oh, just the other dogs." Confused was I.

Quill or be Quilled

The arch enemy of all northern dogs and owners is the dreaded porcupine. For some reason, dogs can't resist messing with the humble rodent. The third largest of all rodents behind the beaver and the capybara, he's a doddering, solitary animal that wishes nothing more than to be left alone.

Unlike the cartoons, porcupines do not throw their quills. Dimwitted canines actually have to impale themselves on the quills. The porcupine's defenses consist entirely of the sharp-barbed spikes, although he does possess a quick tail and uses it to swat interested interlopers.

Some dogs become obsessed and will find every opportunity to harass them, usually ending up with a snoot full of quills. When a dog bites a porcupine and their entire mouth is full of half-broken-off quills, it takes on a whole new dimension.

Over the years many if not all of our dogs had run-ins with the porkies. Most were only curious and after receiving a few quills in the snout, they yelped and ran away, having learned their lesson. Others were slower on the uptake and it took a few negative encounters to learn their lesson. Then there are some that never learned.

The quills, like I said, are barbed; this allows them to continue to penetrate. As the dog moves, the quills work their way farther in, thus necessitating the hasty removal. Broken-off quills are the most dangerous, as they can easily be overlooked.

I was petting our dog Kluane one day and noticed a small bump on top of her muzzle. In a few days, there was the tip of a quill sticking out. It had traveled from her mouth to the top of her snout.

Animals have been known to die from quills working their way to their brains. The wildest of the canine family, wolves, normally stay clear of the porcupine. Although wolves, and even coyotes when hungry enough, have been witnessed flipping a porcupine over and then biting into its unprotected underbelly. Dogs are not that smart.

Atlin did not have a veterinarian, so it was up to the owners to extract the quills. As you can imagine, this is not pleasant for the dogs or the owners. We possessed a few very large Malamutes over the years and it was always an epic battle to remove the quills. Chilkoot in particular turned into a raging beast. I remember once it took my dad and Joe Ackerman to hold him down while my mom pulled the quills with a pair of pliers. Chilkoot didn't have any qualms about biting when he felt threatened, so a chunk of hose was jammed into his mouth and tied off behind his head. With the two burly men lying on top, my mom pulling quills and me holding his back legs, it was a long, bloody battle, but we eventually got them all.

My mother wasn't above drugging in extreme cases. A Gravol motion sickness pill or some rum-laced milk was deployed on occasion with mixed results. She even obtained some illegal ether at one point, but after an hour of chasing the dog around the house trying to shove a stinky rag over its sensitive, quill-filled nose, she realized she was succumbing to the effects of the noxious liquid.

After clearing her head, she gave up on that idea and tossed the ether away.

When something threatens their livestock or crops, farmers and ranchers are known to resort to extreme measures to eliminate the threat. Unfortunately, there was a "shoot-on-sight order" on porcupines in those days. It didn't take long before a porcupine sighting was a rare occurrence in the woods around Atlin.

Porcupines are a bear to skin, but the meat is quite good and much like beef. They are herbivores so are safe to eat raw if one desires porcupine tartare. Roasted over a campfire whole is a fine way to prepare it, but my favorite was porcupine meatballs in gravy.

Thankfully, times have changed; people have fewer dogs and the dogs have less freedom. Once again, the voracious little vegans waddle mostly unmolested throughout the surrounding forest.

Porcupine Bites Dog
Atlin News Miner 1973
Diane S. Smith

It is commonly known that dogs are quite prone to chasing and attacking porcupine, although it is a useless, prickly and painful business. But this summer, so brazen have the porcupines become, that they are now attacking the dogs.

Aishihik', a husky owned by Lance and Leah Fuller, can never tell what actually happened late one night last week at McKee Creek but the facts are this. He was chained securely for the night at his doghouse. All was well. In the morning, Aishihik was still chained but he was sporting a full face of quills that was painful to look at. The evidence is circumstantial; the deductions obvious. A porcupine discovered the captive dog and made the most of a good situation. Porky baited dog. Dog of course, bit at the bait. That the bait was the porky himself was unfortunate for the dog. Sorry we can't report the culprit was apprehended and duly punished; he made a clean getaway. No doubt he giggled all the way home at this lucky turn of events.

Aishihik was dequilled the next morning and that brings to mind there is a present demand in Atlin for a good formula for removing quills from dogs when there is no veterinarian handy with a knock-out shot.

The stories revolving around quill-skewered dogs and the battles to dequill them are too many to count. The recipes for dequilling range from the ridiculous to the sublime—mostly ridiculous. I have asked my slobbering husky to hold his mouth open while I dab vinegar on quills impaling his tongue and jammed to the hilt between his teeth so they will soften up, but I was fixed with such an evil-laden look, I withdrew directly and threw the swab away. "See, Rover, I threw it away."

I have tried, ever so gently, to clip the quills so they would deflate and be easier to pull. Deflate, my foot! The first wave of the scissors turned my quill-filled husky into a canine Mr. Hyde who backed into a corner and snarled blackest murder at me.

There have been tried tranquilizers that wouldn't tranquilize and sleeping pills didn't even make him yawn. And we have used elaborate and diabolical schemes of straight-jacketing to hold him immobile. But do you realize a medium-sized husky with a snoot full of quills can break shackles an enraged elephant couldn't budge?

There is a way, however, and the equipment needed is simple. Here it is. Recipe for dequilling a husky.

One pair of pliers. Four of Atlin's largest, strongest men. Ear plugs are optional. In the largest room in the house, move back all furniture and breakable items. Also remove rug. Lead dog to center of clearing. When he is off guard, flop him on his side on the floor. First strong man holds back legs. Second strong man holds front legs. Third strong man grabs dog by the throat and strangles him slightly. The fourth guy pulls the quills. When done on one side, flop flip over and do the other side. By then dog is so exhausted, he will open his mouth so you can pull the quills in there, too.

When finished, the dog will sit up, scratch a little and walk casually outside. The men usually retreat to the bar.

Although this method of dequilling sounds brutal, it does work and the dogs actually don't mind much. In fact, I have heard of some dogs that will run right after another porcupine so that they can go through it all again. In the long run, the dogs usually hold up very well but whether or not Atlin's largest, strongest men will, remains to be seen.

———

A young Atlin, the dog, sleeping in the sled, mid-1970s.

A Cautionary Tail

If you haven't noticed, my mother had a penchant for naming our dogs after places, in particular Northern places. I was seven or eight when I was given my first husky, a dog of my own that I would be responsible for. I was keen on keeping my mother's naming tradition, and I proudly named my new charge Atlin. After all, it was a place in the North. Atlin (the dog) turned out to be an amiable buffoon of a mutt, but he willingly took his place in our team and performed adequately. He was also a loving and loyal pet.

Atlin was a couple years old and one night I was standing on the back porch screaming, "Atlin!" at the top of my lungs, trying to get him to come home. It suddenly dawned on me the absurdity of yelling out the name of our town indiscriminately throughout the day and night.

Our neighbors and most of the town folks were probably used to it and paid little heed. But I'm sure newcomers and tourists were in wonder at this prideful boy, so full of community spirit that he randomly screamed the name of his town boisterously for all to hear. Poor "Atlin" forever after was confused to be called "Hey, You, get over here" and "Bonehead;" anything but Atlin. A quick note to the wise, when considering a name for a dog, first open the back door and scream the name as loud as you can—if it sounds alright, go with it.

I previously mentioned my mom's complicated dog rotation schedule to decide which dog got to stay inside on any particular night. She also had a similar rotation during the day, but for which dogs spent the day off the chain. Every day there were six or seven dogs loose to wander. Most stayed close to home, but a few went hunting rabbits. Three dogs in particular were quite good at it. We first noticed their hunting prowess when we found a frozen rabbit in the puppy box under the desk. Apparently, motherhood piqued the instinct to provide. Week-old puppies have no idea what to do with a frozen rabbit, but it was quickly added to the freezer-burned fish, moose and caribou scraps, and other items destined to become dog food.

The hunting team consisted of three huskies, two females and one male. It was quickly obvious that the females were the hunters and the male was brought along to pack home the prey. The two females while in heat were mortal enemies but normally coexisted well and made an efficient hunting team. While roaming the bush around the outskirts of town, any dog ran the risk of running into their larger, wilder cousin, the wolf. While the rabbit cycle was high the dogs were fairly safe, but during a down cycle, dogs were fair game for wolves. At times, hungry wolves were known to take dogs right off the chain in the middle of town.

One of the females, Tyee, began her life baptized by the ferocity and gentleness of one of the North's most cunning beasts. Tyee's owner, Rick Halladay, lived for a time in a small cabin a couple miles (3.2km) north of town. Rick's female had recently given birth to a litter. One day after mushing to town, Rick was delayed and forced to spend the night. Upon returning to his cabin the next morning, he discovered the wolves had visited. All that was left of the female was a small chunk of hide so clean it looked as if it had been tanned. Unbelievably, all the pups were left untouched. Tyee was one of those pups.

Although very neurotic and completely obsessed with my mom, firmly believing she was her mom too, Tyee made a fine sled dog and a great mother herself.

Kluane, the other female hunter and integral part of our puppy business, was taken by the wolves. She disappeared one winter day never to be seen again. Arnold Edzerza reported finding wolf scat with gray dog hair in it and the lower part of a leg matching her description.

In those days after butchering their moose or caribou, people often chucked the leg bones out into the yard for any passing dogs to have. We had six or seven dogs roaming around town on any given day. Needless to say, our yard filled up with moose and caribou legs. In the spring as the snow

Beautiful Kluane explores an abandoned mine shaft, early 1970s.

melted, our yard tended to look like a slaughterhouse refuse pile.

Marrow is extremely nutritious and a doggie delicacy. A few times every spring as more and more legs were exposed, my dad and I cracked them open with a maul and metered out the marrow to our drooling mutts.

We had so many dogs over a short period of time, it's impossible to remember them all. Of course, some stood out and remain near and dear to my heart. I think the most amazing thing to take from all of it, is my mom's love for dogs. First, she was exploring Puget Sound on her little sloop with her best friend Lucky, then she immediately acquired a couple of mongrels when arriving in Juneau and soon after, added two husky pups to the brood. She moved to Atlin with those four dogs and acquired more.

Some say it might have bordered on obsession when she brought two full-grown Malamutes and a litter of pups on the only Smith family vacation. We drove our pickup and camper across all the western states. We made quite a splash in most places, but the people we encountered in New Mexico were blown away at these huge hairy beasts. They were the biggest, hairiest Chihuahuas ever seen in those parts.

We boarded our dogs in Denver then flew to Kentucky where I met my grandma for the first time. My parents were sure the kennel was charging admission for people to come and play with the puppies. After a week in Kentucky, we flew back and picked up our bewildered mutts and continued on our road trip.

Mom never went anywhere in her car without three or four dogs, and at times, many more. Two blocks down to the inn, load the dogs. A trip to the grocery store, load the dogs. A visit to a friend's, well, you get it.

Mom walked in the woods most evenings when the weather permitted. She loaded up the dogs in her car and headed out one of the roads, usually toward the gold creeks. When she saw an interesting place to stop, she'd pull over and park, let the dogs out and wander into the woods. The Atlin area was replete with decaying miner's cabins and interesting claim posts and bottle dumps. For years she explored, always feeling safe because she had the dogs with her.

One evening she was following a long-forgotten overgrown lane. The dogs were up ahead around a corner chasing a squirrel. Suddenly one of the dogs hurdled past her and disappeared back toward the car, soon followed by the rest. None of them made a sound or hesitated for a second, they just ran away leaving her standing alone. Needless to say, this was greatly unsettling. Not sure if there was a bear or a pack of wolves or a five-headed gargoyle, she decided it would be prudent to follow the dogs. She said it was the longest short walk of her life. She covered most of the distance walking backward. When she made it to the car, she found all the dogs sitting there looking a little sheepish, waiting anxiously to be let in. She never did figure out what scared them so bad, but it made her think twice about feeling safe because she had dogs with her.

Since we were, for a time, a puppy mill of sorts, there were always a few dogs that weren't yet trained in car etiquette. When left too long, they got bored. What do bored, young dogs do? They chew. The entire interior of the car was ripped, torn or chewed. The sun visors: shredded. Radio and heater knobs: chewed or missing. Door handles and locking knobs: chewed or missing. All the seats: fabric torn and at least some foam missing. The dash and steering wheel: chewed. At times it was hard to see out of the window through the slobber and dog snot. And then there was the hair, oh, the hair—it was everywhere. A single husky while shedding can easily leave a grocery bag of hair a day. When multiplying that by five or six, well, let's just say we were literally swimming in it. If you have smelled even one wet dog, then I've said enough on that subject. Picture a half-dozen dogs entering and exiting a car multiple times a day during the spring thaw. The amount of mud and sand was staggering. Needless to say, my mother wasn't often asked to transport kids to any of the out-of-town school events. That's one way to get out of it, I guess.

We have all seen depictions of the clowns and their tiny car. Well, that was us whenever we went anywhere. Tourists stared in astonishment as two hairy, harried humans and an endless stream of furry beasts disembarked from our tiny car. You rolled down your window at your own risk because the wind stirred up the hair balls. There's nothing more unpleasant than sucking a massive Malamute hair ball into your mouth as you are taking a breath.

Chilkoot, a Wheel Dog's Life

Chilkoot was one of two puppies that came with us when we moved to Atlin. He was a beautiful dog with classic husky features. Growing up, we had a Josephine Crumrine print on our wall. She featured husky and Malamutes in many of her works. For years, the cover of the Alaska Steamship Company's menus featured her dogs. The dog in the print was a dead ringer for Chilkoot. I spent my entire childhood believing it was a portrait of him.

Chilkoot and I grew up together. Over the years, many dogs passed through our doors, but he was with us the longest. From the

Going for a ride with Dad on Atlin Lake. Atlin in the background, early 1970s.

Chilkoot in harness, early 1970s.

time I was a baby till I was an early teen, he was my friend. He was a loyal pet and a great sled dog.

Because of his size, his position in the team was directly in front of the sled, the wheel dog position. Wheel dogs have the most physically demanding jobs and are the powerhouses of the team. They are the first to take on the weight of the load, especially during starts and on hills. They also need to be good-natured to endure the constant slamming of the sled.

Sled dogs do their bodily functions while on the go, so to speak, but not Chilkoot. When he had to pee, he stopped dead in his tracks. Without the wheel dog, the team isn't going anywhere. When Chilkoot stopped, everything stopped. Presumably he found the practice of going while in motion too undignified. Waiting for a break, he'd hold it as long as he possibly could and only stop at the very last second.

My dad and I were taking the team out for a run on the lake one day. As we skirted the end of Third Island, we were traveling horizontally over the sloping beach when suddenly Chilkoot stopped. It was quick reflexes on my dad's part to keep the sled from running over him. Chilkoot immediately began relieving himself; he didn't raise his leg, he just peed where he stood. He continued to pee and he continued to pee. We waited, and the other dogs were restless and whined and yipped, but he wasn't finished. It seemed like he peed for twenty minutes. As there was only a small hole where the stream hit the snow, my dad commented, "I wonder where it's all going." I happened to glance down the lake and approximately fifteen feet (4.5m) away I noticed a small pond of urine forming on the surface of the lake. Man, but that dog could hold it—there must have been several gallons. I believe he hated peeing while in the team because there often wasn't anything to lift his leg on.

Something About a Dog
Atlin News Miner 1974
Diane S. Smith

It would be easy to write a large volume about dogs. In fact, if I devoted just one chapter to each of the many dogs we have owned over the years, my manuscript would equal *War and Peace* and *Gone with the Wind*. Thinking it over, either of those titles would be suitable for my dog book too.

For now, though, I'll just tell you something about one dog named Chilkoot. He is a sled dog whose interests vary greatly from those of his peers. I think it all started when Chilkoot was a pup and received a cruel injury that undoubtedly influenced his future life.

One day when we still lived in Juneau, he tagged after an older dog that was out chasing women. He returned some time later, head down and badly hurt. We determined he had been hit across the nose with what must have been a heavy club or board. Bones were broken, nasal passages crushed and teeth broken, probably by an owner of a female dog in heat, unhappy with the attentions of our Malamutes.

After Dr. Cliff Loubough had carefully patched and wired him together, the only noticeable indication of the encounter was that Chilkoot turned his head aside if anyone reached to touch his face. Outwardly, he was intact but I always suspected his nose didn't work quite right again. For instance, he wasn't particularly interested in the springtime romancing most male dogs pursue with great enthusiasm. He was happy to putter around the house and yard instead and eventually he developed a leaning toward things of a mechanical nature as a substitute for love in the spring.

Along regular lines was his lively interest in pickups and cars, mainly the tires. Once he got loose in a large parking lot, a place he rarely was able to visit, and he squirted thirty-six tires before we chased him, hopping on three legs, out of the place.

Chilkoot is a detached sort of animal and absent-mindedness, along with his unusual penchant for mechanical items, led into two collisions with pickup trucks. In fact, he ran into the trucks rather than the other way around. The first crash resulted in a hip injury that plagues him now in his golden years and shortened his career as a wheel dog on the team. The next time, he stuck his foot under a speeding pickup and had a fat and painful paw for several weeks.

Later on, it occurred to me he was probably trying to squirt the tires of the moving vehicles to set some new record. He didn't try again and as far as I know it was never accomplished with any success.

Chilkoot liked handles, latches and locks and has become expert at opening doors. He mastered most of the house doors wherever we lived and then learned to open the door of my car. The first time he let himself into my car, I was keeping a female husky in it part of the time since it was spring and the male dogs were chasing women as usual. Young son was loudly blamed for carelessly leaving the door open, an accusation he strongly denied while no doubt wondering what the car door could possibly have to do with the black threat of unwanted puppies.

Chilkoot's motivations were not of a romantic nature, however. He just enjoyed pretty Kluane's company in any season and got in the car to pass a sunny afternoon. I am sure his lack of nose power had squelched his normal canine urge to blanket the world with pups.

Finally, we saw him open the door by hooking one broken fang under the latch to release it. The problem was he often invited his muddy cronies to join him and the mess they made in the car was complete. So, to foil his trick, I parked the car on a slant and locked the lower door. Minutes later, Chilkoot was sitting happily behind the wheel. He had unlatched the high side door then pulled it back enough to wiggle inside. He was also witnessed holding the door for his friends before squirming in past the closing door. His entrance was great, but exit, he could not. When it was time to get out and check the tires, he had to bark for help.

After Chilkoot began spending a lot of time sitting in my car, it naturally followed he should try to drive. The dashboard full of gadgets must have intrigued his technical brain and the idea of driving the car may have been one of the reasons he wanted in, in the first place.

Anyway, one day he decided to drive down Discovery Street. First bumping it out of gear, he eased the car away from in front of the house and headed down the three-block-long hill leading to the lake. I think he would have made it all the way to the water if it had not been for Ron Bowden over at the garage, who saw what he was up to and didn't think he should be driving yet. He dashed across the street and jerked the door open so he could take the wheel. This really made Chilkoot cranky and he told Ron to bugger off ... wouldn't even let him ride along.

Ron figured it was best not to argue, even though Chilkoot didn't have many teeth left, so instead he came to tell me my dog was driving my car. In the meantime, the interruption had flustered Chilkoot and he veered across the road and into the corner of Rudy's property.

I was relieved my car hadn't ended up in the lake, but felt that Chilkoot should have been more apologetic about taking the car without asking. Instead, he just sat there scowling and muttering about Ron butting in.

Chilkoot is past ten years old now and he doesn't drive anymore. As a matter of fact, he never did get his driver's license. He did okay on the written exam but couldn't pass the driving test because he saw Ron on the road and got mad all over again.

Mostly Chilkoot sits in the car and waits for summer tourists who like to take pictures of him. But I've noticed something of late. Whenever a plane flies over, he leans out the window and watches it until it disappears from sight. And one day at the airstrip, he hung around the parked planes instead of chasing squirrels like he usually does. Now, you don't suppose that silly old codger is going to try to ...

———

Chilkoot lived a long, happy life and passed away at home in his sleep, although his freedoms were substantially limited as he grew crankier in his old age and developed a propensity for nipping at anyone who startled him. The final straw that ended his free-range rights happened one day as he lay on the front porch admiring the passing trucks and no doubt dreaming of operating some of the equipment in Rudy's yard across the street. Our newly established RCMP Corporal happened along on his daily jog. For some reason, Chilkoot decided it was a good idea to hobble after him and bite him in the ass. Threats of incarceration and even euthanasia were followed by many apologies and ended with an agreement to keep Chilkoot on a leash or in the house at all times.

It was a topic of much discussion as to whether Chilkoot, in his diminished capabilities, thought he was seeing a moose trot by, or was he confused to see any Atlinite running for no good reason? Another theory was he somehow got wind that the Corporal was enforcing Atlin's first "leash and tie up" laws. The jury is out.

I'm happy to report Chilkoot did find love in his old age, albeit with a Sears Roebuck pull-behind vacuum cleaner. While any normal dog has an innate fear of all things loud and mechanical and takes off to parts unknown at the mere mention of the fire-breathing beast, old Chilkoot seemed to find comfort and relaxation whenever we fired up the vac. He'd get that lopsided, toothless grin on his face. When it got anywhere near him, he rolled over on his back in utter contentment, possibly hoping for a good cuddle.

Canines of Consequence

Atlin boasted a number of dogs that reached heights of notoriety. The Goodwin's dog, Rowdy, was an undisputed hero. On a cold Atlin night in the late fall of 1968, the Goodwin family, Mom, Dad and four children, as well as a pregnant friend of the family, Judy Brasseau, were all fast asleep in the old Kootenay Hotel. Fire broke out in the chimney and rapidly spread through the seventy-year-old wooden structure. Rowdy, alerted by the smoke, sounded the alarm, frantically barking as he ran from one room to the next. The Goodwins and Judy escaped in the nick of time with nothing but their bedclothes. The Kootenay was fully engulfed in minutes and Rowdy had given the family the scant seconds needed to reach safety. Rowdy without a doubt saved his family and their friend; he was not just a family pet but an unlikely hero who saved nine lives that night as Judy would have twins. Rowdy was awarded a medal for heroism by the lieutenant governor of British Columbia.

Peggy Milius' dog, Lobo, was another famous Atlin dog, although not in the same heroic league as Rowdy. Lobo was better known for his immense size and gentle demeanor as well as his epic Hollywood good looks. Ensconced on his favorite street corner, he became a landmark and a beloved member of the community. Rescued from the relentless heat of Southern California, Lobo was much better suited for life in the North. His long flowing hair and classic husky markings made him the subject of countless photos and petting sessions. His amiable personality endeared him to almost everyone who met him.

Lobo, like many huskies and Malamutes, had a unique way of greeting friends and strangers alike, consisting of deep bass "woo wooing" and guttural utterances. This was usually accompanied with tail wagging, although that was often missed by the uninitiated. Most Northerners understand this to be a show of affection. The unenlightened, upon first encountering that display of love, have been known to misconstrue the friendly intentions and flee for their lives, often screaming and crying. When that happened, Lobo looked a little insulted and lay back down to wait for his next victim/friend.

One particular story, or rumor, about Lobo goes like this. The names have not been changed to protect the guilty as usual. For some time, Lobo and Peggy lived beside Gary, a young man with possibly too much time on his hands, who decided to teach Lobo a new trick. This consisted of patting his chest or upper arms and encouraging Lobo to rear up and place his front paws on his shoulders. Now, I'm guessing Gary stands five ten to six feet (1.55m to 1.82m) tall. Lobo, when standing on his hind legs, looked Gary in the eyes. Lobo, being of sound intelligence quickly learned this trick and enjoyed it.

This is where the story gets interesting ... and maybe slightly erroneous. One fine summer day an elderly tourist lady from somewhere south happened to wander down Lobo's street, strolling peacefully while soaking up Atlin's historic charm and incredible beauty. Undoubtedly, she had never before witnessed a dog of Lobo's considerable stature. Upon seeing him rise to greet her, she froze in place, mouth open, eyes bulging. Lobo, considering her yet another fan, greeted her in his customary way, "woo wooing" as he approached. When hearing what to her must have sounded like a vicious growl, the lady uttered, "Oh, my God," and brought both hands to her mouth. Now to Lobo's reasoning that looked an awful lot like an invite to show off his newly-mastered trick. Eager to please his new friend, he reared up and placed his large paws on her shoulders, affectionately gazing down at his now apoplectic prey.

It's not clear if Peggy or Gary saved the poor lady, but it was noted that she immediately left town after a quick stop at the liquor store.

Dog team crossing overflow which is caused when water seeps through cracks in the lake or river ice leaving puddles of water on the surface. Overflow is often covered in snow and invisible to the unexpecting. The danger lies in getting wet paws and feet at minus freezing temperatures. Sometimes there is only a matter of minutes to get dry before it's too late.

I believe Peggy had a few choice words for Gary as she was known to speak her mind and often displayed an adeptness at inserting the appropriate vulgarity where needed. I'm sure Gary felt the sting for many days to come.

Lobo, unfazed by these events, went back to his favorite corner and resumed his job as Atlin's unofficial greeter and only living landmark.

Dick Craft's dog, Tippy, had the distinction of traveling by foot over a hundred miles (160km) from Atlin to Whitehorse. Dick left Atlin one Friday morning in his pickup truck heading to town for a busy two-day business and shopping trip. Saturday afternoon, while driving down Main Street, Whitehorse, he was shocked to see Tippy bopping along the sidewalk, seemingly entranced by the big city lights and endless sign posts and telephone poles on which to pee upon. Not only is the distance and timeline impressive, Tippy somehow navigated at least three major intersections, correctly choosing each time. Three of our own dogs tried the same thing, but were slower than, and not as smart as, Tippy. We found them only twenty miles (47km) up the road, sleeping in a ditch, on our return home late that evening.

We often left a number of our dogs unleashed when heading off to Whitehorse for the day. Mostly they stayed close to home and caused little concern to others. As it was our habit to run the dogs out of town behind the truck in the evening, something they loved, what often followed was a comedic and frustrating ordeal for my dad. Escaping town without the unavoidable convoy of mongrels became a madcap dash of absurdity. A circuitous and frenetic race around town preceded every trip to Whitehorse. A few dogs were smart enough, they didn't fall for the faints and trickery. They figured out waiting at the only exit from town was easier and wiser. In this case speed, dust and flying gravel were the best strategy. Upon seeing he had been outsmarted, Dad deployed the only weapon he had left and stomped on the gas pedal.

Once the truck was out of sight, most of our pack lost interest and turned for home. One or two might pursue as far as Como Lake, a couple miles (3.2km). Only the one time that we know of did they follow farther.

I would be remiss if I did not mention a dog of a certain breed, the Tahltan bear dog. The Tahltan (also Nahanni) are a First Nation's people of the Athabasca-speaking group who live in Northern British Columbia. The Tahltan bear dog was originally bred to, as their name indicates, hunt bear. Small in stature but furiously brave, two or three were sent out to confuse and distract a bear so the hunters could safely get close enough to kill it with arrows or spears. Now, a dog that stands roughly twelve inches (3.5cm) tall and weighs around twenty-five pounds (11.5km) that willingly takes on a thousand-pound (453kg) grizzly bear is a creature of a particular nature.

Shortly after moving to Atlin, our dog Tongass wandered into the wrong yard, in search of love, no doubt. One of the young men of the house took exception to the intrusion and dispatched him with his .22 rifle. Now my father, extremely upset, decided to confront the young man's father. In the tête-à-tête that followed, tempers ebbed as it was explained that our dog was in fact in their yard uninvited, but it was also agreed the young man had acted hastily and thus he apologized earnestly, as did his father on his son's behalf. Now, with calmness and reason prevailing, introductions were offered and accepted. The young man's dad's name was Sylvester Jack, and that was the beginning of a long relationship between the two families.

I know you're wondering what any of this has to do with the Tahltan bear dogs. Hold on, I'm getting there. A few days later, my mom heard a knock at the door, and upon opening it found a woman of diminutive stature, a kind face and shy smile. Cupped in her hands was a small, black ball of fur. Without saying a word, she thrust it toward my mom. A bit startled, mom hesitantly accepted the gift, only then realizing it was a tiny puppy. The woman introduced herself as Evelyn Jack, Sylvester's better half. She expressed her condolences and again apologized for her son's actions. She offered the puppy as a gift in hopes it would make up for the loss of Tongass. My mom accepted and invited her in for tea.

Tutshi, named by my mom after Tutshi Lake near Carcross, Yukon, was a Tahltan bear dog. A breed bred for their tenacity and fearlessness and used to antagonize bears is not always a good fit for a home filled with large huskies and Malamutes. But he became a beloved member of our family.

Too small to pull in the team and not of preferred breeding stock, Tutshi was out of place among his larger cousins. He was smart, sly and a bit of a trickster. He often caused problems amongst the sled dogs. He loved inciting chaos. When two or more huskies were posturing and growling at each other, a common occurrence more often than not ending without an actual fight, Tutshi liked to bounce around the antagonist, barking and nipping at their heels trying to get something started. If he did succeed in getting his dumber brothers to fight, he quickly removed himself from the fray and gleefully watched from a safe distance.

Tutshi's favorite pastime was standing at the end of a particular sled dog's chain and barking and darting in and out of their reach, infuriating the chained dog and driving them into a fit of rage. Although Tutshi didn't fit in well with the other dogs and had no real purpose other than pet status, my dad did find one use for him. As most of the sled dogs hated Tutshi and would have loved to sink their fangs into him, my dad brought him along on the trapline and let him run loose lead in front of the team. This seemed to motivate the team greatly as they all dreamed of catching him. It was a different take on the old carrot-and-stick play.

Tutshi was one of the dogs we didn't tie up and he could roam around at will, and he also spent every night in the house. One particularly cold December night, Tutshi didn't return home at

Tutshi running loose lead in front of the team, early 1970s.

feeding time as was his habit. Five days passed and still no Tutshi. The temperature stayed at forty below during the entire five days. It was thought he may have been killed by wolves or even another dog or been injured and frozen to death.

On the night of the Christmas concert as we were bundling up to leave, a faint scratch was heard at the door. My mom opened it and Tutshi slowly dragged himself inside. His neck and chest were covered in frozen blood. My mom inspected him and found a large patch of skin and meat torn away from his neck, exposing the jugular vein and throat. She could not determine if either had been harmed. Joe Ackerman suggested we help him drink some milk and see if any leaked out, but none did. Nothing could be done at the time, so we bundled him up beside the stove and let him rest. The next day, Jessie, our nurse, sewed him up and we used a horse disinfectant to ward off infection. Yes, our nurse sewed him up. The closest vet was over a hundred miles (160km) away. Tutshi recovered fully, and the best deduction was he either zigged when he should have zagged while playing his game of "piss off the husky" or maybe a wolf got him. To survive injured for that long at that temperature is nothing short of miraculous and speaks volumes for the temerity of the breed.

Unfortunately, the Tahltan bear dog is now considered extinct. It is believed that the Connolly family and Winnie Atcheson of Atlin had the last three. Two were of the same sex and the other neutered so no possibility of furthering the species. Variations of the breed still exist, but none pure.

Buck, the Golden Charmer

I remember a dog named Buck. Buck had a peculiar habit that endeared him to a number of people in town as well as frustrating them at the same time. It was a cold, dark evening and my mom and I were in for the night, all settled down with a book or magazine. The dogs were sprawled about the living room, basking in the glow of the wood stove. By now I was in my early teens and we were pared down to only five dogs and the occasional litter of puppies. Although we still had dog houses, they preferred to stay in at night and my mom let them. We heard a rustle and a scratch at the door. Our dogs jumped up and Mom and I did an immediate count, quickly realizing all our mutts were present and accounted for. Mom hesitantly opened the door and Buck confidently pushed his way in. Our dogs greeted him politely; in fact, they acted like they knew him. Neither Mom nor I had ever seen him before, but he was very friendly and came up for an ear scratching and a quick cuddle. If I was to guess, I would say Buck was a long-haired golden retriever/golden lab mix, but we had no way of knowing for sure. Our dogs quickly returned to their lounging and didn't mind in the least when Buck proceeded to clean up all the leftover dog food and drink most of the water. Fearing he was still hungry, we offered him more, but he was polite and seemed to be happy with what he had already consumed. After more petting and ear scratching, Buck took his place on the floor by the stove. Once again, our dogs hardly paid attention to him. My mom and I exchanged curious looks but went back to our reading.

Before bed, we let everyone out for the regularly scheduled bathroom break. Buck went out with the pack. Assuming he might use this opportunity to go home, we were surprised when he came back in with the gang and once again flopped down on the floor. Not ones to throw an animal out into a cold night, we shrugged and went to bed.

The next day, Buck hung out around the yard with the rest of the dogs, doing all the same things our dogs did. At feeding time, my mom put a bowl down for him and he ate with the others. It was odd to us that he acted like he had lived with us for years, and also odd that our dogs acted the same way. Buck's visit went on for a few days, before my mom started asking around if anyone knew where he belonged. Someone thought her description of Buck fit a dog they had seen at Krist Johnson's place. My mom went to his house and Krist was happy and relieved to hear of Buck's well-being. He was the one who told her his name, a name Krist had given him, so probably not his real name; strangely enough, Buck did not belong to him either. As he described it, Buck had just shown up one evening and moved in like he already lived there. Krist said he stayed for a few weeks then disappeared like he had arrived, quietly and mysteriously.

My mom could see that Krist was very smitten and attached to Buck, so she agreed to bring him back. Later that day she loaded him in the car and returned him to Krist. That evening once again, there was a scratch at our door and as smooth and casual as could be, in walked Buck. He said his hellos, cleaned up the dishes, got a drink and flopped down by the fire.

The next day Mom once again talked to Krist and together they agreed to let Buck do what Buck wanted to do. As long as he was okay, they were happy. A few weeks went by and one day Buck just up and vanished. Assuming he was back at Krist's, my mom stopped by to see, but there was no sign of Buck. He had not returned there. Both my mom and Krist were worried something had happened and they began making inquiries around town. It was over a week later they discovered Buck had moved in with Jennifer and Darrel.

It was to become known as Buck's trapline. Along with my mom and me, Krist, Jennifer and Darrel Hansen, Jack and Ollie Green were also on Buck's route and it was never determined if there were more. Buck would just show up one evening and move in for a few weeks or a month, then just like he came, he would suddenly disappear. He always got along well with other dogs, he was respectful of the house rules, he was neat and clean and brought joy and happiness wherever he went. Aside from our dogs, Jack and Ollie had a Chihuahua, but the others had no dogs. As far as I know, no one ever found out where Buck originated. I remember Jennifer showing up on our doorstep one night with a bag of scraps she had saved for Buck—before she could feed them to him, he had moved on to our place. People really cared for him and would have loved it if he stayed permanently, but on the other hand, they realized he was his own dog, doing his own thing, and that was to be honored.

I remember many times my mom calling the other members of Buck's trapline to check on his well-being.

Depletion in the Ranks

I imagine growing up with so many dogs over the years might be like growing up on a farm. It's not wise to get too attached, although that proved impossible for me. I vividly remember the heartbreak when we lost a dog or sold one or gave one away. We lost an amazing dog that I loved so much. His name was Attu. He was so curious and playful and smart, always getting into trouble but bringing so much happiness wherever he went. He was run over and killed right in front of me when I was ten. Attu's back was broken and he had to be

Our Malamute Knik, in front of an abandoned miner's cabin in the early 1980s.

put down. I'll never forget holding him and trying to make him feel better. He just kept looking at me like he had done something wrong and that I was mad at him. That look will never leave me.

When we lost Kluane to the wolves, I was devastated. She was the most beautiful husky I've ever seen; she was gentle and kind and an amazing mother. The pain of not knowing was only slightly alleviated when we figured out what happened to her.

At The Pillman House, we still raised a litter a year to sell, but at times we couldn't resist keeping one. Klondy, short for Klondike, was a pup my mom kept. Klondy attached herself to me and I was completely smitten. She was a pretty Malamute with big feet. Her ears were huge and still floppy so she was only a few months old. At that time, Chilkoot was the only dog we constantly had restrained, the rest stayed close to home and we didn't worry about them. One evening when letting in the gang for dinner, Klondy was absent. Not immediately concerned, we called and waited. Soon after, I went looking. At first I looked for tracks, but it was snowing hard. I went back and got my dog Atlin. Within a block from our house, Atlin found her covered in snow. Someone shot her, an innocent puppy, for no reason.

When my parents split, some of the dogs went to Inuvik with my dad. If I was lucky, I might see them twice a year. These dogs were part of my family and suddenly they were gone. Cassiar, our consummate lead dog, went with my dad. He was a puppy when we moved from Juneau, and like Chilkoot, was with me my entire life up till then. My dad gave away the dogs he took except Cassiar, and it was known (by me) that he wasn't taking good care of him.

Kluane's puppies, mid-1970s. A typical representation of our dogs. I was a lucky kid. We had two to four litters of pups a year. I enjoyed playing with the puppies.

Cassiar lived under the Mad Trapper Bar. My mom insisted that he be returned to us. My dad agreed, but somewhere in the returning, he lost Cassiar in Whitehorse. I'm not sure how much he looked, but my mom and I drove in and looked for two days. He was never found by us and we could only hope someone took him in. It hurt me then and still does to this day. He was such a loving and loyal dog, he didn't deserve that in his old age. The puppies were always hard to see go, but I didn't have time to build up an attachment, so it was easier.

While writing about the dogs and especially the puppies, I started to feel down for one particular reason. I realized I may never again lie down in a box of puppies while they crawl all over me, trying their best to lick my face. The smell of their little puppy breath and their slobbery tongues may forever be a distant memory.

Chapter Nineteen

Hardluck Harvey

Although not a dog, Hardluck Harvey deserves a mention on these pages. Hardluck was, in fact, a burro or donkey. "Asinus" is the burro's scientific name, suggesting certain "assiness" traits that hint at a further truth that burros, asses and donkeys are pretty much the same thing. An argument could easily be won defining Hardluck as an ass in the figurative and literal sense. Asinine was a word often used to describe Hardluck's exploits.

John Harvey decided that in order to completely pull off his new persona as gold miner and prospector, he needed a donkey, thus fully legitimizing his new vocation. John was new in the North, straight out of Toronto, and he may have been harboring delusional, romanticized dreams of what the North and gold mining, in particular, held for him. Many newcomers of the time suffered from the same disorder. For example, my dad and his "trapping by dog team" venture. John learned of a donkey for sale in lower British Columbia. He quickly purchased him and air freighted him to Whitehorse. How many donkeys have flown on a jet, you may ask? This might have contributed to Hardluck's air of superiority.

In the beginning, Hardluck was young, cute, and gentle, and this endeared him to the local population. The kids and adults alike loved Hardluck. The dogs seemed a little wary and held their judgment, as if understanding we weren't yet seeing the donkey's true personality. I'm not sure if all the attention spoiled him or if he was innately an ass, but soon Hardluck began to act out like a spoiled brat. Somewhere along the way, he developed a bad tobacco habit. I suspect some of the young men thought it funny to give him cigarettes, but no matter how it happened, he quickly became addicted. Unlike his human counterparts, he didn't ask for a cigarette but rather took them right out of a person's hand or even mouth, lit or not, he didn't care. He got good at nudging the whole pack from a front pocket and quickly chewing it up, tinfoil and all, while his victim yelled and cursed. Chewing tobacco and snuff were all fair game to Hardluck. Redman was his favorite.

Hardluck's crimes were minor and seen as cute and easily forgivable. As I've mentioned, Atlin and the surrounding area was considered free range, meaning any livestock could roam free, and Hardluck took full advantage.

Horses are used in big-game hunting for packing and transportation. Utilized for a short time every fall, they were a necessity, but expensive to keep all year. In the summer the animals have plenty of food if they can range anywhere they want. They gorge on lush grass, flowers and weeds, fattening up for hunting season and the brutal winter months. In the winter, the animals rely heavily on their owners for food; although scrounging and digging down through the snow does yield a percentage of their food, it isn't enough to sustain them. Our neighbors, John and Pete Wright's family, had many horses. At intervals during the day, the animals were fed hay and grain but then shooed away to forage for the rest of the day. It was the same for the cows. The free-range system allowed ranchers and big-game guides to sustain their animals. There are detriments to the policy, as occasionally a horse or cow is hit on the road and they are known to destroy gardens now and then, but it was the only way to afford them throughout the year.

Hardluck had free-range rights like the horses and cows, and this allowed him constant access to places and things he shouldn't have had access to. Hardluck decided that the bulletins on the bulletin board outside the post office looked like a colorful salad, so he ate

John Harvey in prospector's garb with Hardluck at the Campground after a parade, 1971.

them, many times over. Most looked upon this as funny, but others relied on the messages posted on that board and they may have seen it as less so. My mom was not so happy to lose all the flowers in the flower beds around the house. This was, unfortunately, a frequent occurrence as the local cows also enjoyed flowers. She was more perturbed by losing her entire chive patch, and the culprit was soon discovered as he had the rankest green-onion breath for days to come.

The cows were off the hook that time. Unlike the cows, I don't remember Hardluck destroying gardens, but given time, I'm sure he would have moved up his criminal activity to include the most heartbreaking of all Northern crimes.

Hardluck escalated his mischief by eating laundry off clotheslines, shoving in porch doors to get at the dog food bag and generally

Hardluck posing in front of the Courthouse, 1971.

becoming crankier and more stubborn. It was bad enough to find an uninvited ass standing in your living room upon returning home, but to see he had helped himself to the loaf of fresh bread on the counter and the contents of the entire sugar bowl was too much to take. Worse yet, he might not leave when politely asked/threatened. The ensuing removal of said beast often ended up with some broken furniture and/or a spiteful defecation on the floor.

I'm not sure if Hardluck had a substance-abuse problem or was a glutton or maybe didn't have taste buds, but he drank and ate pretty much everything and anything, including gasoline and diesel on a number of occasions. He also drank linseed oil, but his favorite seemed to be paint. One day, the band office was getting a new coat of white paint and between drinking it, dumping it on himself and brushing up against the newly-painted walls, he managed to change his color from gray to mostly white.

You would think one color change that summer would have been enough for any fashion-conscious ass, but not for Hardluck. Wayne and Cindy Merry were in the middle of painting their house blue when Hardluck paid a visit, and needless to say Hardluck was soon sporting a lovely blue-green swirly look with white trim. As a number of homes that summer were decked out in fields of various blues and trimmed out with white, he fit in well.

Along with his tobacco habit, Hardluck enjoyed a beer whenever he could get his lips on one. I'm guessing some of his smoking buddies introduced beer to him, but he could easily have discovered it on his own. For a time, Hardluck was a sought-after guest at any outdoor party and it wasn't long before he started draining every beer bottle he saw. Once at an outdoor beer garden at the Campground, it was estimated Hardluck polished off upwards of thirty partial beers.

Finding them unattended on the table wasn't enough for him—he got to taking them right out of people's hands.

Whether invited or enticed, he did make at least one appearance in the local watering hole, where it was reported he requested a Labatt's Blue and was served after showing some assuredly asinine ID.

Hardluck quickly found himself being left off

With Hardluck when he was a colt, 1971.

most party invitations as he continually hogged all the beer, stole cigarettes and generally made an ass of himself. Now, no one can say he actually got drunk, as he was pretty much an ass all the time, but it was obvious he suffered from severe hangovers. Cantankerous and moody, for some reason he blamed the dog population for his malady. Hardluck hated dogs and was often seen chasing them down the street braying and gnashing his teeth.

Hardluck became possessive of John's attention, and jealous and rude whenever John spent time with others. At first, he would subtly push himself between John and anyone he was conversing with, and later he took to lowering his head and forcing the person away. When this escalated to butting and biting, even John decided Hardluck might be outstaying his welcome.

I'm not sure how much prospecting John and Hardluck did together; but they shared a bond and Hardluck definitely loved John, although in the face of the growing anti-Hardluck sentiment, John's reciprocation may have waned some.

Several subversive plans were already afoot to remove Hardluck from the population when John was convinced to offer him up as first place prize in the yearly walkathon. Brian Denton was a perennial first place finisher and he lived out of town and had plenty of fenced space for an angry, thieving, destructive donkey. Before the diabolical plan was initiated, Brian got wind of it and was so adamant that he didn't want to win Hardluck, he walked the whole twelve-mile (19km) course backwards. Although he did not place first, the judges were so impressed with this feat they went ahead and awarded Hardluck to him anyway. Brian emphatically refused his prize and Hardluck was once again free to wreak havoc.

Eventually Walter and Barb Erhorn offered John a home for Hardluck at Halfway, an out-of-town, pastoral homestead. Hardluck could at last be a donkey without the distractions and temptations of urban living. With a couple horses and Walter and Barb's kids to keep him company, Hardluck mellowed, reverting to the lovable persona of his youth. Those that missed him were encouraged to visit anytime and many came to scratch his ears and take pictures. He did not want for attention.

Although Hardluck did give up drinking and his use of harder substances, he never quite kicked the tobacco habit and stole cigs and chew at every opportunity.

Sadly, he passed away a couple years later. He was only a teenager, and donkeys are known to live twenty-five to thirty years. He was found deceased beside Pine Creek, lying peacefully on a little patch of snow as if basking in the winter sun's warm rays. With no obvious reason for his demise, it was speculated his previous gluttonous habits may have caught up to him and shut down his system or weakened him enough for pneumonia to do him in.

Loved or hated, but never forgotten, Hardluck will surely go down as one of Atlin's most colorful residents.

John Harvey found this almost 38-ounce nugget on his claim at McKee Creek near Atlin in the late 1970s.

Chapter Twenty

Mushing

As I mentioned, when I was growing up in the North, dog mushing, and racing in particular, was experiencing a comeback. Many Atlinites had a few dogs and a sled to hook them to, enabling a weekend ice-fishing trip down the lake or a sojourn up the creek to have dinner with a friend. Free from the roar of the gasoline engine and without the pungent smell of exhaust, it was a more intimate way to commune with nature's wonders.

Some teams were used on the trapline, others to haul water and groceries around town. There is no greater experience than swooshing down the trail on a moonlit night when the dogs are at a full run with only the sound of paws and sled runners on the hard-packed snow, the subtle jingle of the harness and maybe a distant hoot of a lonely owl. The experience of standing on the runners holding on tight, gazing forward over the backs of the galloping huskies as the forest rushes by evokes an ethereal feeling much like flying.

One Christmas Eve, Mom and I were invited to dinner at Keith and Julie Brunner's, who at the time were staying at Graham's farm a couple miles (3k) south of town. We hitched up five of our

Malamutes, Cassiar as lead, Tyee and Kluane behind him, and Chilkoot and Taku in the wheel dog position. The temperature hovered around thirty below that night. The dogs were excited as they always were before a run. They barked and yipped and strained at their leads.

I untied the sled and quickly jumped aboard. Mom released the break and yelled, "Hike, let's go!" and we shot forward. We called running dogs, mushing, and those that ran dogs, mushers, but no self-respecting musher in those days ever yelled out "mush." Truth be told, one could yell Klingon gibberish to your team as long as you were consistent. Although we started out in the late afternoon, it was already dark. The moon was still well below the horizon. We skimmed across the Alkali Flats and the slough at the end of town, then onto the Ski-Doo trail that led south toward the farm. As most teams are full of energy for the first few miles, we let them run. I hunkered down in the boot of our old freight sled, and my mom rode on the runners, hanging on tight to the handlebars, one foot poised over the brake. Cassiar took commands well and, like all lead dogs, knew "gee" and "haw" for right and left. There was no need to slow as we entered the trails. Cassiar chose the correct paths without being told and we continued at a rapid pace. When we burst out of the brush and onto the old strawberry fields, the dogs were still running at full pace. Mom decided they needed a longer run, so we stopped and loaded up Julie and her baby and headed out on the lake.

The air was still and little clouds of ice crystals rose from the mouths of the panting dogs. After a couple miles, the team began to slow and Mom turned them in a sweeping circle back toward the farm. We quickly noticed the aurora borealis bouncing across the sky behind Monarch Mountain. Mom stopped the team as the dogs were ready for a break, and they lay down without complaint. Within a few minutes, we were entertained by the best northern lights ballet any of us had seen. Before us the sky exploded with the full spectrum of colors as the aurora danced and flitted over the mountain. Long tendrils of vibrant crimson and neon green shot toward us and over our heads to retreat and surge back again. The aurora twisted and turned, darting in and out, up and down. For at least a half hour, we stood spellbound, not noticing our feet growing colder or the icicles forming on our eyelashes. It was a small cry from the large bundle of blankets Julie held in her arms that snapped us back to reality.

Mom on the sled with three-dog team on the lake, 1970.

We reluctantly loaded back on the sled and headed for the distant lone lantern shining through the frosty window of Julie and Keith's tiny home. As we stomped in the doorway, we were met by Keith and the smell of dinner. That night, we gorged ourselves on roasted Canada goose, potatoes and carrots from Julie's garden, homemade stuffing and moss-berry pie. My mom brought her famous low-bush cranberry sauce and some fresh-baked buns.

After dinner, Keith strummed his guitar and we sang Christmas carols. My mom told a not-too-scary ghost story that I'm pretty sure she made up on the fly. It was an intimate, peaceful night that I will never forget.

When it was finally time to go, we bundled up and roused the team. Keith and Julie's dogs sent us off with a boisterous chorus of barks and howls. Once again, we let the team have their head, confident Cassiar would lead us home safe and sound. The northern lights had paled to wispy plumes of lazy smoke slowly drifting across the top of Monarch Mountain. Halfway home, we heard a wolf howling in the not-far distance, then another and another. It was obvious a pack wasn't far away. Our dogs spooked, their ears lay back flat

I'm standing on the frozen lake in front of town on a thirty-below day. When it was that cold, only mukluks could keep my feet warm.

and they cast nervous glances in the direction of the nearby choir. The team quickened their already rapid pace. After we reached the Alkali Flats behind town, my mom hollered for Cassiar to stop as she jumped on the brake. At a full stop, the dogs fidgeted and craned their necks back along the trail. Dogs have an innate fear of wolves—for good reason.

We listened to the back-and-forth howls for a few minutes and speculated on how close they were before we let the dogs off the hook and my mom yelled, "Get up!" It's rare, but not completely unusual, for wolves to be that close to town, especially as I already mentioned, when the rabbit cycle is down and wolves are hungry.

It was only a few days later that Keith and Julie were dealt a cruel blow. As they didn't have electricity at their place, Keith couldn't plug in the block heater on his truck. When the temperature drops to a certain level, the oil in the engine and oil pan thickens into a molasses-like substance. This condition inhibits the starting of the vehicle. Some use a torch to warm up the oil, but Keith took to lighting a small fire under the pan in order to thaw it. Although it was a practice he used on many occasions, for some reason this time, the fire ignited the engine, quickly spreading, and his truck was a total loss. Living out of town without a vehicle can be dangerous in the winter, especially with a small child.

The Way It Used to Be
Atlin News Miner 1976
Diane S. Smith

Dogsled racing is a tough sport today. Interest has increased tremendously over the last few years and, as more people move into the racing circle, the tracks become longer and harder but, by the same token, the winner's purses become fatter.

The Yukon Championship Race in Whitehorse is a forty-five miler (72km) with three fifteen-mile (24km) heats over three days. It draws twenty teams now as compared to six when it was first held six years ago. The World Championship Race held in Anchorage, Alaska, draws the crack teams from the lower forty-eight states, Canada, Europe and Alaska. To win this race, as George Attla, an Athabascan Indian from Huslia, Alaska, has done several times, you drive a team of sixteen dogs at fifteen miles (24km) an hour (this speed wins the Yukon race), then you urge these dogs to hit speeds of twenty miles (32km) per hour in the final grueling home stretch. Most of this race track is within the city limits of Anchorage, through the streets lined with cars and surging with spectators ... bad enough for dogs from the bush, but worse yet, they must run on concrete covered with a hauled-in blanket of snow. This is a race to tax the physical and mental limits of both team and driver ... a test of endurance and skill.

But I wonder what the mushers of yesteryear would think of our races today. How about men like Leonhard Seppala, the diminutive Norwegian who ran the socks off every team in Alaska and in doing so made the Siberian husky famous? Seppala won his first racing notoriety by winning the All Alaska Sweepstakes in 1915 in Nome. This race was a 408-mile (647km) round trip between Nome on the Bering Sea and Candle, Alaska, on the Arctic Ocean. His time in that classic event was 81 hours, 3 minutes and 45 seconds—less than four days.

The course lay along the telephone line so messages raced back and forth and bulletins were posted in Nome so boosters could keep track of their favorite mushers. In a history of races, Esther Birdsall Darling wrote, "... the town waits day and night for reports on the whereabouts and welfare of the racers." Strange spectator sport as compared to today's sprint races where there is scarcely enough time to get a cup of coffee when the first team is sighted heading for the finish line.

Kenai was a descendant from the Seppala line, 1971. Leonhard Seppala, a Norwegian man whose dog racing prowess is legendary in Alaska, was one of the first to use the Siberian sled dogs. He won every race of note in those days. He played a large role in the 1925 serum run to Nome, Alaska, and he ran his team in the Olympics.

The 408-mile (647km) race was sponsored by the Nome Kennel Club and their members maintained relay stations along the route where drivers and teams could get food and rest. The trick was to know how long you could stop without losing too much time. The only required stop was at Candle, where the judges inspected the teams before they headed home on the second leg of the race. The equipment the drivers carried on their sleds was furs and rubber boots for themselves and moccasins for the dogs.

After Seppala won the 1915 All American, the townsfolk of Nome were proud when he received an invitation to compete in the Ruby Derby of 1916. The Ruby race was considered one of the short ones, a marathon run over a fifty-eight-mile (93km) course. Seppala entered and won easily, but to do so he had to mush his team 450 miles (725km) over mountain passes, along the frozen Yukon River and through sub-arctic forests to reach the town of Ruby.

Leonhard Seppala lived to be eighty-nine years old and raced until nearly sixty. He saw the modern-day mushers dashing off to races with their dogs loaded in neat camper kennels aboard comfortable pickup trucks or packed aboard swift airplanes. These sights must have brought vivid pictures of his racing days and his 450-mile (724km) trip by dog team just to reach the starting line.

Probably there were times when Leonhard Seppala felt the same way Norman Fisher felt the other night. Norman, who is eighty-nine, put in hundreds of miles mushing the mail team from Carcross to Atlin and on to Telegraph Creek years ago.

But after listening to an hour of high-powered dog talk at the curling club lounge, he said quietly and with a twinkle in his eye, "You know, I decided I don't know anything about dogs."

———

Like many of the youngsters of that time, I enjoyed hitching up two or three dogs for a run out the road, usually accompanied by my buddy Randy Green. I'm sure my memories glorify our exploits and my adroit adeptness at handling the sled and our surging beasts. Randy may remember things differently, but he's not writing this.

On a crisp winter morning, we'd harness up the dogs and hook them to a sled. I preferred the racing sled, a lightweight nimble craft, easier to manhandle than our clunky, aged, freight sled. As our dogs were easily distracted and may have had less respect for my authority than my mother's, leaving town was always an exercise in frustration and willpower. Dogs are contrary creatures and have been known to leave their masters sitting in the middle of the trail, dazed and confused as they watch their team disappear around a bend. Once successfully navigating the three blocks to the edge of town, skirting neighborhood dogs, horses and cars, it was time to step off the brake and let them run. Most young boys of nine or ten aren't big enough to completely stop a team of even three dogs with the brake alone, but fully applied, it will slow them down and make them a little easier to control.

Ten to fifteen miles (16km to 24km) an hour may sound slow to some, but from the back of a dogsled, it seems break neck. The first few miles, when the dogs are excited and eager to work, is exhilarating to say the least. After they tire a little, they settle in to a more measured pace and the driver can relax a little, but never completely—EVER.

During this brief period of repose is inevitably when a lynx dashes across the road and the age-old "dog chasing cat" scenario enfolds at the speed of light. If your arms aren't wrenched out of their sockets and somehow you manage to hang on, you may find your feet in the air and see your buddy fly over your head when team and sled hurtle over the snowbank along the side of the road. The fleet-footed lynx, with his enormous paws and light frame, effortlessly skims over the top of the snow and disappears in the blink of an eye. Huskies, sled, driver and passenger are not so fortunate. The dogs only make it a

I'm leading Cassiar with Randy Green in the sled, 1976.

I'm on the sled while Randy Green holds Cassiar. We are using a light-weight racing sled made by my dad. Our freight sled was clunky and heavy making it hard to handle. The Discovery Shop is in the background, 1970.

few yards before they are mired in the deep snow. Dog mushing is a series of highs and lows in rapid and unpredictable succession. Many times frustration only begins to express your feelings for your furry friends. They eat dogs in some cultures, don't they?

Turning a team around in deep snow is a chore, to say the least. Greatly appreciated is the assistance of your friend after he extricates himself from the branches of the nearest tree. Of course, he may decide dog mushing is not for him and begin the walk back to town, muttering under his breath, "They're not my dogs," leaving you alone to sort out the mess. With or without help, it's a herculean task and dampers the mood of even the best outings and can push the boundaries of any friendship. To add to the fun, one of your lovely charges may find this an opportune time to act upon a long-harbored grievance and bite his teammate in the ass. The ensuing brawl often reinforces the desire for that new Ski-Doo one's been admiring. Hopefully with your friend pushing, you pulling, some digging, swearing, biting and punching, one or two temper tantrums, not to mention crying, you manage to extricate yourself and your team and friend from the quagmire. Bloodied, battered, cold and fatigued, it's often time to call it a day and head home to a warm fire, chalking it up to another epic mile-and-a-half (2.4km) dogsled journey.

Contrary to my more than vocal denunciations of my budding dog mushing career, I found time to be a wonderful balm that soothed bruised egos and sore backsides. I quickly found myself shaking out the harness and recruiting my reluctant buddy Randy Green for another wonderful northern adventure.

Disasters a mile (1.6km) from town on a sunny day with three dogs and your friend often ended up as amusing anecdotes; but if it's forty below, you're fifteen miles (24km) from town in the middle of nowhere, and something goes wrong, it's a whole other story. It's easy to find yourself in a life-or-death situation in the blink of an eye. Overflow is the arch nemesis of any musher and his team. Whether on a lake or river, deep or shallow, it matters little because getting wet at low temperatures is instantly dangerous. Overflow is surface water often hidden by snow, and it's easy to blunder into a patch. If you can't dry out almost immediately, a situation can turn deadly, fast.

A sudden dogfight can become dire if you receive a bad bite. Rounding a corner in the trail to find a belligerent bull moose standing in the way can result in injury and even death for the dogs and the musher. Moose continue to be the number-one killer of dogs on some of the world's biggest dogsled races. A team can also bolt at any minute, assuredly when you're least expecting it, leaving you alone in the wilderness without a ride, miles from anywhere.

I was very young, maybe four or five, and out with Dad on a romp through the trails in the woods around town. I was all snug in the boot and he was standing on the runners on the back. We'd been out for a couple of hours and were on our way home. Upon cresting the last hill and viewing the town spread out below us, Dad stopped the team to enjoy the view and change the liners in his gauntlet mittens.

All sleds have a brake that's engaged by standing on it. It usually consists of a board or bar with a couple metal prongs at one end, and it's hinged to the sled at the other end. The driver stomps down on brake driving the prongs into the snow to slow or stop the sled. The bar is lashed with strips of rubber to keep it up when it's not used. Many trappers alone in the wilderness dragged a rope behind the sled as an added safety feature. The rope often had knots for better grip. If you're fast enough to grab it and strong enough, you may be able to pull yourself back to the sled. If not, the drag of the body might slow or stop the team.

New to the mushing game, my dad was not aware of the significance of the rope and we didn't have one on our sled. Like horses, dogs are apt to liven up and gain a burst of energy when on the home stretch. I'm not sure why, but my dad stepped off the brake and, at the same time, the team bolted down the trail. Off they went, leaving my dad behind to run after us. Now here's where our stories diverge somewhat. In my memory, I began to climb out of the boot over the back so I could take control of the team by stepping on the brake. For some reason, for years to come, my dad insisted on saying I had panicked and tried to jump off the sled. Of course, only his screaming at me had saved me from certain death. I prefer my version.

Either way, he messed up by being inattentive, even for the briefest of seconds, and I was delusional thinking my little kid body was heavy enough to stop seven huskies heading for home and chow time. I promptly arrived home in the driverless sled, much to my mother's immediate concern. My dad slogged in a half-hour later winded and embarrassed. Of course, some of the old-timers saw that Smith kid flying by in an unattended sled screaming his head off. Heads were shaken and refrains of "those darn newcomers" and "city folk" were muttered none too quietly. All kidding aside, a couple good lessons were learned that might have saved my dad in the future out on the trapline.

Holding Timber, Lorrina Price's lead dog, 1972. I'm wearing a wolf ruff my mom made.

On one of our family outings to the trapline, we decided to all pile on the sled and check part of the line together. Like I said, my dad often used Tutshi, the bear dog, as incentive for the team, and that day was no exception. On this particular outing, Tutshi got too far out in front, beyond where he could hear my dad's verbal commands. The main trail ran along the shoreline, and the traps were set well off it in the woods. As was the routine when approaching a trap, my dad halted the team a distance away. Then he walked ahead on the main trail and into the woods to inspect the cubby. When he was by himself, he deployed a number of anchor methods to hold the team, including flipping the sled on its side. Since my mom and I were there, she stood on the main brake instead. We hadn't seen Tutshi for some time. We approached another trap and my dad got off and traded places with my mom. I stayed bundled up in the boot of the sled. Dad made his way ahead a hundred yards and took the smaller track into the woods. It was never a good idea to get the team too close to a trap. If there was a live animal, it was unpredictable how the dogs would react.

Mom and I chatted and the team took the opportunity to lie down and rest. We were interrupted by my dad yelling. We looked up to see him emerge from the trail with a small black animal in his arms. "It's Tutshi! He got into a trap and I think his foot's broken," he yelled. Realizing we needed to get him back to the cabin so we could attend to his injury, Mom decided to turn the team around and get them ready to go.

Mom had me stand on the brake as she made her way up to the lead dog. Usually when turning the team around, my dad used places he marked along the line where he could take them into the forest under the trees where the snow wasn't as deep. It was possible to turn a team around on the single track, but only if everything went right. My mom reached the leader, Cassiar, took hold of his harness and began to lead him back along the track beside the rest of the team. As Cassiar passed the third dog back on his side, Kenai, he suddenly attacked, sinking his teeth into Kenai's ear. Huskies are often more bark than bite and all of ours got along ninety-five percent of the time. My mom screamed at Cassiar and pulled back on his harness, but it didn't work: he fiercely clung on to Kenai's ear, biting deeper. Chilkoot, Kenai's gang-line mate, decided this was also a good time to attack, and he furiously tore into Kenai's other ear and together they pulled and chewed. Blood was leaking from both sides of Kenai's head.

In the ensuing melee, my mom got knocked off the trail into the deep snow, causing her to lose her grip on Cassiar. The other dogs became agitated, lunging, barking and nipping at each other. The sled jolted sideways on the trail. My dad clutched Tutshi in his arms, screaming at Cassiar and Chilkoot. Every few steps, he broke through the base of the trail and sank up to his crotch. Frustration oozed from his pores as he frantically slogged his way back to the sled. My mom was losing her battle with the dogs and chose to concentrate on extricating herself from the billowy depths of her snowy entanglement.

I continued to clutch the handlebars of the sled, wide-eyed and bawling, scared for myself, my mom, Tutshi and mostly Kenai. More blood poured from Kenai's head and it looked like he was about to be scalped. He could do nothing to save himself, and besides, he was a lover, not a fighter. That might have been the cause of the animosity. Kenai was new to the pack and already held the ardour of our two prominent females.

My mom eventually fought her way out of the snow and onto the sled where she loosened a snowshoe and used it to clobber Chilkoot and Cassiar over the head. I somehow got behind Cassiar and started pulling on his tail. My dad finally arrived and tossed

Tutshi into the boot of the sled. He immediately began pulling at the two antagonists, trying to get them to let loose. It didn't work and only caused Kenai more pain. In my fear for Kenai and my frustration with Cassiar, I bit down as hard as I could on his tail. I can still remember the disgusting texture and taste. Unbeknownst to me, at the same time, my dad punched Cassiar between the eyes. Whether it was the biting or the punch, Cassiar let go and, shortly after, Chilkoot also released his dogged grip.

It took a half-hour of untangling the team, reacquiring our possessions, turning the sled the rest of the way around and bandaging Kenai's head before we were underway. Kenai's injury turned out to be the typical head wound; lots of blood but little damage, although he would have a small tear on one ear for the rest of his life. It didn't seem to deter the girl dogs, as he remained a favorite suitor. Tutshi had a swollen paw for a couple weeks but no permanent damage. My mom broke my dad's snowshoe over Chilkoot's head, and it took me a few days to get the foul taste of dog tail out of my mouth. My dad later noticed his very thick, solid gold ring was cracked all the way through. It was a testament to the hard headedness of Cassiar, who showed no ill effect from the punch or the bite. This was an example of how things can go completely wrong in a matter of seconds. Had my dad been alone, things may have turned out much worse.

Although a few of our Siberian huskies went to racing teams, none would be considered racing dogs today in this climate of smaller, faster dogs. Our dogs tended to be more for the recreational musher

Tutshi, the bear dog, on the lake in front of town, 1969.

I'm on the ice in front of our cabin with Kluane on Atlin Lake at Twelve Mile Bay, 1971.

or trapper. We had Kenai and two other Siberian huskies from the Seppala line. At that time, they were considered racing dogs. Not as big as their Malamute brothers, they were still large dogs. Today racing dogs are bred exclusively for speed and endurance, whereas ours were bred for strength, size and stamina. Because of their size, distinct marking and generally gentle dispositions, our dogs were desired by Northern pet owners and novice mushers. For a number of years, our pups sold throughout the Yukon, British Columbia, and Alaska.

Chapter Twenty-One

Trapping

Living your life in the bush is hard, and making a living is even harder. Many men from town, and some women, ran traplines in the winter to help make ends meet. Whether by dog team or snow machine, trapping was a large part of the economy in those times. Furs were bought and sold by some of the local merchants and others were sold in Whitehorse, but most went to the fur markets in the south, then on to clothiers worldwide.

Fur was used for winter clothing—a wolf or wolverine ruff for a parka or a pair of mink-lined gauntlet mitts for those cold sled rides. Beaver hats were a must for any foray into the winter wilderness. Mukluks were topped with coyote or lynx to keep out the snow and there's nothing like a warm pair of rabbit-lined slippers on a cold cabin floor.

Like most things done in the isolated North, using fur and leather was important and necessary. The trapper traps to survive and feed his family. People wore fur because they needed to. In those days, most anything you could buy commercially was woefully inadequate for survival in the North's brutal environs. If someone could make

*Prime fur
trapped by
Dennis and
Ron Odian,
late 1960s.*

a few thousand dollars over a season and provide needed winter wear, then it was a worthwhile endeavor.

If your dad was a trapper, there was often a frozen lynx or fox thawing out somewhere in the living room. Hides on stretcher boards filled the back room or were stashed under the beds. Some carcasses were used to augment the winter supply of dog food if not used for human consumption. Sheds were full of an array of traps, dog harnesses, sleds and snowshoes. Bundles of beaver pelts might be suspended from the rafters to keep them safe from mice.

We enjoyed our family outings to the cabin and, of course, anytime we took the team out was a great thrill. When he wasn't trapping, my dad turned out to be quite adept at building fine racing sleds—something else he learned from books. He built them in the traditional way, bending the wood and fastening it with wet sinew and binding the joints. No nails or screws.

A lot of the youngsters in Atlin had small snare lines for rabbits and squirrels. For a time, I too tried my hand at the old trapping game, snaring in this case. In the woods just out the Warm Bay Road, a quick walk from our house, I set out a dozen or more snares. In the snow, it's pretty easy to figure out where the rabbits travel. Like any animal, they will take a well-worn trail rather than randomly wander. Although the snowshoe hare can easily travel on top of the snow, they stick to their trail most of the time. So it seemed easy: find a trail, find a tree or branch that's fallen over the trail, anchor your snare and go home. The next day, go harvest your prey.

Our team at the trapline cabin, early 1970s.

I'm checking a Lynx cubby on the trapline, early 1970s.

Well, I quickly learned it wasn't that easy. Even though I had my friend Daniel Connolly, an accomplished trapper at a very early age, as my tutor, I don't think I listened very well. Let's just say that, like my dad, I wasn't cut out to be a trapper. The one winter I set snares by town, I believe I caught a total of three rabbits. I did slightly better near our trapline cabin. It was always a complete surprise to find something in my snare after endless fruitless days.

Like Daniel, some of the kids were quite successful and progressed from squirrels and rabbits to fox, mink, marten and coyote. Remember, these are children aged ten and up. Conditions can be brutal. Trapped animals are very dangerous. Even setting small traps can cause injuries easily.

Trapping is an art form. First you have to know where the animal is, where best to set up your trap and what size trap to use. You have to know what kind of bait or lure to use and how to disguise or camouflage the trap. You have to make sure you don't leave your human scent on the trap or anything you've used to make your set.

If you're skilled enough to catch something, your job is just beginning. The animal needs to be skinned without destroying it. And yes, there is more than one way to skin a whatever. For most small animals, the technique is called "casing," where the hide is mostly peeled off the body whole. "Open skinning" is where the hide is skinned by cutting straight up the belly, like gutting a fish, then it's cut and peeled off the body. Open skinning is always used for larger animals such as bears, moose, and sheep.

After skinning, the hide has to be fleshed by scraping away any fat or flesh. When the hide is clean, it needs to be stretched. Stretcher boards can be purchased, but many trappers make their own. The cased furs are placed over the board fur side in, gently pulled firm but not stretched too far, then fastened and left to dry. Open furs are laid on a flat surface, fastened around the edges and left to dry. In the case of beaver, muskrat and seal, sometimes hoops are used and the hide is stretched inside the hoop. Drying correctly is important; if the temp is too high, the hide can be destroyed.

What I have described is only a quick gloss-over, and any of these maneuvers done incorrectly can decrease the value of your fur or even destroy it. If everything has been done right, the furs still have to be stored and shipped.

Chapter Twenty-Two

The Cabin

My father's foray into the trapping world was short lived and met with little success—not for lack of trying, but more from a lack of experience. Memories are murky, but I believe he purchased the line or took it over after the prior owner abandoned it. Hindsight being prized, there may have been a reason the line was in disuse. Our line stretched around the eastern shore of Teresa Island.

To make it easier for the dog team, a family friend ran our trapline with his snow machine before the season. This provided a base for the sled and team. If we experienced a big snowfall during the winter, the friend once again ran the line for us. Although the trail itself could easily support a sled and dogs, on either side the snow was quite deep.

Teresa Island is considered the second-tallest lake island in the world; Spruce Mountain, on the island, reaches an approximate height of 3,000 feet (914m). Having to wait for the lake to freeze, trapping didn't start for us until early- to mid-January. With the line came an old rundown cabin. Our trapline cabin was twelve miles

Helping Dad repair our trapline cabin roof, 1970. The snow was so high there was no need for a ladder and no danger of falling off.

(19km) from town, across the lake, due south and located in a lovely cove at the base of Spruce Mountain. At night, we could see the lights from town twinkling on the horizon.

Dad ran a section of the line every day with the team. During the spring school break, my mom and I spent time at the cabin. Aside from the odd summer escape from the rain by boaters, the cabin had seen little use in many years and was showing the effects of neglect.

I remember the first trip to the cabin. The snow was up to the roof line and we had to dig down to the door. The floor was so rotten, my parents were falling through in spots. Porcupine, squirrels, mice, pack rats and who knows what other creatures had long used the cabin for shelter and, in some cases, food.

The log structure was roughly twelve by twelve (3.5m x 3.5m) with a slanting shed roof, two tiny windows and one door. It had a small wood-burning barrel stove in the middle of the floor. The stove was in fair condition and immediately usable. My dad quickly got a fire going as my mom and I inspected the rest of the tiny shack. Within a few seconds, the whole place filled with smoke. It was obvious something was blocking the chimney. We discovered someone had placed a bucket on top of the chimney to keep the rain from rusting out the stove, a common practice and we should have remembered to look.

In one corner, standing a few inches off the floor was a crude bed made from saplings and axe-hewn boards, and beside it was an oil can crate, presumably used as a nightstand. Close to the stove in the middle of the room stood a rough-sawn table and a worn bench. The kitchen consisted of a wide shelf at waist height

I'm with Dad on the trapline cabin roof, 1970.

and two narrower shelves above. There were a few more shelves and some nails in a log by the bed serving as a wardrobe. All the shelves and furniture had rounded corners where the animals had gnawed on them. The oil crate housed a family of mice and one of the shelves was obviously being used as a home for a much larger animal; although we never saw what it was, we assumed it was a pack rat from our findings in the nest.

After digging our way in and lighting a fire in the stove, we began clearing out the cobwebs and pine cones. By that evening, we were nestled in our cozy domicile, the little wood stove burning bright, warding off the frigid night air. A Coleman lantern provided our light. Mom prepared our dinner on a portable camp stove. We ate moose stew and homemade bread brought from home. We sipped wine and watched the occasional mouse scurry by ... okay, I had powdered milk, come on, I was kid.

Unfortunately, as the cabin became warmer and warmer, the layer of snow on the roof began to melt and leak through the weathered roofing, at first a drop here and there, then in places a rivulet and soon it was raining inside. In the scramble to cover our belongings, my parents periodically fell through the floor. Cursing, laughing and stopping long enough to gulp their wine, they did their best.

I guess mice don't appreciate a spring shower either, so in an agitated state, they were scurrying about and climbing up the walls, much to the delight of my mother. We slept under a tarp my dad rigged up. Mom and Dad scrunched into the rickety bed and I slept on a cot beside them. The wood stove hissed all night as drops of water landed on it. Mom, spatula in hand and one eye open, didn't sleep at all that first night. The next day, we shoveled off the snow and covered the roof with a tarp. Later that spring, I helped my dad repair the floor and apply a new tar paper roof.

Snowshoes on our feet, Mom and I explored the number of small islands in the bay in front of the cabin while my dad was out checking the traps. I set out rabbit and squirrel snares in the woods and we tried our hand at ice fishing. Our evenings were spent popping corn, sipping hot cocoa and dashing outside to see how the moon and stars looked, or to catch a northern light display. My mom made a checkerboard on a piece of cardboard and we used white and black beans for the pieces. Our dogs broke into impromptu concerts of howls, perhaps answering a distant wolf's lament.

On the sides of our tunnel-like entryway, I used a spoon to dig a complicated series of intersecting roadways for some Hot Wheel cars I brought from home. I was never bored. I learned from my dad how to skin small animals and the best places to set my snares. He taught me how to flesh a hide and stretch it, readying it for drying. While I mostly caught squirrels and a couple of rabbits, he caught fox, coyote, mink and marten, with the occasional lynx. The big-money fur proved to be elusive. Wolves and wolverine are smart and very wary; not only hard to catch, but great thieves. Many times, Dad came upon looted traps, and by the tracks, he could tell a wolverine had outsmarted him, stolen the bait and sprung the trap.

As a kid, of course I thought my dad was all-knowing and I never questioned his knowledge. It was many years later that I wondered how a guy raised in Kentucky knew how to catch, skin, flesh and stretch a lynx. It turns out he was reading books and asking old-timers. Unfortunately for him, some things can only be mastered through experience and diligence; so it turned out the wolf, the wolverine and, for the most part, the lynx remained unattainable. I will also add that our line was strung along the base of a steep mountain with the lake on the other side. This may have limited the number of animals the area could support. With a family to think about, he moved on to other pursuits.

The Tradition of the Latch String
Atlin News Miner 1974
Diane S. Smith

When the latch string is out on the cabin door it means, "Welcome, stranger, be my guest. Use my cabin and help yourself to my supplies. I may have to call at your cabin sometime when you are away, and I will expect the same hospitality." But the symbolic unlocked cabin door has a deeper meaning. It signifies a faith in fellow Northerners and cheechakos (newcomers to the North) as well as an interest in their well-being. It is a pledge that personal property be respected and that generosity is reciprocal. It is a northern tradition that in recent years has been badly abused.

One winter night when the mercury lurked at minus fifty, a young man was driving the Atlin Road. He had arrived in Whitehorse that day by plane and had neglected to change to appropriate warm clothing before starting for Atlin. About sixteen miles (26km) from his destination, he succumbed to drowsiness and road hypnosis and his vehicle plunged into the deep snow at the side of the road. The billowing cascade filled his engine compartment and smothered the engine. It would not start, so he could not use the heater. Two miles (3.2km) farther on was an emergency shelter, his only hope, and he made a desperate dash for it. Soon in its black interior, he fumbled with matches and wood and was able to get a lifesaving fire going.

These shelters with their latch strings always out were built and maintained by the Atlin Highway Department. Their vital importance is recognized by Atlinites who travel the sixty-mile (97km) deserted Atlin Road in winter. Others are not so concerned, and the next summer, windows and a stove were destroyed in one of the shelters. Why? Winnie Atcheson, Atlin correspondent for the *Whitehorse Star*, made a plea in her column that these cabins be respected and so they are by most.

But her words fell on deaf ears of the pranksters, the weirdo's, the sickies who find their way into the North.

One summer a man who was establishing a wilderness home for his family at the end of Atlin Lake cached food supplies at a friend's trapline cabin on the lakeshore. Returning later to retrieve his goods, he discovered they had been stolen. Gone also were the cabin owner's lanterns and gas supply. None of these things were ever replaced. Why?

On the other hand, some Atlinites used the same cabin for a summer holiday. When they left, the grounds were clean and orderly, wood was stacked near the stove and food was ready for the next visitor. They understood the tradition of the latch string. As Atlin grows steadily in population, more residents are going off the beaten trails into the wild for various reasons. Some are trapping; others are just looking for spots away from it all. Many have repaired abandoned cabins and registered them for taxes. Some have built new cabins. Each of these places is important to the owner. Each cabin is also important as an emergency shelter. Even a cabin suffering from disrepair could save the life of a lost or stranded man. Once, a man could leave his cabin vacant and unlocked for long periods secure in the knowledge it might be used but never abused.

Now a man leaves his place with certain misgivings. The latch string is out, but he wonders how things will be when he returns. Often his fears are realized and he returns to a damaged cabin and pilfered belongings. Why? Certainly the percentage of destruction-bent individuals is no greater than years past. Maybe we are to blame because we let the tradition of the latch string drift into the dusty past when it should always be a part of the present. Maybe we should dig it out. Dust it off and put it back in use again. It is, after all, one of the best of the old Northern traditions.

We adhered to the tradition of the latch string. Our cabin door was never locked. Even when leaving it for the season we made sure there was wood, kindling, dry matches, a lantern or candles, more than likely some canned food or dried goods, and, of course, an old handmade checkerboard and those black and white beans. Mom never locked her door even in town; when she got older, I finally got her to lock it at night and she did, although begrudgingly, I'm sure.

Chapter Twenty-Three

Fishing for Fords

The next story goes in the trapping category ... or possibly fishing ... you be the judge. For a time, my dad ran a small trapline just north of town, as well as the Teresa Island line across the lake. On one particularly warm and sunny January morning not long after freeze up, Dad decided to drive down the lake in his new Ford crew cab truck to check his traps. It was a lot of work hooking up the team for the short trip, so driving made more sense. The lake ice was plenty thick to support a vehicle and there wasn't much snow yet, so in effect, the lake was a virtual super highway. People had been driving on it for a few weeks.

Now, that's not to say there are not hazards to be aware of, especially pressure ridges or cracks. Some locations have recurring pressure cracks every year. Most Atlinites are aware of the dangers and take extreme caution when traversing these areas. It can be deceiving even when you know what you're doing. The first winter after we moved to Atlin, a man and his wife, son and entire dog team were victim to one of the pressure cracks. This was a man who grew up traveling the lake and had intimate knowledge of its dangers.

I'm sitting on a pressure ridge on Atlin Lake, late 1960s.

Pressure ridges or cracks are caused when two flows or sheets of ice collide or regress; at times, a ridge is formed where two flows push against each other. Other times, there can be open water when they pull away. My dad was fully aware that he would be crossing a pressure crack on his trip to check his traps. As he neared the danger area, he could see there wasn't a ridge, so he got out and approached on foot. He found where there had recently been a separation, leaving roughly twenty feet (6m) of newly frozen ice. He tested the new ice and determined it thick enough to cross.

Carefully crossing, he proceeded down the lake to his traps. Reaching the location of his first set, he discovered the trap missing. Although there wasn't evidence, he thought maybe a large animal was able to drag the trap away, toggle and all. He quickly checked the rest of his line only to find the same thing repeated at every set. Someone had stolen his traps. On rare occasions a trapper might come across a looted trap, but to steal the trap as well was adding insult to injury and jeopardizing a man's means to make a living. My dad was understandably furious and in a rush to get back to town to report the robbery to the RCMP. He approached the familiar pressure crack, believing he was in the same location he crossed previously. He thought he was following his own tire tracks in the occasional patch of snow; although there were many others, he believed he recognized his own. He went ahead without first checking. As he gingerly crossed the suspect area, the front end of the truck abruptly crashed through the thin ice. He quickly realized he couldn't exit the front doors with the water already at his window. He jumped into the back seat only to find the rear doors also blocked by the ice. His only escape was the rear door window. He rapidly rolled it down and squirmed out to safety.

Atlin Lake frozen before a snowfall. A ninety-mile-long (145km) skating rink, mid-1970s.

Our dog Tyee in the back seat needed little coaxing and she wiggled out just as the entire truck settled beneath the surface. Neither got a foot wet. With a subtle splash, a gurgle or two and a few large bubbles, his new truck was gone, swallowed by the lake's icy depths. A couple of cardboard boxes and a red gas can floated to the surface. Dad stacked the boxes and gas can beside the opening as a warning to others and, with Tyee in tow, began the walk back to town. Having spotted him walking in off the lake, a couple friends were waiting on the shore and it wasn't hard to convince him he needed a stiff drink and time to tell his story. Considering his loss, as well as the exertion of the walk, a drink seemed appropriate to him. While he was entertaining his buddies with his tale of woe and vigorously attempting to wear off the rough edges of his epically bad day, our RCMP Constable Ed Michaluk came across the open water and the items stacked beside it. As one of the boxes had my parents' name and address on the top, he quickly deduced it was my dad who had gone through the ice.

He did not notice the meandering tracks of a man and a dog leading away from the hole or wonder who had stacked the boxes. He quickly rushed to town to notify my mother that my dad was surely drowned beneath the ice of Atlin Lake.

A group of friends help my dad retrieve our Ford from the bottom of Atlin Lake, early 1970s. The truck rested on its wheels roughly three hundred feet (91m) from shore in seventy-five feet (23m) of water. Photos by Clive Aspinall.

As Mom was attempting to absorb the devastating news, my dad rushed into the house, assuming something was terribly wrong at home upon seeing the RCMP truck outside. Both shocked and angry, my parents made no attempt to control their displeasure with the Constable. He made a hasty retreat, no doubt considering pressing charges of littering, polluting, fishing out of season and verbal assault as he left.

The next day, they used chainsaws to cut a channel in the ice for the cable all the way to shore where they cut an opening big enough to pull the truck through. A bulldozer was brought to the shore, the cable was connected and they slowly pulled the truck across the lakebed to the opening at the shore.
Photo by Clive Aspinall.

With emotions back in check, Dad immediately set about planning how to retrieve his truck. Armed with a generator, a long cord with a light bulb coated in wax and a couple friends, he returned to the scene of the crime that night. After lowering the light into the water, they could see the truck, sitting on its wheels facing away from shore, roughly seventy-five feet (23m) below the surface. Lowering a hook down on a wire cable, they were able to hook the bumper. That night they secured the cable and readied for the following day. The idea was to somehow winch the truck along the bottom to the lakeshore. The lake ice wouldn't hold the weight of something as heavy as a bulldozer, but that was exactly what they needed. Jack McKenzie, a good friend of the family, figured he could take his dozer across country to the lakeshore where the truck lay submerged. While Jack was working his way toward the site, my dad and friends Joe Ackerman, Ted Carlson and Clive Aspinall sawed a long slit in the ice with chainsaws for the cable to travel. They began where the truck went in and cut all the way to shore, where they carved out an opening big enough for a Ford crew cab truck to fit through.

With Dad in front of our Ford shortly after it was pulled from the lake bottom.

Everything worked exactly as planned; Jack made it with his dozer, the truck rolled easily across the lake bed, the bumper stayed attached and it came out of the hole with a minimum of fuss. The truck was quickly towed to town, stripped, cleaned, oiled and lubed.

In less than a month's time, the Smith family plus two adult Malamutes and five puppies embarked on an epic western United States tour in that same truck. Traveling across thirteen states there was never a hiccup. The only residual damage was a bent bumper, a dented-in roof from the pressure, and as we discovered on our trip, the radio didn't work, which mattered little as we had no radio service in Atlin.

Part IV — The Community Way

Made by the Erie Steam Shovel Company, this shovel and others like it were brought from middle America to Atlin in the 1920s. It was shipped in pieces over the frozen lake ice and assembled on the creeks. This steam shovel is fully restored and operational, and has become the centerpiece of the Atlin Museum Yard.

Chapter Twenty-Four

The Women

It's hard to express awe of the average Atlin woman and not appear sexist toward them, as most didn't see any big deal in the things they did. But when you compare them to the typical urban dwellers of that day, the disparity is tremendous. I can't imagine many of their southern counterparts knowing how to jump-start the family pickup truck or drive a stick shift, for that matter. How many hunted for a moose or caribou every fall, or fished for trout through the ice, or tanned animal hides, or sewed parkas for the entire family, or chopped the winter's wood supply, or built a green house?

Atlin Women worked in the gold mines, they operated equipment and fought forest fires. They fished for salmon on the Taku River and they built log cabins. They repaired their children's bikes and planted gardens, and they quietly and unassumingly kept the town alive. The men preferred the peacock roll and were good at it. They were often the face of an event whether an MC or Grand Marshall. But behind every fundraiser, every association, society, club or committee was a dedicated, hardworking core of women often leading from the rear. I'm not saying the men weren't involved in the trenches, because they were. I'm just saying the women were often the structure and bones of most, if not all, of Atlin's functions and associations.

Average Woman – Atlin Variety
Atlin News Miner 1973
Diane S. Smith

From the kitchen of a snug log house comes a loud thud and a smack. A quick look reveals a young woman with a smudge of flour on her cheek dressed in blue jeans and a blouse—tails hanging out, she is expertly beating gobs of elastic brown dough into oblong shapes and popping them into pans. Soon they will emerge from her oven—beautiful, rich loaves of bread. A tendril of hair trails in one eye as the young woman turns to other chores. She slips outside to hang a large sign near her front door. It says simply "Water." Then she sits down to agonize over a large stack of catalogs, making out orders for things she hopes will be sent quickly and correctly. Since she does about a fourth of her shopping by mail order, she knows well the black labyrinth of paperwork encountered if she has to return, reorder or track down a missing item.

The flour-dusted face seen on this particular weekday morning is only one of many faces of the Average Woman, Atlin variety. This young woman leads a life different than that of a stereotypical housewife and she often faces situations unknown in the predictable lives of her sister city dwellers.

If she smokes, she probably rolls her own, but this act, usually associated with range-riding cowboys, loses all essence of masculinity in her hands. It is an economic measure.

To come here, she and her husband gave up jobs which provided a comfortable joint income. Now small savings make a sporadic income stretch farther.

Her closet is a variable paradox. A quick inventory would baffle her city sister. It might read something like this: One pair of muddy leather shoe packs, a beautiful mini-length dress, two or three pair of faded blue jeans, a stunning velveteen parka trimmed with wolf that she made herself, a pair of over-the-knee boots and a pair of beaded mukluks. Her lingerie may be one-half frilly bikinis, one-half long johns. She wears sexy black pantyhose or grey wool socks with equal aplomb.

The Average Atlin Gal is an outdoor woman. She likes a riotous Ski-Doo ride over a moonlit lake. She may be learning the graceful swinging glide of cross-country skiing under the expert guidance of Francoise and Stephen Shearer, Atlin instructors and advocates of ski touring. She can hurl a forty-pound curling rock with fair accuracy and ease.

Although at this time she doesn't present a picture of glamour, if the occasion demands, the Average Atlin Woman can transform herself into a dazzling creature that could easily hold her own at any social function.

The Average Atlin Woman is somewhere under thirty and has two small children. One child may be a baby of less than a year; since Atlin has long been omitted from the stork's itinerary, it has suddenly become one of his prime targets.

The Average Atlin Woman is not Atlin-born. She has been here less than five years and came originally from a heavily populated area. She and her husband abandoned their former home for a smaller town and larger wilderness. Atlin seemed a better environment for a growing family.

Atlin's Average Woman doesn't enjoy all the conveniences she took for granted in her city life. No tiled bathroom for her now. More than likely a small, traditional building in the backyard has replaced the usual bathroom fixtures. The sign she hung out this morning is her assurance of a continuing water supply. It signals Ron Bowden, the water man, to fill her storage barrels. Running water and sewer systems are things of the past.

Our gal has acquired new skills since moving here. She drives a pickup truck with the same finesse she used to wheel her sedan through the 5:00 o'clock traffic. She is handy with an axe since her kitchen range is a wood burner. Although not a dead-eye shot yet, she sometimes bags a moose or caribou for the family freezer and she enjoys a lone horseback ride through the pines.

There are frustrations in her life. Fifty pounds of spuds freeze then thaw and run a black mess all over the pantry floor. Mud tracks in by the ton during the spring thaw. There are times of quiet apprehension. Her oldest kid goes out to play at twenty below (-29°C). A lost mitten could mean a frozen hand. A tiny knot forms in her stomach when someone close is late coming home from Whitehorse on a minus-forty-degree night.

The fire siren sounds and her blood runs cold. Vivid memories of Atlin fires crowd her brain. And when winter stretches long, the four walls may close in and cabin fever is near.

These times occupy a small part of her life and mostly she is too busy to be worried long. Atlin Mountain wreathed in morning mist can dispel cabin fever and a boisterous curling bout will make the time whiz by until the late arrival gets home.

It is evening now. The kids are ready for bed and a babysitter is settled in with her homework. There is a dance at the new Recreation Centre tonight and it's almost time to go. Average Atlin Gal suddenly steps from the bedroom. "WOW!" Our floury moth has become a glittering butterfly. Her new hairdo sparkles with gold dust. A stylish mini dress barely peeks below the velveteen parka. She wears mukluks and carries a pair of platform sandals. Her husband gives an appraising look at legs that are usually encased in jeans. Then she takes his arm and disappears into the crisp Atlin night.

———

It was a time and place where people did extraordinary things as if they were ordinary. It was a time and place traditional gender roles were obliterated. If a couple starting out or a new family were to survive and prosper in the wilderness, then they did things daily that pushed them past their comfort level.

It was a time when two women transformed a couple of derelict buildings into a fine home and a quaint gift shop. They did this not because they were carpenters or contractors—they did it out of necessity. A carpenter couldn't be afforded, but a friend was inexpensive and for a few bucks, a little bartering and promises of reciprocation, the job got done.

My mom never dreamed she could make fine kitchen cabinets from old, weathered barn board, but we needed cabinets, so the choice was fairly obvious: build it herself or put our dishes on the floor. This was a common attitude of Atlin women and men. There wasn't much time wasted wondering how something was going to be done, it just was. If you didn't have lumber, then maybe you made a deal to tear down an unwanted shed for the salvage, or you traded something to the sawmill owner. If you didn't know how to build it, you looked in a book or you sought advice from a friend who always had time to help.

Atlin was a town where all the mothers were your mother; well, at least you'd better listen as though they were. If you were playing with friends and it was lunchtime, their moms fed you as if you lived there. For some reason, food at your friend's place always tasted better even though it came out of the same can. I had many a bowl of chicken noodle soup and grilled cheese sandwiches

Mom cuddles with Sitka, mid-1970s.

at the Colwell's. If you were acting out or being an ass, then you were scolded and told to go home, and you did. You didn't sass back. If you were at Keith's house, you were instantly part of the family. His mom, Sue Carlick fed half the kids at her end of town at one time or another. I still remember her bannock—best ever. If a kid needed a place to stay, she let them stay no questions asked. Pete and John's mom Pam Edzerza was a nurse. It was a good thing, too, because her boys were pretty rowdy. She also patched me up on a number of occasions.

My Other Mother

Ev Colwell, a wife and mother to five children, ran a successful business, was an accomplished artisan and craftswoman, was involved in every town function, shared gardening, hunting and fishing duties with her husband, chaperoned and drove for all of our school outings, was an avid curler and still had time to keep track of all of the town's kids. She offered guidance, discipline and motherly support when needed.

Mrs. Colwell often collected me and took me on their family outings, knowing my mom was busy trying to make us a living and could little spare the time. I remember she was the one who showed me how to tie a fisherman's knot.

I will always remember the summer beer bottle hunting trips led by Mrs. Colwell. British Columbia had a bounty on beer bottles at the time; it was ten cents a bottle. People saved their bottles and returned them to the liquor store to redeem their payoff. As kids, it was a source of income.

The Yukon didn't have such a bounty and your average Yukoner wasn't used to keeping their beer bottles. Unfortunately, some thought it good sport to fling their bottles at signs and anything else they saw on the trip back to Whitehorse.

A few times a summer, Mrs. Colwell loaded up her five kids in the family Suburban, gathered a few more strays from around town and we all headed out the road to hunt for beer bottles. She parked on the side of the road and we spread out along both sides and in both directions and began our search.

We took buckets, and when they were full, we dumped them into galvanized washtubs in the back of the car and went out for more. We didn't get rich, but we always got enough for an orange float at the café or a round of Nutty Buddy ice cream bars from the Trading Post, and we helped beautify the Atlin Road.

Casual Competence

The women were more often than not the school bus drivers (family vehicle) on any of our school outings to other communities. They were chaperones for the school dances, they were judges and timers at the track meets, and they were coaches and mentors, teachers and bosses.

Atlin was replete with female artists and craftswomen. From a bone and stone carver to watercolor and oil painters, to fashion designers who created works of art with fur and leather. There were jewelers working with gold and jade and even moose poop. Wood burning, weaving, intricate traditional beading and leather work were all in the repertoire of Atlin's women artists.

Marina Wallace's store, The Cache, made parkas for most of the children and half of the adult population of Atlin throughout the 1970s. Ev Colwell's store, The Boofus Shop, provided the town with leather belts, wallets, purses and tack for the equestrian folk. A hand-woven and intricately-knitted sweater or hat from Claudia was a must-have winter apparel necessity, both fashionable and functional. Mom's shop turned out anything and everything leather and fur, specializing in refurbishing old, out-of-date fur coats and turning them into modern, functional parkas. The Discovery Shop's leather vests, pants, buckskin shirts and the popular-at-the-time leather hot pants were all worn by Atlinites. Not so much the hot pants—those went more to the tourists. Shhhhhhh!

Atlin boasted a number of female pilots, which at that time was much more of a rarity than now. One Atlin lady and her husband built small planes in their garage. Atlin women were business owners and entrepreneurs, writers, teachers and caregivers. These are only a few examples.

Peggy Milius

You will undoubtedly notice some of the same names keep appearing throughout the book. All I can say is they are people of note that impressed me even as a child. One of those names is Peggy. Yes, the owner of Lobo and yes, my mom's friend, the interior decorator, designer and carpenter extraordinaire.

Most notably, Peggy was an amazing artist. Her paintings adorn walls in countless Atlin homes and many more abroad. Peggy's pieces are considered treasured family heirlooms by anyone fortunate enough to own one. She found her inspiration in her surroundings. A landscape artist of exceptional talent, Atlin was ideal for her with its boundless subject matter.

Peggy became frustrated with her limited access to some of the area's most beautiful scenery. Like most Atlinites, she set out to remedy this problem on her own. She desired to spend more time out on Atlin Lake, in particular the southern end. The periodic overnight boat trips were not long enough for her to create her masterpieces. Unlike some, Peggy preferred to paint in sight of her subject, not from a reproduction. She said being in the presence of her inspiration made her a better artist and kept her humble.

Peggy designed and built a raft, complete with a stern paddle wheel and a comfortable wall tent—a home away from home. She designed and built the furnishings and did her own upholstery. With a water pump, a small wood stove and a few Coleman lanterns, she was ready to spend the summer down the lake amidst the beautiful wilderness she adeptly reproduced on canvas.

Nestled in a small cove on Teresa Island, a place that will forever remain known as Peggy's Cove, Peggy spent many a summer happily painting her magnificent surroundings. With her dog

Peggy Milius, early 1980s. Interior designer, upholsterer, fashion designer and tailor, a carpenter, an amazing artist and raft builder extraordinaire.

Nahanni, she entertained guests and chased off the odd marauding bear with the same aplomb.

Peggy was known for her entertaining prowess, and guests on her humble raft home might be surprised to be served lake trout with orange-saffron sauce on a bed of wild greens, sprinkled with fresh onions from nearby Onion Cove, or stuffed grouse breast with mixed wild mushrooms picked not far from her raft. Of course, there was usually a low-bush cranberry scone or mossberry cobbler for dessert. No gourmet meal would be complete without wine and there was always a selection. Peggy was known to enjoy a good cigar and a snort of scotch for a nightcap.

Peggy's Raft in the early 1980s.

Peggy, to me, embodied the Average Atlin Woman; she was a true renaissance lady indicative of most Atlin women of the time—in no way average at all.

Lorrina Price
From letters to a friend 1971
Diane S. Smith

I have a young friend, a girl of about fifteen or sixteen, who comes in once a week and scrubs my kitchen floor, etc. I can use some help and she could use some money. She is a real outdoor gal and this winter she and her younger brother Mike are running a trapline just north of town. They have about five miles (8km) to go each way on their line so far but will be adding more trail and traps right along. I gave Lorrina a puppy last winter, a half German Shepherd/half Siberian husky male. She taught the dog to pull and pack and this winter my husband rigged her small toboggan with handlebars and a brake so she could use the dog to pull her gear and sometimes herself along the trapline trail. It was obvious right away she needed more dog power, so I loaned her a Siberian of ours. With two dogs things went better and she and Mike Price could ride on the slopes and the flats but she was interested in using a regular team. So we have gradually added dogs and now she uses our big black leader, Cassiar. He is a real fireball and Lorrina took a few headlong dives into the snow before she got used to him. But now she is driving four dogs and just a few minutes ago, she and Mike took off on their ten-mile (16km) jaunt. Kids are tough

Lorrina leading her team. Minto Mountain in the background, early 1970s.

creatures but just the same, I gave them an extra parka and blanket and checked to make sure they had plenty of matches along. I'll keep track of the time and if they don't get back in the usual four or five hours, we can send a snow machine out after them. The reason for the precautions is because with a temperature of minus 25°F (-32°C) and a wind of fifteen miles (24km) per hour, the wind chill factor is around 60°F (-51°C) below. This is not weather to act foolish in.

———

Lorrina – Trapper and Dog Musher
Atlin News Miner 1973
Diane S. Smith

One cold day a year ago, a slender, dark-haired girl and her younger brother were carefully making their way across a frozen lake two miles (3.2km) north of Atlin. Mike broke trail on snowshoes while close behind, Lorrina walked in his tracks. At her heels followed two dogs, Timber and Cassiar, hauling a toboggan with a small cargo of trapping gear. It was twenty below (-29°C).

Suddenly there was the sickening crack of ice and in that instant, Lorrina, dogs and toboggan plunged through the deceptive overflow into a foot of frigid water. The terrified dogs, instinctively trying to protect their feet, pulled their paws up underneath themselves and lay flat and shaken on the fragile ice. Mike quickly tramped a trail to shore then walked cautiously back and threw the snowshoes to Lorrina. There was no other way for her to navigate the thin ice during the nightmare of getting dogs and toboggan off of the lake. But already, the insidious water was seeping into Lorrina's mukluks. Working against the inevitable danger of frozen feet and handicapped further because the frightened Cassiar refused to work, Lorrina pulled with Timber and slowly moved the toboggan, heavily encrusted with unyielding ice, to the beach where Mike already had a fire burning.

The dogs' feet were dangerously iced, but something told them to paw furiously in the dry pine needles under the trees and soon they freed themselves of the disabling ice. Lorrina, using her axe, battered the ice from the toboggan's sliding surface,

*I'm in the sled riding
with Lorrina on
frozen Twelve Mile
Bay, Teresa Island,
early 1970s.*

then, not realizing her mukluks were thoroughly wet, she and
Mike hitched up the dogs and headed swiftly back to Atlin.

What followed for Lorrina is the unfortunate tale of many
a sourdough; the excruciating pain as her frozen feet thawed,
the restless days limping tenderly around the house as the slow
healing process took place, and worse, the gnawing thought of
her trapline going unattended during the best part of the fur
season.

Lorrina, at sixteen, is an accomplished trapper. She caught
her first small fur bearer five years ago and since that time she
has trapped each winter for the market, and the furs she sells
are well skinned and professionally stretched.

Last year Lorrina, Mike and another younger brother, Carl,
worked the trapline north of town. Early in the season Lorrina
discovered that Timber, the only trained dog she had for pulling
her sled, was not enough. Someone always had to walk, and
checking the traps was a time-consuming business. Then
someone loaned her a second dog and with two dogs working
she could make the trip faster but was still under-powered. She
borrowed another dog and then a couple more. Soon she was
managing five or six rambunctious sled animals with reasonable
skill. The work on the line had been cut in half and the challenge
of driving dogs had captured her. She had decided that traveling
by dog team was the only way to go for her.

Working during the summer with a training cart, Lorrina continued with Timber's lessons. Soon he was geeing and hawing and generally working well ahead of three other dogs she had acquired: Taku, a snowy Samoyed, Akala, a handsome, burly Malamute and speedy little Trapper, a fire ball of mixed husky background.

Timber, she admits, is stubborn, but by the same token he is willing to bow to a superior force. He is half German Shepherd and half Siberian husky. His German ancestry comes on strong in appearance and temperament, but his Russian half is all sled dog.

When there is pulling to be done, Timber is more than willing. He proved this fact quite effectively at an impromptu one-dog pull at the Atlin Fun Day last April. At Lorrina's command, he literally dug in and pulled a freight sled full of squirming kids from a dead stop over a course of sticky spring snow. This was an estimated 500 pounds (227kg)—a surprising accomplishment for a dog just a year old. He had never been asked to do a job of this sort before.

Things are going smoothly on the trapline this winter. Lorrina's four dogs and two loaners, Kenai and Cassiar, are eager and well behaved, for the most part. She realized how much her team had improved when she hitched a new dog with them one day and discovered it was much like running with one flat tire.

For Lorrina, trapping is a business; the money made from her furs pays for her clothes and incidentals, food and rigging for the dogs, and some must go back into traps. So this winter when she found that an otter had blundered into one of her beaver sets, her mind automatically registered sixty dollars. The animal had to be clubbed and it kept disappearing beneath the creek ice. Each time it vanished, she saw the hard-won sixty dollars slipping away. Since there was not enough snow on the trail for the team that day, she could also imagine an eight-mile (13km) hike for nothing. Happily, she got the otter and it counts among the numerous lynx and beaver and several mink and marten she has scored so far this season.

Although a competent trapper and woodsman, Lorrina, by law, is not old enough to carry a rifle with her on the trapline. This presents problems with which the other trappers of the area, all men, need not concern themselves. If an animal is found alive in a trap, she has to kill it. She must use a pole. "The longest pole I can find," she said. So far there have been no mishaps, but a potentially dangerous situation is always at hand. Someday she may find a live wolverine in a trap. Here would be a $100 fur wrapped around a notoriously vicious animal. The prospect of approaching this valuable but menacing creature armed only with a pole puts a burden on the young trappers the others need not worry about. What would you do? Turn away from $100 or take your chance with a club?

The Number 4 trap is the largest and toughest of the commonly used flat traps. It is set for beaver, wolverine and formerly for wolves. Most men, but not all, can set a Number 4 by breaking it open over a knee. Lorrina sets hers this way. But it took a long time to learn the trick. She said, "It used to take three of us—one on each spring and one in the middle praying like mad no one else would let go."

This winter, along with regular trips to the trapline, Lorrina is taking advantage of every free afternoon to work with her team. She has decided that her working dogs may very well double as racing dogs. On their days off she runs them, twelve or fifteen miles (19km/24km) against the clock, noting with great enthusiasm they are getting faster.

Lorrina carries a wicked bull whip on her sled. The dogs never feel its sting unless they fight. She uses it mainly to get their attention when they begin to doddle. When it whistles overhead and pops loudly, the most delinquent dog snaps to.

One day the whip got her into a ticklish situation. She had given it two mighty swings around her head to get the loitering dogs into action. But on the second circuit, the whip neatly picked the toque off her head and sent it flying into the air. It landed in the trail twenty or thirty feet (6m or 9m) behind the sled, while up front, six highly-spooked dogs were raring to go. It wasn't easy convincing them they should "hold" while she gingerly walked back to retrieve her cap. It's always embarrassing for a musher to return on foot.

Lorrina is going to try racing January 28 in Whitehorse when the Yukon Dog Mushers hold one of their scheduled races over a twelve-mile (19km) course. Then, at the end of February, the big one! The Sourdough Rendezvous in Whitehorse—three days of hard racing over a fifteen-mile (24km) course. Lorrina will be pitting her team and skill against other new mushers and veteran dog drivers, a big order for a sixteen-year-old girl, but one she will surely handle with a tough determination and casual good humor. Very important to this town is that this bright, fleet-footed girl and her dogs will be the first representatives that Atlin has ever had in the big Yukon race.

One Girl's Dog Sled Race
Atlin News Miner 1973
Diane S. Smith

It was a cloudy, ten-below (-12°C) morning in Whitehorse. A sparse, shivering crowd lined the fences along the Yukon River. They stomped mukluks and waited while nineteen dog teams assembled on the ice. It was the first day of the 1973 Yukon Championship Dog Sled Race.

Lorrina, Atlin's sixteen-year-old trapper, dog musher and now race driver, waited too. With just one twelve-mile (19km) competition her sole store of racing experience, she was about to match her six working dogs against a formidable field of seasoned teams and men mushers.

There was "Iron Man" Wilfred Charley of Carmacks, famed for his fumbling starts and flashy finishes. Wilfred had won the championship four times and was defending the title this year. Stephen Frost, dashing musher from Old Crow, has raced in every Rendezvous since 1962. He nabbed the title once and is consistently in the top five contenders.

Ed Bauman, cool, calm and easy with his dogs, was a new face. He held an impressive string of wins during the pre-Rendezvous races. He was a new musher entering his first championship race. He proved his prowess as a musher by urging his hounds on to the coveted 1973 title. Unusual too, was that he finished first in each of the three-day heats and walked away with $800 for best aggregate time as well as $450 day money.

Then there was loose belt Bob Erlam, publisher of the *Atlin News Miner* and the *Whitehorse Star*. Bob was the oldest musher in the race, Lorrina, the youngest, and between them they waged a good-natured feud during the entire event. In the end, it cost Bob a big box of chocolate because Lorrina beat him in each of the three fifteen-mile (24km) races.

There were four tough contenders from Fort Nelson, British Columbia, and Nick Molofoy was there with his team from Edmonton, Alberta. Molofoy took the title to Alberta two different years and he still holds the track record of 55 minutes 51 seconds, one Bauman came close to breaking on the first day of the races.

Then Lorrina experienced the stomach-knotting tremors all racers encounter just before the "go" signal. She was in the starting shoot; sled tied to the snubbing post, her mother Joan, acting as handler, holding Trapper and Taku, the lead dogs. "15 seconds," the starter yelled. Trapper, who is usually screaming to be off, sat placidly surveying the spectators. Taku contemplated a spot on the snow. "10 seconds," came the ominous warning. Get up Trapper. "9 ..." The countdown started. "8-7-6 ..." Joan stepped away from the team. "5-4-3 ..." Akala looked vaguely interested but Cassiar and Kenai were yawning. Get up, Trapper. "2-1-mush." "Hike Trapper, Hike."

He was up, they were all up and running, not full out but dead on the trail going the easy lope they use to cover the trapline. It was this steady lope and Lorrina's skill that brought her novice racers in with good respectable times in each of the three fifteen-mile (24km) heats: (1:20:36), (1:20:49) and (1:17). Her consistent pace also won her $35.00 each day for finishing within forty minutes of the winning team. She managed to cut this margin in half.

Lorrina's small team of work dogs ranged greatly in size and age. Taku, a registered Samoyed weighs forty-five pounds—a good racing weight. Trapper, bright and fast, is a yearling. Usually, dogs aren't considered adult enough to race until they reach their second year. In wheel position is big Akala, a registered Malamute weighing ninety pounds. He works next to Kenai, a registered Siberian from the Seppala line who is over six years old. Another old-timer is Cassiar, Malamute-Siberian and blind in one eye. He works point position with Timber, Lorrina's first sled dog, a Siberian-German Shepherd cross.

Lorrina's comments on the race shed light on some of the advantages and difficulties her "soup to nuts" team offered. She found the four-mile (6.5km) uphill stretch hard. Where the larger teams could take the grade at a lope with their drivers riding the runners, Lorrina did a lot of running to give the dogs a break. When she climbed aboard, the team slowed, but big

Lorrina before the big race at the Yukon Sourdough Rendezvous in Whitehorse, 1973.

Akala kept things moving ahead anyway when he threw his weight into the harness.

Lorrina's dogs do a lot of traveling on the lake and are familiar with ice, so when she hit the river, she could keep her dogs at a fast run and gain valuable time. Other teams, unused to ice, spooked somewhat or missed the interest a trail offers and slowed to a trot. Trapper picked his trail on a pre-run of the course and during the three heats, stuck stubbornly to it to avoid overflow and other distractions that caused trouble for some of the other drivers. The dogs passed other teams easily and went obediently around a pile of teams near the starting line on the third day.

Lorrina plans to race again next year. She wants to try some of the other competitions around the North. She plans to run a larger team of better-matched and faster dogs. In the future, as at the Yukon Championship Race just past, it is a good bet Lorrina will continue to capture the attention and admiration of those who see her. And win, lose or draw, she will always be Atlin's Number-One Dog Musher.

––––––

Lorrina – Honored by Fellow Mushers
The Whitehorse Star February 1973
Bob Erlam – Editor-Publisher-Owner

The second-best thing to winning the big Yukon Championship Sled Dog Race is to win the admiration and respect of your fellow mushers. Lorrina, sixteen years old, the only female competing in the three-day classic in Whitehorse and the first musher from Atlin ever to enter a team in the big event, was chosen by the other race drivers to receive the trophy for sportsmanship.

Not only did Lorrina perform as a competent and cooperative dog musher, but a particular event occurred that led to her receiving this important honor.

During the last race day, Lorrina was well along the course when the team of John Capot Blanc of Fort Nelson overtook her on the trail minus its driver. The team was traveling at a terrific clip and a turn off the trail could spell disaster to dogs harnessed together like that. Lorrina stopped her team, managed to halt the runaway dogs and tied them to a nearby tree. This is a difficult maneuver in any musher's book and one that could easily result in a pileup of dogs and it cost her precious minutes.

———

Although not average in any way, Lorrina personified the can-do spirit of the Average Atlin Woman. Confronted with a difficult and dangerous situation, she didn't ponder or contemplate the options, she instinctively reacted; she quickly saw what needed to be done and, without hesitation, did it. End of story. I was in awe of her, even though it wasn't cool to like girls yet.

Note of interest: in 1972, having won Atlin's First of July Princess Contest with a one-year tenure, Lorrina held that title during the time of the race. Did the guys she beat realize they were bested by a princess?

Jessie James

Jessie James. No, not the old west outlaw. Atlin had our own Jessie James, Jessie with an *I*. From my point of view, she was much more accomplished, more interesting, more notorious and the complete antithesis of the Jesse James without an I. But like the other one, our Jessie James's legend continues to grow. Jessie was our nurse—the nurse. Working out of the tiny one-room outpost building beside the school, she tended to the town's medical needs. A petite woman with enormous drive, Jessie was easy to distinguish from a distance by her rapid pace. She never learned to drive and had no interest. She enjoyed walking and did so with alacrity, much like her nursing. She didn't take crap from anyone. Jessie dealt with a large, intoxicated miner the same way she did a newborn with diaper rash: kindly, skillfully and straightforwardly.

When it was time for whatever shots were needed that year, we all left school, walked the few yards to the outpost and lined up outside. Jessie ran us through like an assembly line. Quickly and efficiently, she processed the entire school in a couple hours. She didn't give us time to worry—if you were next, you better step up and do it fast.

I had just started grade one and it was shot time. My class lined up in front of the outpost like good little minions. While we waited, I alarmingly realized I was first in line. How did that happen? This was not good. I felt I needed more time to prepare myself and/or to see if the other kids made it out alive. I tried to change positions, but teacher wasn't having any of that. As I worked myself closer to full-blown panic, the door flew open and Jessie yelled at me to get inside. I didn't hear her. Apparently, I didn't hear her a few times. Then I was being pushed from behind. My so-called friends all said I was backing up but I don't believe them.

I felt a pair of hands on my back as I was shoved aside. My classmate Maureen Wallace brushed past me, walked right up the steps and in the door as cool as an orange creamsicle. My goose was cooked. There was no way out now, a girl had just shown me up.

For some stupid reason I thought Jessie would be sympathetic to my very real phobia of invasive sharp spears of honed steel. I was wrong. She spent the entire time calling me names. Scaredy Cat and You Big Baby are memorable. It didn't help my cause that I was bawling before I even got the shot.

The worst part was having to go back outside all red eyed and sniffy. I was met with a line of cheesy grins and muffled giggles. I later tried to claim that I had unusually thick skin and Jessie needed to use ... Never mind, I was a complete wimp. Damn that Maureen and her six-year-old fearless approach to life.

My dad had a couple interesting encounters with Jessie. One night, late, he managed to run the palm of his hand through a table saw. Mom called Jessie at home. That was what you did after hours. Jessie, in her usual calm demeanor, asked a couple questions then said she would meet my dad at the outpost. Knowing Jessie didn't drive and concerned for my dad, Mom asked her if she needed a ride.

She declined, adding she thought my dad could use the time while he waited to read the instruction manual for the saw. I don't know if my mom relayed Jessie's comment to my dad at that time or not.

Dad walked the block to the outpost with his hand wrapped in a towel, meeting Jessie on the way. The cut was deep but in the fleshy heel of the palm and didn't sever any nerves. She informed him that she was out of local anesthetic. I'm not sure if Jessie had some whiskey (for sterilizing?) or my dad brought his own. Either way she said it might help if he had a quick drink before she started the stitching. I'm pretty sure Dad had already self-medicated a little before he left home, but he gratefully agreed.

Jessie readied her needle and a pair of pliers, cleaned the wound and proceeded. The inner stitching was easy enough, but as she got to the thick, callused skin of the palm she began using the pliers to push and pull the needle. It was hard work, but as with everything, she accomplished it with competence. My dad commented that she was pretty good at it and Jessie casually commented back, "I've been practicing." It might have been the whiskey, but my dad said that comment took a moment to sink in. As if she could see the wheels turning, Jessie blurted out, "Not on humans, dummy, on moose hide." It turned out she was in the process of hand sewing a moose-hide jacket for her husband. They had a good laugh and a running joke over that for a long time to come.

My dad and Pastor Dave got the job of shoring up the old one-room schoolhouse when it was moved to where it sits today. The job entailed jacking, and leveling and shoring. Long timbers and short blocks were placed in strategic locations. Toward the end of the project a number of the timbers protruded past the blocking and needed to be cut off.

Dad crawled under the building with his chainsaw and started cutting. Laying on his back and cutting above his head, sawdust falling in his eyes, wasn't ideal but apparently was necessary. As luck would have it, and as he was unable to see properly, the saw blade hit a bolt and kicked back in his face. He was cut from the top of his head down the forehead, across his eyebrow and into the corner of his eye, just nicking his eyelid.

Not knowing how bad he was cut and blinded by the blood and sawdust, he yelled out for help. Pastor Dave managed to drag him out from under the building and lay him in the grass. Fearing the worst, he flagged down help and did his best to staunch the blood flow with his shirt.

With help from others, they half-carried half-dragged my dad to the outpost. Jessie immediately assessed the damage and tried to slow the bleeding. She was able to ascertain that it was not life-threatening and got the bleeding mostly stopped within minutes. A chainsaw leaves a pretty nasty wound, and as it was so close to the eye, Jessie wanted my dad to get to the hospital in Whitehorse in case he needed surgery.

My mom was notified and while she was preparing for the trip and finding someone to watch me, Jessie cleaned and wrapped my dad's head. Although in pain and still woozy, Dad asked if she was glad she didn't have to sew him up again. Jessie immediately retorted that all the practice in the world wouldn't help her sew up his thick skull. Once again, he had no pain killer because she was worried he might be concussed. She also warned against whiskey as it might put him to sleep. She gave him a few aspirin and sent him on his way.

After a long, nightmarish trip, my parents got to the hospital and my dad was repaired. The doctor did a great job, and after his eyebrow grew back, the scarring was noticeable but faint.

Jessie also acted as Atlin's emergency vet on occasion. Although I believe she detested it, she understood the need and I think she did it more for the well-being of the owners than the animal.

It was just another way of taking care of her people, and when it came to medical care, we were all her people. She truly cared about each and every one of us.

Jessie was occasionally relieved by other highly qualified nurses from the community, but when I was small she was always the one that looked at my pink eye or poked and prodded my neck when I had the mumps, issued that nasty-tasting cough medication when I had strep throat or listened to my lungs rattle when I had bronchitis. I can't imagine how taxing it must have been for her during a measles or mumps outbreak.

Jessie randomly handed out advice as she hastened past: "You need a hat, it's cold, and you'll freeze your ears." "Where's your coat? You're going to catch a cold." "You need to get home and get some dry clothes on right now." "I better not see you at the outpost next week." When Jessie told us to do something, we did it.

Chapter Twenty-Five

Curling: The Great Canadian Pastime

The year was 1968, the temperatures fluttered between fifteen (-26°C) and twenty below (-29°C), and a brisk, northerly breeze penetrated parkas and sweaters alike. Ringlets of ice fog wafted in off the lake, swirling in ghostly eddies across the icebound slough. Hearty bellows of "sweep, sweep" and the muted applause of mitten-clad hands echoed across the ice. With much enthusiasm, a set of borrowed rocks and a little elbow grease, the Gold Nugget Bonspiel was born and curling was back in Atlin for good. With lots of antifreeze consumed by curlers and boosters equally, everyone survived the brisk January weather and thoroughly enjoyed the games. Coupled with a full house for a banquet and dance at the Old Moose Hall, the Bonspiel was deemed a raucous success.

With visiting teams heading back home, word spread that Atlin put on one heck of a Bonspiel and promises of next year's return resounded up and down the Alaska Highway. With the success of that first spiel, a need was created for a club and rink. On an evening of reflection in the wake of recent revelries, four couples germinated the idea of the Atlin Curling Club. Never from these humble beginnings could anyone imagine the magnitude of effect this small spark of an idea could hold for the future of one small Northern town. An argument could easily be made that this innocent gathering of friends was the start of Atlin's modern metamorphosis from sleepy, dusty ghost town to thriving, cohesive community.

A meeting was quickly scheduled and attended by many. Officers were elected, or more likely volunteered with no objections. A set of bylaws were drawn up and, by July of that year, the Club became a registered society and could hold real estate property. A scramble for a site to erect the rink took place and culminated in the purchase of a piece of land made available by the Crown.

Plans were drawn up for a building that would house two sheets of ice and a cozy spectator room. With a small loan from the Board of Trade, ideas began to turn into realizations. The local RCMP Constable volunteered to spearhead construction, a foreman was hired and volunteers worked under his guidance. Lumber and logs were supplied at cost from a local sawmill, wall board and ceiling tiles were donated, and local electricians wired in the lights at no charge. A fifty-cup coffee urn fell off a truck and found its way to the new rink, plastic sheeting covered the roof until roofing material could be afforded, and, by December of that year, the first rocks were sailing down the ice. Everything was ready for the second Gold Nugget Bonspiel. More importantly, a fine example had been displayed as to what a community could accomplish by pulling together and working hard.

As funds were required for such ambitions, a Ways and Means Committee was formed during the building of the rink. Bingo, pie and cake sales, turkey shoots, dances and banquets were held to raise money. Raffles for gold nugget jewelry, local artwork and even snow machines were a constant, Nabob coffee coupons were saved and donated to get items needed for the future kitchen. Through these endeavors the First of July Parade and celebration came alive again. Discovery Days, a midsummer fishing derby, BBQ supper and family get-together, was born. An honorary membership plaque was made and friends and curlers far and wide paid twenty dollars each to get their name etched onto the plaque. Prizes and trophies were donated from Whitehorse, Teslin, Watson Lake and Atlin businesses.

With the rink in one location and the banquet and dance hall in another, a growing desire to house all the Bonspiel events under the

The first modern Atlin Gold Nugget Bonspiel on the slough, 1968.

In January 1968 with borrowed rocks and truck headlights for lighting, the small slough at the south end of town became the venue for what would become the historic and long-lived annual Atlin Gold Nugget Bonspiel. The event celebrated its fiftieth anniversary in 2018.

same roof concluded with plans for a 30' x 60' (9m x 18m) hall. With a bank loan of seven thousand dollars, phase one, a 30' x 30' (9m x 9m) partial cement basement, was erected to house the clubroom bar. Permits were obtained and the bar was opened in time for the next Bonspiel. For the next two years, the club pursued different avenues of funding to start phase two, the 30' x 60' (9m x 18m) hall above the bar. The hall project was proving insurmountable, and no matter how big the fundraising schemes and volunteer effort, the project was too big for the small town.

Upon discovering that Canadian Manpower grants were available for local initiative programs, the then-president of the Board of Trade, Tom Kirkwood, brought this information to the Atlin Curling Club. At a 1971 curling club meeting, a vote was taken to become involved in the program. The size of the hall was increased to 40' x 60' (12m x 18m) and a full basement was included.

The initiative program paid wages for fifteen workers for ten weeks and a $15,000 bank loan guaranteed by club members finished the construction. Let that sink in for a minute. If that is not community confidence, I don't know what is. What it means is individuals and families put their necks on the block for the betterment of all Atlin's citizens. I would say that kind of commitment to one's community has become rare. Construction began in minus forty degree weather. Within six months, the first dance was held in the new hall.

Rules of the initiative stated that the development had to service the whole community. With the curling club in essence a private club, although open to all for a small fee, it did not fit the grant's criteria; so the Atlin Recreation Centre Association was formed. Upon the Association becoming a registered society, the curling club turned over the title to the land and building. Immediately afterwards, the Gun Club and Community Club joined the Recreation Centre. The Ways and Means Committee and Bar Committee became elected groups in the Rec. Centre Association, thus leaving the curling club to curling and bonspiels, although it remained the biggest supporter, bringing in roughly three thousand dollars in profit annually those first years.

In the ensuing years, improvements to the complex were made, including better lighting, running water and a sewage system. A stairway was added from the bar to the hall; the stairs came from the old Atlin Inn. The Moose Hall donated a piano and a pool table, both originally came from Nolan's Mine. A bar and kitchen were added upstairs and a pumping station for fire suppression was also added. The library was housed beside the shooting range in the basement, and later, artificial ice machinery was installed for the rink.

Many of these accomplishments could never have been achieved had it not been for the endless hours of volunteerism. Not only did the citizens come together to build a beautiful community center that became the beating heart of town, they also put in the enormous amount of time and effort to sustain it.

Curling continued to thrive and bonspieling flourished. The Gold Nugget Bonspiel quickly became the can't-miss event of the year for Atlinites and curlers up and down the Alaska Highway. By year six, the Gold Nugget was attracting over thirty teams and reaching epic fame throughout the North. The now familiar refrain, "Atlin puts on one heck of a bonspiel," was heard far and wide.

Although the Gold Nugget was the king of bonspiels, the town also held men's and women's and youth spiels, as well as school and family events. Emphasis was never put on winning but more on inclusion and enjoyment. For many spiels, teams were encouraged to include at least one novice curler. When the students traveled to other towns for curling, we balanced the teams with more and less experienced players, never stacking all the talent on one team.

I remember one particular student outing to Cassiar. We put our usual ragtag teams together, loaded up our borrowed brooms and tumbled into parents' cars and trucks. We headed out in the dark morning hours of a thirty-below (-34°C) day. We traveled 350 miles (565km) on less than optimum roads to arrive tired and fidgety late in the afternoon. A couple of our teams were surprised to find out they were scheduled to curl within minutes of arrival. Quickly shuffling into the venue, we were immediately impressed and intimidated by the rinks and viewing area. It was cavernous and bright, and the seating area held what seemed to us a hundred spectators. We had never played in front of anyone other than a handful of our friends and family.

The local teams had matching sweaters and slacks; they had curling shoes, new brooms, sliders and kneepads. Most of us had our jeans with holes in the knees and a hodgepodge of gym shoes and runners. When we first took the ice, there was some tittering and muffled laughter—even some mild taunting from a few of the other teams. It soon faded away and was replaced by grumbling and in-fighting and maybe a little begrudging admiration. Even though some of our players were complete novices and our opposition looked like they had been teamed together for years, we slaughtered them. We won everything: first in the A, second in the A, first in the B, second in the B and so on.

They had all the fancy trappings, but we had community and friendship and we viewed curling as fun, not something serious that we had to win. I'm not saying we didn't have a competitive spirit; we definitely enjoyed kicking their tails, but we would have had fun no matter the outcome.

Any bonspiel was exciting even if you weren't playing. It was a chance to get a hot dog or cheeseburger at the concession stand. It was a chance to help out in the community, maybe set up the tables and chairs for the banquet or dance, or clean up the mess after. It was an excuse to stay up late and watch your parents or friends curl. For a young person, it was an electric atmosphere; the town came alive, and it added warmth to a cold winter.

Curling and bonspieling, symbiotic in nature, involved the entire community in some way or another and added a much-needed boost to Atlin's sluggish winter economy. Drawing teams from as far away as Dawson City some 450 miles (725km) north, accommodations, meals, and refreshments were all required. Curlers and non-curlers alike turned out to support the spiels in any way they could. Concession workers, bartenders and organizers were kept busy night and day. The cooking and baking for the banquet had local home kitchens working overtime. Countless days were spent fine tuning and perfecting the ice, well before the out-of-town team's arrival. Set up and clean up for the dance, banquet and award ceremony, and washing dishes and cleaning toilets all needed doing and were happily performed by volunteers.

Some of the local teams began the round-robin tournament on Thursday night before the out-of-town teams pulled in Friday afternoon and evening. Bonspiels are a twenty-four-hour affair to get all the games played in time for Sunday's award celebration. The rink fee for the Gold Nugget Spiel in 1973 was twenty-four dollars per team. This included a banquet featuring home-cooked fare Saturday evening followed by a dance with a live band. At midnight, a cold-cut buffet was made available to soak up a bit of the liquid revelry in case your team had a game at three o'clock in the morning.

The concession stand was manned all night, providing gallons of coffee for clarity of mind and body in the early morning hours. Of course, who knew when a hot dog or cheeseburger or steaming bowl of chili with toast craving might take hold?

Sunday morning started off with Uncle Dave Goodwin's famous pancake breakfast, something few Atlinites or visitors missed—and was the

Brian Jack is giving me a shovel ride at the first modern Gold Nugget Bonspiel, held in 1968, outdoors on the slough.

highlight for many. With the games wrapping up Sunday afternoon in time for the award ceremony, visitors prepared for departure. Prizes were awarded not only for the obvious wins but also best sportsman, best newcomer and best or worst curling sweater. I remember at a young age winning in some dubious category or another, and unfortunately the prize was a case of Molson's beer. I hardly had time to get to the podium before my mother materialized from the ether to whisk away my hard-earned prize.

I was fortunate enough to be on the winning team of the 13th or 14th Gold Nugget Bonspiel, I can't remember which. I say fortunate because I was a last-minute pickup by a team from Watson Lake when a member had a sudden family emergency and could not attend. Although I was used to being the skip on our school rinks, I was delegated to the position of first on my new team. I have to say, I lent little to our win compared to my more skilled teammates, but they treated me like I was an integral part of our success and we all had a great time.

The prizes for first in the A were nothing to scoff at. Along with a rather impressive trophy, I also received a top-of-the-line float coat, a rod and reel with a full tackle box and a beautiful Zippo lighter with a 24-karat gold-nugget dogsled and team depicted on its side. There were a number of other prizes, but those were the standouts for me.

Atlin was a town that saw most of its annual income in the summer months only from tourism and mining, so it was always amazing to see the continuous outpouring of goods, money and time from Atlin businesses. For every fundraiser, and there were many, every business was hit up, over and over, and never did they disappoint. The prizes for the Gold Nugget Spiel were some of the best in the North and, of course, featured its namesake, gold nuggets, in one form or another. As all Atlinites spent a fair amount of money in Whitehorse in those days, Whitehorse businesses were generous supporters of events in Atlin and provided many of the prizes and trophies.

Lifetime friendships were forged on and off the ice. Often visiting curlers were housed in local homes and gladly reciprocated when Atlinites bonspieled in neighboring towns. Not only did the Curling Club and the bonspiels bring the Atlin community together, they also brought the greater Northern community together.

The Dry Facts on Curling
Atlin News Miner 1972
Diane S. Smith

The origin of curling is not known for sure. Some think the Flemings originated the game and in Teslin, they are positive this is true.

The Scots have been credited with sophisticating the game and spreading its popularity to other countries. The Flemings are credited with spreading its popularity up and down the Alaska Highway.

It is known the Scots curled early in the sixteenth century. They called the stones "kuting stones" or "loofies." Nowadays, Atlin curlers have other names for the stones but none can be printed in the *News Miner.*

A Scottish museum displays a stone which bears the date 1510. Atlin used to have an old stone that dated to the gold rush. It rested for years on the front porch of the Government Building. When the Atlin Curling Club held its first Gold Nugget Bonspiel in 1967, Tom Connolly was awarded this stone for some feat or other. No one told Tom it was a joke and he thought it would make a nice addition to his new fireplace. He cemented it securely and prominently into the fireplace facade. When he found he couldn't keep the stone, he had to chip the damned thing loose and it left an unsightly scar in his masonry. For some reason, that stone has never been seen again.

The very first stones were water-worn boulders with natural holes for thumb and fingers. Later on, handles were added, much to the delight of curlers who no longer had to wear steel-toed shoes. Some of the early stones weighed over a hundred pounds. They were in use before the advent of the bonspiel. As its popularity grew, the heavy stones were abandoned in favor of stones weighing around forty pounds. They prevented players from becoming exhausted with playing the game and left them more time for bonspieling.

The first curling games were played on natural ice on ponds or lakes; however, cold weather and the need to play during the nighttime soon led to the building of covered rinks. The first Gold Nugget Bonspiel was played on the slough near the Atlin Street Bridge. At this event, coldness and lack of light was remedied with moose milk (an alcoholic concoction of a variety of ingredients) and pickup truck headlights. Although this worked effectively, the Atlin Curling Club soon built a covered rink with artificial lighting. The problem of cold and light was solved, but the popularity of moose milk and similar libations like sluice spiel spunch prevailed when they were found great for dispelling the gloom of losing or to celebrate a hard-fought victory.

Canada was one of the early followers of curling, and in 1852, the first Canadian branch of the Royal Caledonian Curling Club was established. The present Atlin Curling Club was established in 1967 and since has grown in membership and flourished as one of Atlin's most active organizations. It is probably safe to predict that this club will continue hale and hardy as long as curling and moose milk exist.

Chapter Twenty-Six

Fun Days

Fun Days is another of those obvious names Atlinites are fond of. Fun Days, innocent-sounding enough, unequivocally became the biggest weekend of the year, surpassing the Gold Nugget Bonspiel. It was a spring festival and release of winter's pent-up enthusiasm. Fun Days was a chance to unwind and say hi to neighbors last seen at the Bonspiel and to shake out the cobwebs of cabin fever and to renew thoughts of long-dormant passions like gardening and fishing and picnicking.

Fun Days started when the Atlin Gun Club decided to organize a day that gathered snow machine owners together to offer rides to the young and old for twenty-five cents. Hot dogs were also sold, and it turned out to be a great way to usher in the spring. The annual Trapper's Ball and gun shoot were scheduled for a couple weeks later. These two events held at the end of March were combined, and an invite was sent to neighboring towns to come participate, thus creating what would become the biggest small-town spring festival for miles around. At first called Atlin Family Fun Day, it quickly became three days and the name was shortened to Fun Days.

Teams readying for a race on the lake in front of town, mid-1970s. Teresa Island is in the background.

The first combined Fun Days, a two-day affair, was held the last weekend of March 1973. On Saturday morning, people gathered at the new shooting range in the basement of the Rec. Centre. Youth shooting took up the morning, with boys and girls shooting for top prizes of cakes and pies. All afternoon, the adults competed for turkeys and hams. Simultaneously, upstairs at the curling rink for the non-shooters, drawing a rock closest to the bull's eye could also win a cake, pie or turkey.

Around noon, town folks and visitors gathered in front of the post office to greet the snow machiners racing in from Carcross. The race commemorated the Carcross-Atlin mail run from the days before the road. Actual mail and commemorative stamped envelopes were brought in by dog teams later in the afternoon. To greet the teams, Delin Sawatzky, Atlin's postmistress, along with long-time resident eighty-nine-year-old Norman Fisher, were on hand to receive the mail. Norman himself ran the mail by dog team for thirteen years to and from Carcross, Atlin and Telegraph Creek. The Carcross-Atlin run was considered the most dangerous mail run in Canada. Atlin did not have a road until 1951, so everything was brought in over the ice in the winter and by lake boat in the summer. The first regular flights began in the early 1930s.

That evening, a banquet was held at the Rec. Centre. After that the Trappers Ball kicked off and local musicians played into the night. The hall was decorated with furs, snowshoes and fresh-cut pine boughs. It resonated with a woodsy charm. It was estimated three hundred and fifty people attended that dance, more or less the entire population of the town. Of course, many out-of-town people were there, and as it was sixteen and up for that dance, none of the youngsters were in attendance.

Sunday morning was a beautiful sunny morning with a mild thirty-five-degree temperature. The early birds were on hand to send off the dog racers as they started a timed fourteen-mile (23km) race around the islands and down to Fourth of July Creek and back. The afternoon was eaten up with snowshoe and ski races, the one-dog pull, sprint races for kids and their three-dog teams as well as events for the snow machiners. Everyone gathered at the Rec. Centre for the prize ceremony that evening.

The first combined Fun Days was a raving success and the event would only grow in prestige and notoriety in the years to come. Just three years later, Atlin's humble, little spring fling was being heralded and attended by folks from the Yukon, British Columbia and Alaska. Atlin folks just aren't capable of half-assing anything; it's either go big and be excellent or it's not worth doing in the first place.

Fun Days were spilling out at the seams. Two days was no longer enough, so Friday evening was now incorporated into the event.

Gambling and Glitz

Friday night, called Miller and McLaren Night, named after the two prospectors credited with the first gold strike on Pine Creek, started with casino games. Roulette, Blackjack, Craps and Five-Card Draw were popular with the seasoned gambler and novices alike. Many a high-rolling nine-year-old broke the piggy bank on Miller and McLaren Night. Young and old alike got to try their luck at beating the house, and we all know how that ends. Worry not, all proceeds went back into next year's Fun Days event. The smallest kids were kept busy at the fish pond or bean bag toss where everyone left a winner.

Although my mom warned me of the follies of gambling, she seemed to think losing money to a good cause was expected and added five dollars to my entire net worth of five dollars. With two crisp five-dollar bills tucked securely in my Boofus Shop wallet, a new sleeve garter, and sporting a jaunty bowler on my head, I was poised to strike it rich at the world's second oldest profession.

I strode in with my best girl on my arm. Okay that part was fantasy, but I was with a few friends and at least one was a girl. I surveyed the room looking for a seat, but every table was full and people were waiting. What I was witnessing resembled little the games we played in Pete and John's basement with poker chips and sometimes pennies. I noticed they were not using any wild cards. Where were the jokers and the one-eyed jacks or red threes or black twos? That makes it a lot harder; maybe I didn't know as much about poker as I thought. I didn't have a clue what was going on and decided I wasn't going to submit myself to a most certain embarrassment. Black Jack as well was an entirely different game than the one we played. Although alluring, I was too old for the fish pond or the bean bag toss.

That left the roulette wheel. Knowing nothing about roulette, I cautiously approached and observed. It seemed easy enough. Pick a number and place your bet. Or even easier, pick red or black. This was my game and I was determined I would beat the house. I boldly placed a whole five-dollar bill on black. One quick spin and half my money disappeared. That made me angry so I placed my other five on red, determined to get my money back and then some. A fool and his money is soon parted.

That sums up my gambling career, the entire thirty-five seconds. I didn't get the girl either. The silver lining was a ten dollar donation to the Rec. Centre.

The Entertainment

Capping off the evening of gambling, the tables and chairs were quickly realigned in preparation for the entertainment portion of the night. It was an opportunity for anyone who had long suppressed an affinity for the raucous and bawdy genre of showbiz known as vaudeville: "without as much skin, in most cases."

I propose an innocent question. Where on earth can you get the town's welder, the water man, the fish and wildlife officer, an equipment operator, the telephone repairman, a couple of gold

Jack Green, Ron Odian and unidentified contestant (possibly John Thoma) all vied for the title of Queen of the Creeks, early 1980s. I believe it was won by Ron Bowden the same year he was Miss Boulder Creek. Originally published in the Atlin News Miner, photo by Tom Kirkwood.

miners and a hardware store owner to dress as gay nineties Queen of the Creeks contestants? Among others, Miss Ruby Creek, Miss Pine Creek and the most popular Miss Boulder Creek all vied for the coveted title of Queen of the Creeks. Another year many of these same sequined starlets performed an all-male, unshaven rendition of Tchaikovsky's Swan Lake.

Although women were outnumbered, there were plenty. After all, this wasn't an outback sheep station and they weren't in a Monty Python troupe, although very Pythonesque at times. I guess Atlin harbored a number of comedic geniuses hiding as everyday folks, all with a penchant for dressing in drag. Could it have been the water? As far as I know none were even English.

Over the years, notable Miller and McLaren Night productions included The Baby and the Bathwater, staring Jack Green who worked for the highway department. Jack played a baby with a very hairy chest, sporting nothing but a bonnet and a diaper. He sat in a galvanized tub while an inebriated Ron Bowden, our town's water man dressed as a bald Mother Hubbard, poured water over his head from an old chamber pot. All while being serenaded by a giggling, drunken barbershop quartet with only three members, singing about a baby washing down the drain hole.

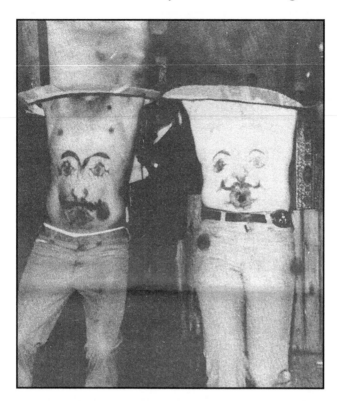

Two unidentified belly button whistlers entertain the crowd at Miller and McLaren Night at the Rec. Centre, Fun Days, late 1970s. Originally published in the Atlin News Miner. Photo by Tom Kirkwood.

The Jug Band made a couple of appearances. I played the spoons one year because I couldn't play anything else. Our bass was comprised of an upside down washtub, a broom stick, and a string. We had two washboard players, a kazoo section, three or four jug blowers and an improvised xylophone consisting of tin cans and bottles. Anyone could join in until the stage overflowed with "musicians," many with nothing to play but their feet and hands. I'm not sure if it was fun to watch, but it sure was a blast to participate.

The whistling belly dancers will always be remembered—a number of men wearing nothing but pants and huge top hats that hid everything but their naked bellies. On their bellies they had painted faces with the belly button as the mouth, and they moved their guts in and out in time to The *Bridge on the River Kwai* soundtrack: "Colonel Bogey March."

I can't stress enough that the average actor in these farces was middle-aged at least, usually carrying a few extra pounds and more often than not, sported a long, shaggy beard or droopy mustache. And that's just the women. I'm joking, of course; in fact, it was usually the opposite for the women. Fun Days seemed to be a good occasion to polish the diamonds.

The entertainment was open to all ages, although at times slightly bawdy and assuredly a demonstration in inebriation. It was hilarious to young and old. I often wondered at the confusion and ensuing questions when young Johnny suddenly realized that was his dad he just witnessed up on that stage in a pink tutu cavorting and pirouetting about as if he was channeling a drunken Anna Pavlova. Harder to explain than discovering your dad is Santa, I bet. I'm still working on that one.

I was spared such a horror, but I often wondered how long it took a child of one of the lovely queens or ballerinas to scour away the image of seeing their father with makeup and a wig, dressed in a slinky black dress, beard, hairy legs and all.

Although the men tended to steal the show, the women accounted for themselves magnificently, including the most popular event of the evening. These were real women, mind you: "Ladies and gentlemen, I give you Atlin's famous can-can girls." It was quite amazing to see your friend's mom, the one who wore ripped jeans, a sweatshirt and rubber boots everywhere she went, suddenly had metamorphosed into a beautiful, bedazzling showgirl.

All the dresses were made locally, many in my mom's shop. They were as intricate as they were colorful, combining multiple layers of frills and ruffles and bejeweled in sequins and rhinestones. The dancers wore their hair up adorned with brilliant feathers. They accessorized with sequin and feather chokers, fishnet stockings, boas, ankle boots, and garters.

One couldn't help but be mesmerized as you recognized your teacher and the lady who worked at the store and the local accountant and the cook at the café all transformed—and they could dance. Wow, where did they learn that?

Some of the most memorable skits were performed by the gals, even though I remember they too were often dressed as the opposite sex. Was this a case of gender confusion or comic beguiling, or as I originally assumed, the water?

Usually, a woman was found behind the scenes pulling the levers. My mom was in charge of the entertainment for a couple years, and many other Atlin luminaries filled that role before and after her tenure.

Haberdasher and Finery

After the entertainment and before the ensuing dance, a costume judging contest with categories for most authentic, best lady's dresses and hats, and best family was held.

The Historical Society became a big part in the Fun Days Festival, playing up the 1898 gold rush theme. The museum opened up in the days before to sell hats, boas and other haberdashery reminiscent of the era. Soon the men folk and boys of town were sporting top hats, boaters, bowlers and sleeve garters. Mothers were busy sewing vests and dresses as well as constructing the great floppy-brim lady's hats popular at the time. Entire families dressed the part. The men and boys were dressed as gamblers, saloon keepers and miners fresh off the creek, and there were always a few decked out in buckskins and furs. A typical male's attire might consist of a sporty top hat, a neat black bow tie on a white shirt and sleeve garters on both sleeves, topped off with a colorful vest. Some of the dandier fellows might have spats and a pocket watch with a gold-nugget fob and jade and gold-nugget cufflinks.

The women were high society ladies adorned in flowing gowns layered with ruffles and tulle, complete with puffy shoulders and corseted waists. Some were dressed as dance hall girls bedecked in sequins and costume jewelry, fishnet stockings and garter belts.

At that time, my mom's shop, like Fun Days, had expanded from its humble beginnings. With a full-time seamstress employed, they were inundated with orders for dresses for ladies of town and the can-can dresses and others needed for the Miller and McLaren skits. For months before Fun Days, Mom's workshop was filled with enormous dresses, large floppy hats, frills and sequins.

My mom and her friend, Leah Fuller, sewed until their fingers hurt, trying to keep up with the vests, dresses, garters and hats. The year the men did Swan Lake, a couple of weeks prior, I received a large pack of white long johns for my birthday and most had yet to be worn. I came home from school to find all my new long johns dyed pink and hanging in the kitchen to dry. Later I got to see them worn by a troupe of drunken old men dressed as ballerinas. Of course, money was always short and I had to wear stretched-out pink long johns for the next few years. Explain that to your therapist, I dare you.

Fun Days crowd on the ice in front of the Tarahne, late 1970s. Originally published in the Atlin News Miner. Photo by Tom Kirkwood.

Teams ready for the beginning of the Atlin to Carcross mail run in front of the Atlin Post Office, late 1970s. Originally published in the Atlin News Miner. Photo by Tom Kirkwood.

Plug Hole Dance

By 1976, the Historical Society added Popcorn Kate's parlor to the Fun Day's menagerie. Popcorn Kate's was housed in the Old Moose Hall, once again resurrected to serve its community. Named after gold rush character of note, Popcorn Kate first established a bunkhouse at Log Cabin on the early route into Atlin. Later she opened the Discovery, a hotel in Atlin, only to give it away and leave town for parts unknown after being denied a liquor license because she was a woman.

The modern-day Popcorn Kate's sold old-fashioned candy, lemonade, coffee, tea, sweets and savories, and of course, popcorn. As I mentioned, Fun Days was held at the end of March, meaning spring thaw and runoff was often in full swing. The first year of Popcorn Kate's, there was an early thaw and the streets were running with water during the day and frozen at night. Water seeped into the Moose Hall and soon the floor was covered with a couple of inches of muddy runoff. Someone had the idea to drill a few holes in the floor and let the water drain out, and it worked.

That Saturday, with the water drained and the floor cleaned, business was brisk. By early evening all was prepared for that night's festivities. The Trapper's Ball was a complete sellout weeks before the event, so it was hastily determined to have an overflow dance at the Moose Hall/Popcorn Kate's. Local musicians were hired to play, and anticipation ran high.

As the band struck up and the dancers began shaking off the winter cobwebs, the floor sagged under their weight and water began seeping back up through the recently drilled holes. An annoyance at first soon turned into a unique attraction. Unlike Popcorn Kate herself, the Historical Society had no problem obtaining a liquor license and many of their patrons were well lubricated.

Trading high heels for rubber boots, the dancing went on into the wee hours of the morning. During particularly raucous songs, the floor got to bouncing and water shot to the ceiling. Dancing began to take on a combination of musical chairs, Jack in the Box and a wet T-shirt contest.

As the story goes, one well-oiled patron was inspired to take a reversed shower. He stripped down to his skivvies and pantomimed a good lathering up, while being serenaded by the infamous barbershop quartet of recent Miller and McLaren Night fame. For reasons unknown, the quartet now had five members. "Can anyone count around here?" Their repertoire of one song had undergone a hasty rewrite to change the lyric to "my baby went down the plug hole." After witnessing and encouraging the shower participant, most watchers were silently thankful he wasn't French.

That night will forever be known as the "Plug Hole Dance." The Historical Society would later start a "Plug the Plug Hole" campaign in an attempt to raise money to restore the Moose Hall.

Sled dogs, Ski-Doos and Smoos

The bright, unyielding spring sun was almost more than some could bear, but a great portion of Atlinites and visitors were down on the ice in front of town bright eyed, if not bushy tailed, by eight o'clock for the commencing of Saturday's events.

The morning started off with the kid's events, as they were clear of mind and raring to go. There was a boy and girl's snowshoe race around First Island and then the kids' three-dog sled race around Third Island. Cross-country ski races of various lengths were held, and fire building and tea making proved to be a popular spectator's sport. As the day progressed, cabin spike driving, cross-cut log sawing and even squirrel skinning drew competitors. I think the tobacco spitting contest only lasted one year, as a woman won it and the men took their toys and went home.

The student travel club operated a concession stand on the shore at the bottom of Pearl Avenue where they turned out coffee and hot cocoa by the bucket load. They say everything tastes better outside when it's cold and that may be so, because I still remember the cheeseburgers and hot dogs with grilled onions being the best I've ever tasted.

By mid-morning, the longer distance dog sled races were off to their usual raucous start and it was time to fire up the snow machines. A number of unusual races and competitions were scheduled and eagerly participated in.

The slalom race was exciting, but the blindfold slalom was not only exciting, but extremely humorous and more than dangerous. It is a two-person event where the driver is, you guessed it, blindfolded

Mass start sprint race on lake in front of town. Atlin Mountain in the background, late 1970s.

and his partner riding behind is the navigator. As you can imagine, much confusion, frustration and at times sheer terror ensued.

Tube serpentine proved to be another great spectator sport and also quite humorous. It was a high-speed affair set out much like the slalom, but with greater distances. A tire tube on a long rope was attached to a snow machine, a rider mounted the tube and off they went. Many a rider was quickly and violently ejected from their tube and often had a short, but exhilarating, flight before their body slammed back to the ice. A number of snow machine races of various lengths and durations also took place, but none as exciting as blindfold slalom and tube serpentine. Strange that we would never think of riding a dirt bike without a helmet but very few people ever wore one snow machining.

Snow machine broom ball was popular. Teams were made up of three or four machines per side, each with a driver and rider armed with a curling broom. The teams raced back and forth on a vaguely defined playing pitch trying to hit a medium-sized rubber ball into the opposing team's hockey net. Sounds easy enough. Crazy antics and blatant cheating were the norm and overlooked by the referee. Snow machines, although fleet, aren't always the most agile. Hitting a ball with a small broom at a high rate of speed proved to be much harder than anticipated and passing the ball was almost non-existent.

As the afternoon wore on, snowshoe softball was showcased beside the *Tarahne*. The ball was painted a bright purple to distinguish it from the landscape of white. Snowshoes were donned and a ball diamond marked out with spray paint. Hitting proved to be easy enough, but fielding was another matter altogether. Fun to participate and funny to watch as the players tripped and fell around the bases and across the outfield.

Tug of war between communities always drew a big crowd. Leg wrestling, snow sculpturing, hammering cabin spikes, sawing logs, fire building, and tea brewing were open to all who wanted to give them a try. From a spectator's and participant's point of view, the Schmoo race had to be the most hilarious competition ever invented. A team consisted of four people armed with two long two by four (5cm x 10cm) boards with attached loops for the feet. Participants slipped their boots into the loops, thus binding all four people to the two boards. Mind you, to get anywhere all four people had to move in perfect unison—as in, all left legs forward together then all right legs forward together. Although described as a race, it more often than not began and ended at the starting line in a jumble of giggling, helpless, hungover, possibly still inebriated participants.

Power and Puff

Sunday morning saw more snow machine races, including the two-man, long-distance poker race where the racers had to navigate to certain locations where they collected a playing card sealed in an envelope. Upon their return, if they didn't have all the cards, they were disqualified. There were two ways to win. One was to finish first, and second was to have the best poker hand.

The one-dog pull was also a Sunday event and always a favorite. It drew a huge crowd. For those not familiar, this event, as its name suggests, is where a single dog pulls as much weight as it can. With two categories, smaller dogs and larger dogs, the weights pulled in both categories are always mind blowing. From a dead stop, mind you, and no assistance other than verbal encouragement from its owner, a dog must break the sled free and pull it a pre-determined distance. The smaller dogs are usually around sixty (27kg) to seventy pounds (31kg) with the larger dogs up to one hundred pounds (50kg) or more. Six hundred pounds (270kg) and one thousand pounds (450kg) pulled, respectively, were not unusual.

At some point, my mom and I acquired an enormous Malamute. We called him Knik. Knik had long, luxurious hair and massive ears that only stood up halfway and flopped over at the top. He was mostly black with white facial markings, his paws were enormous and he towered over our other dogs.

We didn't know his past, as he had come to us as a stray, but we quickly found he was well trained. Someone had spent a lot of time teaching him commands. He knew the usual "sit" and "lay down," but he also knew "stay," "come" and "heel," among others. He was better trained than all of our other mutts.

I was watching the one-dog pull at Fun Days one year and my friends were bugging me to enter Knik. They assured me he would clean up with little effort. As far as I knew, Knik had never been in harness. Eventually, they convinced me. I retrieved Knik, borrowed a harness and hooked him to the weighted sled. We started him at a weight well below the final total pulled by the smaller dogs. I was ready, Knik was ready, and the crowd, anticipating a great show of doggie brawn, stood hushed. I began to call him: "Come on, Knik, come on, Buddy," and "Let's go." I gestured, beckoned, called and whistled, all to no avail.

Knik was the kind of dog that would die trying to adhere to a command. I called him to a roof top and he climbed a ladder to get there. I called him across a raging creek and without hesitation he dove in and swam across. He heeled as I waded through swamps and deep snow. Knik lived to be loyal and do what was asked of him.

Apparently somewhere in Knik's past, he'd spent a good amount of time tied up. As soon as he felt any tension on the line, he promptly sat down, wagged his tail and loudly "woo wooed." Knik was not to be a puller. We both took the snickers and gentle joking in stride. We later watched a dog half Knik's size pull just over a thousand pounds.

Sunday afternoon at Fun Days was set aside for the trophy ceremony at the Rec. Centre. The winners collected their prizes and received accolades and ribbing from the crowd. People said goodbye to friends and new acquaintances. Snow machines, kids and dogs were loaded up, and preparations were made for the trip home. Proud, satisfied and satiated, Atlinites dragged their weary bones home for some much-needed and deserved rest, confident that once again Atlin had shown their amazing community spirit and warm hospitality.

Chapter Twenty-Seven

Dominion Day / First of July

Dominion Day, later named Canada Day, marked the anniversary of Confederation in 1867. As in the United States and their celebration of independence on the fourth of July, the date became the familiar name of the event, First of July. Although the Gold Nugget Bonspiel and Fun Days were the two biggest events of the year, they were in no way the only thing going on in our little town. Dominion Day always proved to be a great time and a greater way to kick off the summer. Horse owners hitched up buggies and wagons and adorned their best steeds in first-class tack. Dog teams pulled carts or sleds on wheels. Businesses sponsored floats of all sizes and sorts. The RCMP Constable donned his beautiful red serge, mounted a magnificent stallion flanked by mounted flag bearers and led the procession.

After winding through town a couple times, passing the judge's stand at least twice, the parade concluded at the Campground. The judges tallied the votes and awarded trophies and prizes for best boy's or girl's bike, best float or horse and rider. Horse races and games for the children and adults ensued. The Community Club ran a concession

Fire truck in Dominion Day Parade, early 1970s.

stand with delicious fare of hot dogs and burgers. A beer garden sponsored by the curling club kept the adults entertained while the kids were competing in the sack race, three-legged race or tug o' war. Often a guitar, fiddle or accordion materialized and an impromptu jam session entertained the crowd.

The floats were imaginative, depicting humorous scenes of mining, trapping or logging. Kids decorated their own bikes with streamers and flowers. Kids and adults dressed themselves up in all sorts of costumes.

The summer forestry crew always turned out in full forest-fire fighter mode with hoses, pumps, chainsaws, axes and Pulaski's, their truck draped in brush, trees and stumps.

**Ed Smith watches the parade's modern convenience
wobble its way along.**

My outhouse costume for Dominion Day Parade, 1972. Published originally in the Atlin News Miner. Photograph by Tom Kirkwood.

Riding in the parade sponsored as usual by The Discovery Shop, 1970.

The Atlin Volunteer Fire Department rolled out with their pumper truck, then later their first engine. The youngsters were encouraged to ride on the engine, an exciting treat.

One year with help from my parents, I built a cardboard outhouse complete with the half-moon cut out in the door. Don't ask why I chose to go as an outhouse. They were an integral part of everyday life in Atlin, but knowing my mom's strange sense of humor, she was most likely behind it.

My biffy proved to be quite heavy, and every hundred feet (30m) or so I needed to rest. Mom supplied me with a bag of peanuts in the shell to leave behind in neat piles wherever I stopped. I tottered along the parade route depositing small piles of "poonuts," much to the delight of the dogs and horses and the few kids that weren't in the parade. I later realized it was one of the few times I wasn't sponsored by The Discovery Shop. I wonder why? Noted, peanuts in the shell were enough of a novelty to be considered good giveaway treats at a parade.

Edith Nelson and a friend ride on a skidder in the Dominion Day Parade First of July, mid-1970s.

My friend Lance Shaw portrays a grizzled old miner and I'm his pet Sasquatch, mid-1970s. My mom may have lacked confidence in her Sasquatch-costume expertise, thus the sign. Published originally in the Atlin News Miner. Photograph by Tom Kirkwood.

Another year my buddy Lance dressed as an old prospector and led me through town at the end of a rope. I was adorned in fur and made up to look like a Sasquatch. More than once I feared a dog would attack me. I seemed to rile the dog population ... who knew they hated fake Sasquatch?

It became necessary to invite out-of-towners. As most of Atlin's population was in the parade, it left few to view it. After the prizes were handed out, the horse races kicked off in the sawdust pit. Men, women and youth barrel races showed off the skill of the rider and the horse. Roping demonstrations were presented with some of the men roping runaway sawhorses as they galloped past.

Even pillow fighting made a showing when two opponents scooted to the middle of a large, smoothly-worn log suspended five feet (1.5m) above the ground on two posts. When the combatants met in the middle, they locked their legs around the log the best they could and commenced pummeling each other about the head in the hopes of knocking their challenger to the ground. "Pillow fight" sounds so gentle, but I would say this event was anything but. The festivities culminated with a dance at the Rec. Centre with the music supplied by local musicians.

The Gun Club, Community Club, and Curling Club all sponsored young ladies for the princess contest. Usually reserved for the senior girls at school, the number of contestants coincided with the number of senior girls. Our school was small so there were usually no more than four. The winner officiated and handed out prizes at the bonspiels and Fun Days and acted as Atlin's goodwill ambassador throughout the year. During the Dominion Day festivities, the girls sold raffle tickets, helped judge and assisted with the events after the parade. Called a contest in name only, the winner was picked by chance, their name drawn out of a hat.

Chapter Twenty-Eight

An Excuse Was Never Needed

Every month had at least one reason to have a dance and, if none were obvious, one was quickly invented. The Community Club decided Atlin needed a midsummer shindig, so Discovery Days was born and held on the first Saturday in August. Originally consisting of a lake trout and grayling BBQ, the Gun Club joined a couple years later and a one-day fishing derby was added. Prizes for largest, smallest and tallest fish tales were awarded at the BBQ held at the Campground. As well as the wonderful fish fare, fresh local vegetables and salads helped round out the meal. Potatoes were roasted in the coals and a bevy of fresh baked goods were offered. Everything was donated.

The Gun Club held chicken and pie shoots. No, we didn't shoot chickens, or pies. The chickens were frozen and the pies, homemade. They were the prizes for the best shot. My mom may have blundered our first summer in Atlin—a chicken shoot was held as part of the First of July celebration. Mom had been shooting and hunting her entire life and was a dead-eye shot. She ended up out-shooting a few of the proud menfolk of town, including one big-game guide who did not take kindly to this female interloper besting him at his own game. Not wanting to make waves, she thereafter kept her shooting skills to picking the heads off grouse with her old Sears Roebuck 22. She joked that she chose not to curl as to not ruffle any more fragile male egos in case she beat them.

The Historical Society manned the horseshoe pitch and awarded prizes for ringers. Carnival games for the kids entertained them for hours. Small prizes could be won in the dart throw, the fish pond or bean bag toss.

Never should an event escape without ending in a rambunctious dance at the Rec. Centre. Local musicians and midnight cold cuts helped ingratiate locals and visitors alike to Atlin's wonderful hospitality.

Halloween for the adults was just as anticipated as it was for the kids. Costumes were made, never bought, and were often intricate works of art, although I was most fooled by the subtlest of disguises.

I was in my teens and excited to go to the Halloween dance that night. I asked my mom if she was going and she said she would not be as her friend, Ron Bowden, wasn't feeling well. When she did attend one of the dances, she often went with Ron, our neighbor. He was a long-time bachelor while she was a long-time divorcee. They enjoyed one another's company and rather than go alone, they chose to pair up for such events.

That night after I arrived and upon making my rounds, I saw Ron standing at the bar with a raven-haired woman. Surprised to see him, I approached and asked about my mom. He looked at me and said, "Oh, she's sick and couldn't make it." Now I was thinking that was odd, as she said the same of him. Not the sharpest tool in the drawer, it finally dawned on me that Ron had ditched my mom for this raven-haired hussy. Couldn't he have told her he preferred dark hair over blonds. She would have understood totally; after all, they were just neighbors and friends.

As I was growing angrier at Ron, I subtly tried getting a look at his date, the whole time shooting daggers at the both of them. The obvious trollop was partially turned away in conversation with another patron. Every time I tried to peek at her, she flipped her long black tresses, further covering her features. I made small talk with Ron for a couple of minutes and just as I was about to move away, I noticed out of the corner of my eye that the floozy was turning toward me. I quickly looked to see who Ron had jilted my mother for. Glad I didn't have a mouth full of liquid, but as it was, I almost choked on my tongue because there before me stood my mom.

With a borrowed wig, outfit, and subtle makeup changes, she had transformed herself into a completely different person. At least twelve emotions coursed through me at once. Wow, great one, Mom, you got me good and others, too. The entire night, she pulled off her new persona, fooling many.

After a parade, I'm still wearing my costume, 1970. My mom created every costume I ever needed growing up. Sometimes it was my idea, sometimes it was hers. Like this one, I'm sure.

I insisted on being a clown for Halloween when I was seven. Mom, the master seamstress, speedily produced a wonderful clown outfit complete with a tall, pointed hat with a tassel on the end. I'm guessing she used up some undesirable cloth, as the costume was yellow and brown, two colors not usually associated with the bright, gay colors of clowndom. It was better suited for the uniform of the septic-pumper guy, perhaps. No matter to me, though, I was seven. I wore the outfit one year and it went into a box or trunk or wherever used clown outfits go.

Let's jump ahead a little. I'm seventeen or eighteen, I'm home visiting Mom, it's Halloween night and I decide to stay home and help hand out candy. In the middle of the endless stream of little curmudgeon beggars, I see my clown outfit shuffling up the steps. All bedecked in brown and yellow, a small boy is, sure enough, wearing my old clown costume. There is no way in the world two brown and yellow clown costumes exist, hat, tassel and all.

The poor kid must have thought I was insane, drilling him on where he got the costume. He turned out to be no fountain of knowledge and ended up running away as I threw candy at him yelling, "Don't forget your candy." Pictures bore out the truth that it was indeed my old costume, but my mom was no help as she didn't remember getting rid of it.

The Big Game Dinner was one of my favorite events. Sponsored by the Gun Club and held every year around the time of Thanksgiving, it was a huge potluck-style dinner featuring wild game and foraged items from the surrounding wilderness and local gardens. Held at the Rec. Centre Hall, dinner kicked off at six and went on until eight when everything was cleaned up and preparations were hastily made for the inevitable dance.

The bountiful fare included such delicacies as pickled moose nose, mountain goat fricassee, lake trout stuffed with wild rice, wild onions and local mushrooms. Black bear backstrap, porcupine stew, maple-barbecued caribou ribs, Taku River salmon marinated in wild herbs and baked in coals all made it to the table. Fowl of various types were well represented with grouse-breast dumpling soup, crispy mallard in orange sauce, roasted ptarmigan, and what Northern Canadian dinner would be complete without a big, fat Canada goose in the center of the table? Too many meat dishes made their way to that wonderful dinner over the years to even begin to list. Let's just say that at times over my life, I've found opportunity to say, "Yeah, I ate wolf pie or lynx stew or otter mulligan," only to have people promptly move away and immediately chalk me up as a future serial killer. I can safely say I have eaten close to all of the North's wild animals at one time or another thanks to that annual feast—yup, even pack rat.

Vegetable dishes from local gardens were plentiful and every type of salad was represented. Homemade condiments like mustards and ketchups, chutneys and relishes, wild berry jams, jellies and sauces were on every table. Fresh watercress from the grotto made its way into many of the salads. If one had room, and you were crazy if you didn't, dessert was a wonder to behold. An entire table held such delights as moss-berry cobbler, low-bush cranberry muffins, blueberry and rhubarb pie, strawberry shortcake, gooseberry crisp and hand-churned ice cream with sweet rose hip sauce, and no legitimate dinner in Canada at that time was complete without Nanimo Bars.

If one could waddle after dinner, the opportunity was provided to shake off the calories on, you guessed it, the dance floor.

Chapter Twenty-Nine

Duty to Community

Atlin averaged a dance a month in those days, often accompanying another activity, but for a town of such limited resources, Atlin was alive and vibrant throughout the entire year. This speaks to the acute sense of community and dedication to volunteerism, both traits ingrained in Atlin's citizens from an early age. Children did their part, rarely shirked a task, and were continually encouraged to pitch in and help until it became second nature and asking was no longer needed.

Most, if not all, events were thinly-veiled fundraisers, a necessity to ensure the continued survival of the community entities that sponsored them. The Rec. Centre, the heart of the community, needed constant upkeep and care and none of it was cheap, so money had to be continually raised.

The annual walkathon raised money for the Rec. Centre. Organized by the Community Club and held in June, it was a grand event to start off the summer with a little exercise and community spirit. Sometimes the course was from Surprise Lake back to town, which is roughly twelve miles (19km). Other years the course was from town out to the Warm Springs, also roughly twelve miles (19km). I say roughly because I don't know for sure, and if you ask any Atlinite, you will undoubtedly get a different answer. This goes for the written word as well. I have read in the local Atlin papers, as well as other publications, many different distances for various destinations in the area. I'll include the length of Atlin Lake in this discussion.

The premise for the walkathon is simple—a person gets as many sponsors as they can and walks as far as they can. A sponsor pledges a certain amount of money for every mile/km walked by the sponsored. Once again, like the Christmas concert and Halloween, every student participated.

Our school was always involved in the community events and fundraisers, and time was set aside for organization and assisting. I remember receiving our little pledge log sheets at school. On them was a place for the sponsor's name and the amount sponsored, address and phone number. The last two weren't needed, everyone knew who you were and how to find you. Log sheet in hand, school out, look out town, here we come. Kids immediately ran from the school to the closest house and started pounding on the door. I always thought the walkathon, in particular, showed the patience and continuing goodwill of Atlin folks.

For example, let's say there were fifty students. All fifty students hit every house and business in town, and none were turned away. You multiply that by twelve miles (19km), it adds up fast. Most pledges were a few cents, but even at three cents a mile per pledge times fifty, times twelve, it adds up to eighteen dollars a household and more for the businesses, who were also hit up for a prize or a donation.

Of course, your aunt or uncle or grandparents were expected to pony up more. Eighteen dollars isn't a lot in this day and age, but then, when forty-five dollars could buy you a pair of moose hide pants at The Discovery Shop, it was a lot of money. Add that to the fact that most families were often recovering from a long winter with limited income.

Adults also sponsored and pledged amongst themselves, often for substantial amounts, and even businesses challenged each other. Not everyone made the whole course, but it was a challenge not taken lightly and most walked the entire distance. Some jogged and

Atlin Volunteer Fire Department Chief Wayne Merry surveys the aged fleet. Shortly after this photograph was taken in the 1970s, a new fire hall was erected on this site and a new pumper truck was obtained. Originally published in the Atlin News Miner. Photo by Tom Kirkwood.

some flat-out ran. Willy Jack did the twelve miles (19km) in from Surprise Lake in one hour and twenty-five minutes. The youngest finisher was eight, and the oldest eighty-two. Drink stands were set up along the route offering water, Kool-Aid, compassion, and inspiration to those in need.

Whether it ended at the Warm Springs or the Campground, hot dogs and refreshments were provided for the weary participants. For a couple years, the local government agent toured the course in his vintage convertible, handing out cookies, soft drinks, bandages and sympathy. The most famous contestant had to be Brian Denton, who I mentioned previously walked the entire Surprise Lake to town course backwards in order to get out of winning Hardluck the donkey.

Every May, Atlin held a town cleanup. Garbage bags were handed out to willing enthusiasts and another can't-miss event kicked off. The ditches and vacant lots were scoured, moose leg bones picked up and bags were filled and placed on the side of the road. Those who had pickup trucks loaded the bags and took them to the dump. People were prideful of their little town and wanted it to look good for the summer's visitors.

As usual, our school encouraged and facilitated the involvement of their students in many of the local events over the year. The students spearheaded the walkathon pledge drive, and they went

Bonnie, Roberta, and Billie Shepard helping during the annual town clean up, 1972. Originally published in the Atlin News Miner. Photo by Tom Kirkwood.

door to door handing out poppies and collecting donations for Remembrance Day, and all proudly wore one of their own. Children knew the reason for the various holidays and understood the significance and sacrifice others made. Holidays weren't marked by retail sales of one preposterous kind or another. Students volunteered to prep, serve and clean up for the Old-Timers Dinner and the Big Game Dinner. The town cleanup was a success because of the students and teachers. We felt it an honor to serve our town and we had pride.

If ATLIN was in the dictionary, this is what it would say: Volunteerism: The policy or practice of volunteering one's time or talents for charitable, educational, or other worthwhile activities, especially in one's community.

This definition personified the typical attitude of Atlin residents young and old. As children, we were surrounded by great examples and it was ingrained in the fabric of our daily existence. That town lived, breathed and survived through volunteerism.

The Atlin Volunteer Fire Department was arguably the most important and crucial of all the volunteer efforts in Atlin. In the beginning, men risked their lives to save Atlin's citizens with little or no personal protection, antiquated pumps and out-of-date equipment. They made do with what they had and the lack of all these aforementioned items didn't stop them from doing their best.

Thursday, August 5, 1976 was a tragic day in Atlin. Three children and their mother were lost to fire. The alarm was sounded by a neighbor and the fire department responded. The first men on the scene made several forays into that smoke- and fire-filled home, but were quickly overcome and ultimately unsuccessful. With no personal protection, these acts were extremely brave but futile.

Although struggling valiantly, frustrated firefighters were unable to prime the pumps on the 1952 truck and it wasn't until the other pumping unit arrived on scene that the fire was contained and extinguished.

Anger, shock and frustration prevailed but were quickly replaced by a determination that this horrific lesson would not go unheeded. An emergency meeting was immediately called by the department president. A new structure was adopted, one that saw a chief and four captains. The captains would each be responsible for four firefighters.

Wayne Merry agreed to take on the role of chief after current Chief Alex McConnell stepped down. Alex himself had broken out a back window and made a number of entries as the fire raged, helping retrieve the bodies of the three young boys. Alex remained in the department but ceded his position to the more experienced Wayne. Wayne immediately demanded regular meetings and practices with mandatory attendance required. Training movies and guest speakers were scheduled, first-aid classes introduced and maintenance and inventory regularly done. Various Yukon fire departments offered training and suggestions that were greatly appreciated.

The call-out system was revamped by the local telephone service technician. Every firefighter had a red phone in their home. When a fire was reported, it was routed to these phones so the men had an immediate heads up on the fire's location. A concern of access to water in the winter months was remedied by setting up a permanent heated pump house on the shore of the lake. Determined to be inclusive, it was deemed the women would act as fire spotters to make sure other buildings were not in danger, act as crowd control and to make sure vehicles stayed off fire hoses. I'm sure the lady firefighters currently in the department might find this a tad sexist, but it was the 1970s—no excuse, just an explanation.

It was determined that fire prevention was the most important approach, as Atlin is largely comprised of old, dry, wooden structures. Jack Green donated a chimney sweep brush and it was made available to everyone in the community. The importance of proper smoke detectors and fire extinguishers was imparted to the public, and firefighters came to the school to explain prevention and what to do in the case of fire in our homes. Little tot stickers were handed out to parents and applied to the bedroom windows of small children.

Ladies headed the auxiliary and once again became the driving force behind the scenes. Fundraisers were planned and executed, including a raffle for gold donated by local miners. The Fireman's Ball and the spring plant sale also added money to the coffers. A donation of used protective gear from Smithers and Coquitlam, two southern B.C. towns, allowed every Atlin volunteer to have a heavy fire coat and a proper helmet by November of that year. The Ladies' Auxiliary made all necessary repairs to the used but serviceable coats.

The first nugget raffle netted close to twenty-five hundred dollars and it went a long way toward much-needed equipment. Determining a need for a tanker truck to better service any fires away from the endless supply of Atlin Lake water, the search went out for a used truck. The two trucks could easily knock down a residential fire if caught soon enough and Ron's water truck was a great backup, but relying on three different vehicles was less than efficient at best, considering the conditions.

With a new truck, the need to house it properly, *i.e.*, a heated space, would become critical. Already too crowded in the existing building, it was clear a new fire hall was needed. A Canada Works grant would take care of the labor and the Atlin Volunteer Fire Department footed some of the cost, but it left a major portion unfulfilled. The call went out for suggestions.

By March, with the Canada Works grant along with a Low Impact Development grant for materials, a local draftswoman (Mom) drew up the plans. With a volunteer group of young adults visiting from back east ready to help, the project moved forward. Less than a year later, Atlin had a fire hall and a new, used tanker truck. Local volunteers added the finishing touches to the hall and the tanker and once again Atlinites proved undefeatable.

In only a few months of that tragic event in the wee hours of an August morning, the Atlin Volunteer Fire Department modernized and upgraded to a first-class outfit. It would only continue to get better and would soon add an ambulance corps.

————

A common conversation at that time between an Atlin husband and wife might have gone something like this:

Husband: "I thought we were going to have a romantic night at home without the kids soon—how about Friday?"

Wife: "I know, it's long overdue and my sister said she would take the kids anytime, but Friday is my can-can practice and I can't miss it. We're learning a new routine. Let's do Saturday night."

Husband: "Saturday night's no good for me. The Rec. Centre is having a work bee and I'm helping wax the floor. Sunday night's out, it's bath night and the boys will need help with their homework as usual. What are you doing Monday night?"

Wife: "Monday night I've got the Historical Society meeting. We're electing new officers and if I don't show up, I'll end up being the treasurer again. Do you have your usual Tuesday night fire practice?"

Husband: "Yes, and it's mandatory, we're practicing on one of Bill's old shacks. He's letting us burn it and practice putting it out. It's a can't-miss. What about Wednesday night?"

Wife: "Sorry, I'm volunteering at the library; we just got a new shipment of books in from the Yukon Library Association. They were nice enough to send us some of their overflow. The boys are coming to help. When's your Board of Trade meeting?"

Husband: "This coming Thursday night. Don't you have Cub Scouts with the boys the same night anyway?"

Wife: "Yes, every other Thursday night till summer break. And next Thursday night I've got the Atlin Arts meeting; I volunteered to help with the next gallery showing. So now we're back to Friday night and can-can practice again. Maybe after Fun Days we can find time."

Husband: "That seems so far away. I'm afraid we will never get any alone time. How about this as a compromise—what about a quiet breakfast together one day this week?"

Wife: "That sounds wonderful, how about Saturday morning, before the boys get up?"

Husband: "Yeah, Saturday's no good for me, we're doing our winter search and rescue training at Surprise Lake, and I need to be up and out before first light."

Wife: "Oh, my God! 'Move to a quiet little town,' they said. 'You'll have so much quality time with your husband, they said.'"

Husband: "We're going to have to cut this short, Honey. I'm on my way to the Gun Club. The boys and I are shooting for our silver tonight. Leave me a note on the fridge."

Wife: "After you shoot, come upstairs to the curling club. It's ladies' night, maybe we can sneak in a quick cup of coffee between ends."

Husband: "Sounds good. I've gotta run now."

Chapter Thirty

Across the Great Divide

I am honored to have known many of the pioneers in Atlin when I grew up. Men and women of distinction who led humble lives of great accomplishment, but who took no notice of the respect and awe they instilled in others. To them, they lived their life like countless others of the day. That may have been true, but for following generations, they easily instilled a sense of wonder and even inadequacy. To have known these unassuming giants of a bygone time was a privilege indeed. The following list is short, but I have chosen a few, to represent the many. Although I was a small child, I have fond memories of these larger-than-life icons.

Ira Bennett

He was born in Tarbolton, Ontario, in 1899 and raised on a farm in Saskatchewan. At the age of seventeen, Ira and fifteen-year-old brother Joe, struck out on their own. The boys left home with ten cents each in their pocket, one change of clothes and an overcoat. Farming was all they knew, so they worked their way across the

Canadian plains and into the farm belt of America, moving from one odd job to another, usually walking from town to town.

Growing weary of farm work, the boys found jobs laying cobblestones in Chicago, they fired boilers on the Pennsylvania railroad, worked the rigs in the Turner oil fields of Alberta, and helped build the railroad into Lesser Slave Lake in Northern Alberta where they ran a horse team skidding logs for the railroad.

Ira's younger brother, Joe, headed south to take a job in Edmonton and Ira stayed in the North to log. This is where a group of men approached Ira and told him he looked just like a friend of theirs, Roy Bennett. Ira was shocked to find his older brother Roy in such an isolated place. Roy had moved out a few years before Ira and Joe and little was known of his whereabouts. That winter Ira and Roy teamed up to trap, prospect and fish. They ended the winter with a little money and decided to team up permanently.

The boys headed off to Manitoba, thinking it better country for trapping and prospecting. Once again, they walked. The brothers spent a number of years in Northern Manitoba and Ontario canoeing the routes of the voyagers and mushing dogs along their traplines. One winter the brothers went through the ice. Ira froze his feet and ended up losing most of his toes. Never to be idle, Ira limped a little but continued his life of wanderlust. The brothers worked, building the railroad into Churchill, Manitoba and ran cat trains into the Arctic territories.

Ira and Roy were in Vancouver in 1938 and decided it would be a good opportunity to join up for service in WWII. The brothers were continually turned down. Roy had received serious wounds in WWI, but Ira could not understand why he was being refused. Upon request, he was told he was flat footed and could not possibly march great distances. Ira thought this funny as he had walked across the country many times, logging thousands of miles on foot and half of that with most of his toes missing.

Roy eventually took a full-time job with the government and Ira headed off to Northern Quebec to prospect. After a time working in an underground hard rock mine, he eventually teamed up with a pilot and together they prospected from Northern Alberta to Labrador. Ira was dropped off in the spring at an isolated destination, he then made his way on foot over land to be picked up in the fall. Ira easily covered several hundred miles a summer by himself, exploring and analyzing minerals in his search for the big strike. For many years Ira walked and prospected throughout the Canadian North.

For a time, he ended up in Arctic Alaska, then, in the mid-1950s, he somehow found his way to Atlin. Atlin made an indelible impression on Ira, and when finding the constant wear and tear of bush life tiring, he decided to settle down. In 1964, he set up residence in Atlin, his first permanent home in nearly fifty years. He continued to prospect around the area most summers, and for a while he was the caretaker at Nolan Mine.

Ira endeared himself to the children of Atlin, shelling out hard candy and welcoming his young guests into his home where he always had cookies and plenty of stories. With Tagish, his faithful dog, at his side, Ira was a fixture on Atlin streets where he offered advice and showed off tricks he taught Tagish.

When my dad started dog mushing, mistakes were made which were often hilarious to some of the old-timers. Few offered help and most only shrugged their shoulders. My dad told a story about Ira that he found endearing. One afternoon our rider-less sled and three dogs shot down the street past Ira's house. A block behind, my dad was running, swearing and shaking his fist.

Later that day, Ira approached and asked if he could offer some advice. With a straight face, he looked at my dad and said, "You've got to hold on tight to them dogs or they'll leave you sitting on your arse." Although he was stating the obvious, my dad appreciated any advice at that time and later appreciated the humor.

Along with candy, cookies, dog tricks and epic stories, Ira was known to buy lotto tickets and hand them out to the neighborhood kids. It was fitting that on the day of his death one of his little pals won a hundred dollars.

Ollie Osborn Jack McKenzie

Just Jack to all that knew him, he was born in 1910 in Moyie, British Columbia, a silver-mining town. By the time he reached his early teens, his hometown was in decline as the silver had run out. Jobs were scarce and Jack had to leave home to seek work, starting a life of wandering from log camp, gold mine or trapline throughout Northern Canada. A long-time trapper, logger and boatman of renown, Jack was known as a hard worker and man of his word.

Jack McKenzie with lynx pelt, 1968.

Jack was an expert white-water navigator, among other things, running the mail by river boat up the dangerous White River in the Yukon and into Alaska. The White River is a tributary of the Yukon River and is glacier-fed. The White moves tons of glacier sediment every year, turning the Yukon brown from their confluence to its mouth. This sediment made the river particularly hard to navigate and lives were lost while delivering supplies and mail to the mines along its banks.

Like many of the men of the North, trapping filled the winter months and provided support through those long cold days. Jack became an expert trapper while he traveled throughout the Yukon and Northern British Columbia. Preferring logging and saw milling, he sought those jobs, but always returned to trapping.

When my parents met Jack, he lived in one of Arnold Edzerza's tiny trapline cabins near Gladys Lake, accessible in the summer only by a half day, rugged, truck sojourn followed by a boat trip, or in the winter by dog team or Ski-Doo. Forty miles (65km) from town, the isolated life suited Jack, and he enjoyed the days of solitude with his dogs.

To help fill his idle time, Jack loved to draw, cartoon characters in particular. He filled large scrapbooks with his humorous characters, which he then brought to town and gave to some of the children. I was a lucky recipient of more than one. They were of a quality that could easily have been syndicated in the best newspapers of the day, but Jack had no desire to gain anything but the smiles of the children.

My mom met Jack when she purchased some of his furs for sale in The Discovery Shop. That was the beginning of a friendship that lasted until he passed away in 1971. When Jack made it to town, he stayed with us or at Arnold's. I know Pete and John, Arnold and Pam's sons, also received Jack's drawings. Like many of the old bachelor pioneers, Jack loved kids and they loved him. I was always excited to see Jack's old beat-up Ski-Doo parked outside the house. I remember no matter the temperature, he always had his top three or four buttons undone, his bare chest exposed to the bitter conditions.

Jack spent summers in town taking odd jobs here and there. A regular at our dinner table, he never came empty-handed and always brought a block of vanilla ice cream—he loved his vanilla ice cream. Jack had a mission to rid Atlin's gravel streets of all nails and screws. When walking the streets, he constantly stopped to pick up nails, filling his pockets with the rusty tire assassins. In Atlin, after surviving two great fires and many buildings salvaged for their lumber, the streets had their fair share of nails.

I had a constant banter with Jack. I often saw him strolling down the street with a block of ice cream in a paper bag, usually toward our house or Arnold's. I'd ask him, "Hey Jack, what's in the bag?" He always answered the same way: "A pound of nails."

Long before Jack moved to the Atlin area sometime in the 1930s, he spent a few winters trapping along the Yukon River. On Henderson Creek, roughly eighty miles (129km) south of Dawson City, he found and fixed up a long-abandoned cabin. Jack noticed a name carved in a log on the back wall of the cabin. It was famed author Jack London's signature and date. Jack realized the significance immediately. Fearing that after he moved on, the cabin would decay and possibly be lost forever, he carefully sliced the writing out of the log. The closest authority was the mining recording commissioner in Mayo, Yukon. Jack brought the signature there, turned it over to the commissioner and promptly forgot about it.

In 1965, Dick North, famed Yukon author and a friend of our family, contacted Jack through my parents. Dick was researching Jack London's time in the Yukon and was fascinated with finding London's cabin. Through the mukluk telegraph, Dick heard a rumor

Jack might know where the cabin was. Jack told Dick about carving out the name and date and what he'd done with it. Amazingly, almost forty years later, Dick was able to obtain the chunk of log with London's signature. Dick and others searched Henderson Creek and ultimately found Jack London's cabin. The carved-out signature fit perfectly into the void in the log, thus confirming that it was indeed London's cabin.

The cabin was disassembled log by log and taken to Dawson City. Half of the logs were used to build a cabin in Dawson City that eventually became the tourist center where Dick North later served as Dawson's historian and tourist information guru for many years. The other half of the logs were sent to Oakland, California, London's birthplace. Those logs were used to build another cabin in Oakland's Jack London Square.

Jack McKenzie passed away in 1971, a young sixty-one years old. He was found alone on his trapline at Rose Creek.

Norman Fisher

Born in Alma, Ontario, in 1884, Norman was raised on a farm. Like many men of the time, he left home at an early age to seek his fortune or at the least a good wage. Norman moved across the country to Vancouver Island where in 1901, he got the gold bug and he and a partner headed off to Dawson City, Yukon.

Disillusioned with the lack of prospects and the brutally-harsh winters, he split with his partner and, pairing with another man, headed back south. Both men, completely broke, starving and needing work, headed into the Atlin area hoping to find a job at a gold mine.

Norman told the story of when he and his new partner made it into Whitehorse after their long trip south from Dawson. The two men had fourteen cents between them. With the last of their money, they bought two sandwiches and two beers. The sandwiches were old and were crawling with worms. Norman said he was thankful for having the beer as it helped wash the worms down.

When he first saw Atlin in 1902, Norman immediately fell in love with the spectacular landscape and especially the beautiful lake. At first, Norman took odd jobs saw milling for a while and cooking at various mines on Spruce and Boulder Creeks. Norman quickly built a reputation as a hard worker and Louis Schulz hired him to run the mail from Carcross to Atlin.

Considered the most dangerous mail run in Canada, Norman fought bitter cold, stubborn dogs, rotten ice, wild animals and whiteouts in order to deliver the mail, every isolated town's lifeblood, for thirteen years. Considering it an honor, Norman took great pride in getting the mail through no matter the conditions. Only once did Norman lose a sack of mail when his dogs bolted after a caribou and took off over rotten ice. Another man died in the attempted retrieval of that bag.

Norman didn't think much of his exploits and didn't revel in his adventures, but one story he did tell was of a time one late spring when he couldn't trust the ice anymore and there wasn't enough snow for the sled. With dog packs loaded and more mail on his own back, he was forced to skirt around the lakes, walking on the shore and game trails. Norman was a small man, barely five feet (1.5m) tall and maybe a hundred and twenty pounds (55kg) soaking wet.

Somewhere along the shore of Atlin Lake, he stopped to take a break. Unloading his pack, he stepped off the trail to relieve himself. He leaned against a tree preparing to do his business when he was suddenly lifted up and flung through the air. He landed in the deep snow a few yards away, flat on his back. Bewildered, he picked himself up, dusted off his clothes and turned to find a sprung bear trap. Luckily for Norman, he must have stepped on the very edge of the trap, setting it off but not getting caught in it. A man cannot release a bear trap by himself and definitely not if it's on his leg— another inch and it would have certainly spelled Norman's doom.

In 1916, Norman and a number of other Atlin men joined the 72nd Seaforth Highlanders and shipped out to fight in the trenches of France. Of all the men who went from Atlin, only three were to return, Norman among them. Upon his return to Canada, Norman did a number of jobs, but always gravitated to gold mining, finally teaming up with his good friend and mining engineer Mac White. Together they successfully mined on Boulder Creek for a number of years.

In the 1940s, with another war looming and mining in decline, Norman took on a different role, a little more relaxing and one he enjoyed immensely. In his boat, the Prowler, he offered guided fishing and sightseeing trips on Atlin Lake. Norman loved the lake and enjoyed showing it off to strangers and friends alike. Even in his last year, he was readying the Prowler for another season.

Norman was Atlin's longest resident when he passed away at the age of ninety-three. He was put to rest in the new Atlin cemetery overlooking the lake he loved so much. On a sparkling winter's day as a lone piper played, Atlin said goodbye to one of its greatest sons.

Richard (Dick) Craft, Sr.

Originally from Virginia, Dick's family moved to Timmons, Ontario, when he was a young boy. There, Dick became a policeman and later the chief of police. Becoming bored, he eventually headed out west and started a new life—that of a prospector.

Dick passed away when I was very young, but I do have good memories of him. He ran a very small tobacco, candy and magazine stand in the front of his house. Often surrounded by his grandkids, he enjoyed the company his little store provided him. It was where I bought my first comic book. I remember you could barely turn around in there and it was always filled with cigarette and cigar smoke. Whether you bought something or not, he gave all the kids a penny candy. He always wanted to know who your parents were so he could keep track of the different boys and girls who frequented his store. "Oh, you're the Smith kid," he would say in his gravely smoker's voice.

Dick was the oldest licensed driver in Canada at the age of 100. He drove a beat-up pickup truck and when you saw that bright-red truck meandering toward you, it was best to move off to the side of the road, way off, something our mothers constantly reminded us.

At the age of 101, he decided he wanted to take a prospecting trip back to Ontario for one last look at some ground that held his interest. He confided in more than a few that he was in fact on a courting mission, as he had received word that an old flame recently became widowed. He figured it might be his chance for a little love prospecting of a sort.

Off he drove in his red pickup to Whitehorse, and from there he flew to Ontario. It was indeed his last prospecting trip, as he passed away shortly after arriving. No word on the prospects of either kind. But one thing is for sure, nothing ever slowed Dick down and he did what he wanted right up until the very end. Dick was the epitome of the eternal optimist.

Leo Taku Jack

Leo, son of Chief Taku Jack, was quite a character from my point of view. As many of the people of the North, Leo lived a diverse, interesting life. He was a trapper, big-game and fishing guide, and in his youth he too, like Norman, ran the treacherous mail by dog team route from Carcross to Atlin and Telegraph Creek.

I first met Leo when I was three or four, upon bursting into the kitchen in the Old Government Building to find my mom and Leo in the middle of a war dance or something akin. There they were, stomping around waving their arms, singing out and grunting. My mom was fascinated with the Tlingit culture and Leo was happy to answer questions and demonstrate rituals. He was a friendly, outgoing man, who always had a big smile spread across his weathered, kind face. I felt strength from Leo, a calm wisdom, a man who understood things but didn't feel the desire to intercede his opinion unless asked.

I'll never forget the day Mom and I heard a loud crash on the first floor. We raced down to find Leo spread eagle on his back surrounded by oranges. His mukluks were frozen solid on the bottom and had no grip on our slick linoleum floor. Try as he might, he couldn't stand up; every time he attempted it, one leg or the other flew out from under him and back down he went. The whole time he was laughing and soon we all were. As he crawled back to the door herding his oranges like a flock of misbehaving sheep, we followed behind corralling up the strays. Leo was aware of my mom's longing for fresh fruit, and as fruit of any kind was rare in the winter, he bought her a bag of oranges and was attempting to deliver them.

Leo and my mom shared a concern. They worried that many of the Tlingit ceremonial items and artifacts were leaving the area with the tourists and summer residents, whether by legitimate commerce or downright criminal activity, including grave robbery.

The impromptu museum my parents had started in the Courtroom was about to be handed over to the newly-formed Historical Society. Between the two of them, they agreed that anything that came up for sale or anything that just needed preserving, if at all possible, would come to my mom first. She would buy or gladly accept donations and, in turn, guarantee the items be preserved, protected and displayed in the museum to someday be repatriated to the Taku River Tlingit Band.

One afternoon I was trying to learn how to ride my bike down the little alley beside the Old Government Building. I had frustrated my dad and he was taking a break. His technique of giving me a big shove wasn't working. He thought I was being a baby and I thought he was a meanie. I was about to give up, and was pushing my bike and crying. Leo suddenly appeared out of nowhere and encouraged me to keep trying; he ran beside me holding on to my seat, helping me keep my balance. Up and down the alley we went. I finally realized he wasn't there and I had done it on my own. I turned to thank him, but he was gone.

Leo was like a friendly grandpa. I remember he always smelled like wood smoke and fresh baked cookies—not a bad combination if you ask me. Gunalcheesh, Leo.

Anais Lyraud (Auntie) Roxborough

Born in 1889 in central France, "Auntie," as she was affectionately known by all, wanted to become a nurse. She studied for two years and loved tending to the sick. One day the doctor called her father and stated that she would never be a good nurse as she was too quick tempered. Devastated, she quit nursing that day. She took up sewing and quickly mastered it. For a time, she even worked for Coco Chanel in Paris.

In Paris she met John Boyer, a young mining engineer. He regaled her with stories of a far-off land in Northern Canada where he went every summer to work in the gold fields. They fell in love and decided to marry in Canada. Auntie followed John that next spring. First crossing the Atlantic and arriving in Nova Scotia, she traveled from there by train across the vastness of the entire country to Vancouver, B.C. From Vancouver, she boarded a steamship to Skagway, Alaska. From Skagway, she crossed the Coast Mountains on the White Pass Railway, arriving in Canada at Carcross, then known as Caribou Crossing. In Carcross, she boarded the SS Tutshi for the cruise up Tagish Lake and along Taku Arm to the small community of Taku. From Taku, she took a short ride on the narrow-gauge railroad to

Scotia Bay on Atlin Lake. Finally, she crossed the lake to Atlin on the frail spring ice by dog team. "Imagine my thrill," she said. "From Paris to the northern snow fields of Canada and to be surrounded by such beauty. From the very beginning, I fell in love with this country."

Before she could get married, she had to wait ten days for the proper authority. Jules Eggert and family, who were of Swiss descent and spoke French, offered to put her up while she waited. After they were married, she and John moved out to the mine on Boulder Creek. As there was already a cook and she didn't know English, Auntie had little to do, so she walked the high country every day, sometimes all the way to town, every minute falling more in love with her new home. She was in awe of the wilderness, the space and the friendly people. Never missing Paris, she accepted her new challenges with confidence and adapted quickly.

In 1915, John was drafted and left for France. Auntie stayed behind and tended the mine. Soon after, tragedy struck, as she received news John was killed in a trench on the front line. The thought of returning to France after the war was heartbreaking. Auntie moved from the mine into town and attempted to start a sewing business, but it didn't take. Her family offered a position in their silk business in Saint-Etienne, France, but she couldn't see herself living in a small polluted industrial town after experiencing the stark beauty of Northern Canada.

It wasn't long before she met Bill Roxborough, who had recently returned to Atlin to help his father rebuild The Kootenay Hotel after it burned to the ground in the fire of 1914. Bill and Auntie married in 1916. It was a small wedding attended by friends and family, including Norman Fisher.

Auntie found her calling in the hotel business. The nurturing role denied to her earlier in life was fulfilled in her new role as hostess, cook, confidant and mother to her patrons. Auntie and Bill, or Uncle, as he became known, never had children of their own but raised a number of Bill's brother Bob's kids, as his wife died young. "Those years with Bill in that hotel raising all those kids were the happiest years of my life," she recalled later.

Boarding miners in the winter and travelers in the summer, it wasn't long before word spread about the great hospitality of The Kootenay Hotel and the woman everyone lovingly called Auntie.

After retiring from the hotel, Auntie's house was constantly filled with nieces, nephews, great-nieces and great-nephews and random neighborhood kids, all with a cookie in hand and a smile on their face. Auntie was a gentle and caring soul who met her perfect match in Uncle. Theirs was a classic story of love and happiness born from respect and generosity toward each other and anyone fortunate enough to know them. They truly were Atlin's Aunt and Uncle.

Veneration and Admiration

I am fascinated with the lives these early pioneers led and the risks so casually taken. The grand endeavors they embraced on a whim and their daily accomplishments most would not dream of attempting today. Hard to imagine in this time someone like Ira walking thousands of miles across wild country, many of those miles with most of his toes missing; or Norman and Leo risking their lives to deliver the mail across miles of perilous wilderness; and what of Auntie following her heart from the bright city gaslights of Paris to the flickering flame of a single candle in an isolated miner's cabin deep in the hinterland of Canada's North Country?

Who does these things nowadays? Today I am certain few would venture up the White River in any type of boat, or live forty miles (65km) from nearest town alone all winter. How about Dick Craft at the age of 101 still searching for that elusive yellow curse called gold or possibly that more elusive curse, true love?

Atlin old-timer, Russel Crowe, who in his seventies thought nothing of rowing his tiny dinghy thirty miles (50km) down the lake to spend the summer camping and fishing by himself. This is a lake that can see seven-foot waves and turn violent in a matter of minutes.

Krist Johnson who, up into his eighties, climbed Monarch Mountain every year just to say he did it; or (Whispering) Bill Husselbee who, well into old age, spent his winters isolated across the lake where he shot and killed a bear in his cabin after it chased his dog inside.

The list goes on, and there are too many to cover. These are just a few that left an indelible impression on me. All those old-timers lived life as it should be lived, boldly but humbly, fiercely but with compassion, with measured risk and no regrets.

Old-timer (Whispering) Bill Husselbee's summer home in Atlin, 1996. Well into old age, he spent his winters across the lake in a small, isolated cabin with his dog Blackie, where he often contended with bears for the path to the outhouse.

These were the casual examples of greatness I was fortunate enough to grow up around. These were the men and women that helped me understand the type of person I wanted to be. My heroes were not in the pages of my comic books or on the tattered screen at the Rec. Centre, seen twice a month. My heroes were authentic and they were a fundamental part of my early life. They were tangible and accessible, not an imagined being from another universe, a sports star or rock-and-roll god. My heroes walked our streets, they offered advice, told stories, and lead by example with kindness.

Rest in Peace

Atlin has three cemeteries: the Tlingit graveyard on their ancestral land featuring traditional above-ground burial houses and quaint picket fences, the Pioneer Cemetery where Atlin's earliest residents were laid to rest, and the new cemetery situated on a high bench beside Pine Creek with a view in every direction.

I'm not certain when they stopped using the Pioneer Cemetery, but the reason is obvious as it lies in low land and becomes partially flooded in the spring. The Historical Society has refurbished and

Alliott, William S.
born
Eccles, Lancashire England
died
March 25, 1908
Killed in a mining accident
on
Spruce Creek
age 32 years

Bowley, Edward St. George
born
Clapham, London England
died
March 25, 1908
Killed in a mining accident
on
Spruce Creek
age 29 years

These men didn't even warrant their own headboard. Most likely their remains weren't recovered and all that was known of them came from the payroll office of the mine where they worked. Pioneer Cemetery in 1996

Joseph Pepio
died
Nov. 1908
found Dead
in the woods
Age 25 years

In Memory
of
John McIntyre
Aged 27 years
Mail Carrier
was drowned
in Taku Arm
Nov. 28th 1902
Erected by
Fritz Miller,
Atlin Co-Founder

Alex Olson
born
June 4, 1862
in Norway
found dead
on the trail
May 11, 1934
age 72 years

Charley William Rudolf
born
July 2, 1923
died
May 21, 1940
age 16 years
Died from
gunshot wounds
mistaken for
a bear

reclaimed many graves and markers over the years, but unfortunately a few were lost to time and nature. A small group of aviators and history buffs from Juneau flew over every year to cut back the brush and weeds and to tidy up the graves. Many markers were crude pine boards with a carved or painted description of the person's origin and how they died.

Most men didn't have their family near, and many families were oceans away. Atlin, like most gold-rush towns, was a temporary stop on the way to a better job or a better claim. Whether it was a respite or an unintended final repose, the truth remains that many men were unknown. Lucky to be acknowledged in death at all, they could only hope for a few scratched words on an old board driven into the ground at the head of their grave.

There were few places on the planet that escaped the pandemic of influenza, and Atlin was no exception. In 1920, it hit with a vengeance. Nineteen whites were struck down by the insidious disease and are buried in the Pioneer Cemetery. Many were children. The Tlingit people were also hit hard, losing fifteen souls, all buried in the Tlingit cemetery.

FREEZE UP
Atlin News Miner Sept. 21, 1972
Diane S. Smith

The leaves are yellow. The blue-red blaze of the fireweed has gone out. Left in the dying embers are little wisps of smoky seed things floating on crisp air. Fall is here and if this be true, close behind it blowing down the necks of Atlinites is freeze up.

Freeze up—the very words can strike terror into any heart. Freeze up! The man who has yet to install a septic tank is stopped dead in his path at the sight of frost on his neighbors' roof. Freeze up! The house painter throws down his fishing rod and runs desperately with bucket and ladder knowing full well the latex will freeze on his brush before the job is done. Freeze up! The old lead ball forms in the stomach pit of the summer idler and jolts him rudely from his warm weather lethargy. As if for the first time, he sees the carefully compiled list of summer projects tacked to the kitchen door. All season it waved unnoticed as he steamed with cold beers and picnic basket. Now, as though emblazoned with neon, it taunts him. Hey Dad, it sneers. You have twenty-three major projects to complete before freeze up. Would you like to start with number one, cut eighteen cords of wood? Or would you prefer item number five, install backyard fence. That one only requires the digging of twenty-seven post holes.

With a forced smile of nonchalance, Mr. Summer Fun and Games scuttles out of town to the nearest burn with his chainsaw clutched in a clammy hand. He passes a neighbor casually starting to put in a concrete foundation for a new garage. He detects the frantic "I'll never make it" look in the man's eyes and tries to glean some small bit of comfort from another's misery.

About town, the pace quickens. Coffee klatches become short and a leisurely chat with the guy next door may end abruptly when his eyes wander to his roof and he remembers there is a large, leaky place to be patched up before the snow flies. There is a regular conversation in the berry patch as flying fingers fill yawning lard pails. Item Number six: Make forty-eight jars of jam and freeze forty-five pounds of berries.

Catalogs are worn to crumpled rags as pages are thumbed in desperate search for warm caps and mitts even though hope is dim they will still be available. Why didn't you order everything last July when the winter catalogue first arrived? But back in those balmy, palmy days who could consider things like ice and snow and ... Freeze Up!

Unless life in Atlin has changed, this fall will be like all the falls before it. The zero-hour race will prevail until about October 18th. Then one morning the ground will be very white and very stiff but out in the new garage, the freezer will be humming merrily, full of moose meat and berries. Eighteen cords of wood will be stacked by the kitchen door which is no longer graced with that menacing decree of blood-red letters. Summer clothes will be stored and dressers stuffed with woolly long johns and socks because Arthur and Nancy down at the General Store remembered to order enough for everybody. Two sides of the house won't be painted but down under that frozen ground the new septic tank will be busy doing its thing. The coffee klatches again grow long and stimulating as conversation turns easily to winter things. The frantic eyes have a new "we did it again" smirk about them and the once-dreaded words Freeze Up! bring to mind only things like Ski-Dooing, dog mushing and ... curling, anyone?

Epilogue

Atlin has a habit of scraping away pretenses and veneers and exposing the real person beneath. There were people who were in love with the ideal of Atlin and what it represented in those days, there were those who were in love with Atlin itself, the scenery, the buildings, the history. Many of the people in love with the concept eventually slipped away in search of greener fields or whiter snow—a predictable income is important to some.

With limited educational opportunities, and for many years not even a high school, a lot of families moved so their children could have all the advantages available. But there are those that stayed because they couldn't imagine living anywhere else. They stayed no matter the hardship or isolation, in some cases because of it. At times, they even left so that they could stay. Many have had to pursue work out of town, but that lonely hardship allowed them to continue to live in Atlin.

My mom was one that left temporarily so she could stay. She moved back to Alaska for a short period, allowing her the ability to retire in Atlin and survive on a meager pension. She chose to live on the

343

land and in the town, surrounded by the people she loved. She faced many hardships in her life in Atlin and she could have assuredly had a more prosperous, more comfortable life somewhere else. But she never lost the wonder she felt that day so long ago when cresting that final rise on Atlin Road and beholding the magnificent scenery that would become the backdrop of the rest of her life.

Unfortunately, couples do not always share the same ideals. As it turned out, my mother and father came up on opposite sides, and they parted ways. My father chose the more urban, comfortable way of life. My mother chose to be in the place she loved, no matter the struggle. I've always held great respect for the families that made a life in Atlin and were able to forever call it their home.

I, too, left Atlin, first to attend high school in Whitehorse, and then because I could not see the economic opportunities I thought I needed. The truth is I needed to see what the bigger picture looked like. Like the restless spirits that were searching when they found Atlin, I needed to search. I also felt a little smothered by the small-town familiarity.

High school in Whitehorse allowed a slow severing of the Atlin umbilical cord as I was able to come home most weekends, and Whitehorse offered a wider lens and gave a small taste of future possibilities.

At twenty, I moved back to Alaska and started what would become a diverse and somewhat restless life, with stays in Homer, Alaska; Monroe, Everett, Redmond and Bothel, Washington; Juneau, Alaska, and many rural villages across Arctic Alaska. Now home base is back in beautiful British Columbia, Canada. Many moves, many jobs and many amazing experiences combined have all made me what I am today, but my formative years in Atlin made me who I am every day.

My first trip back to Atlin, only a few years after moving to Alaska, was disheartening to say the least. I pulled into town in the early afternoon, intending to stay for three days. I drove all the streets in a matter of minutes, had coffee at the café and dinner at the Inn. I stopped by one of the grocery stores and throughout, I never saw a friend. Believe it or not, I did recognize a few dogs but didn't see their owners. The suffocating feeling was still prevalent, and I also had a sense of loss and loneliness. That evening, I left. I didn't get it yet.

I'm on the back of our freight sled, 1970.

I realized that all my peers had also left for various reasons, mostly economic. The very few that remained were most likely working out of town for the summer. It wasn't until I returned with my children that it became obvious to me what Atlin was and is. Seeing it through the eyes of my boys helped me understand how very lucky I was. At the time, they were city kids, and although we camped most every weekend, they had experienced nothing like Atlin. My boys lived in a time and place where I could ill afford letting them out of my sight. Atlin was bewildering and magical to them.

On one particular day, having recently arrived back, we were at the Garrett Store chatting with Caroline Moore. Both boys were bugging me to take them to the Campground, now sporting an enormous play area. Not yet ready to leave, I told them to go ahead and we would meet them there. They both looked at me as if I had lost my mind. My older boy finally understood what I was saying, but my youngest was hesitant to be that far away from us. It took some coaxing, but they did go on their own. Of course, that opened the floodgates and they quickly became free-range Atlin kids.

For many summers, we came to visit Grandma in Atlin. My boys loved it, and to this day value that time greatly and will never forget the freedom they experienced. They also laugh at their old dad when the enormous hill behind the school turned out to be a little smaller than the stories I'd told and the Black Rocks now had a house in the middle of the boulders.

Between our summer visits, Grandma's history lessons and constant Randy Green stories, I am happy a little of Atlin wore off on them and they continue to cherish their time there.

I have attempted to depict and explain a time, a place and a sense of community that I have never experienced again in my life. I have taken a small slice of time as seen through the eyes of a young boy who lived it. I chose to see and tell my story in a bright light, understanding every community has darkness; but while in no way would I minimize it, I don't see value in recounting it at this time. Although I refer to the past, I don't mean to infer Atlin has lost any of the inclusiveness and sense of community that I write about. So many have given so much to keep that town great over the years, and to all I applaud and say job well done. I would not and do not attempt to speak of any time but the time I lived there.

Atlin has seen booms and busts in its young life, the first boom during the gold rush, and then it slowly ebbed away to its lowest bust during the 1950s. It saw its second boom from the mid-1960s to the early 1980s and that is the time I recall in these writings. I was part of the slow drain of the second bust, although nothing as climactic as the first. Atlin has had and continues to maintain a robust and progressive existence with one eye to the future and one eye on its storied past.

I am happy to report that Atlin seems to be in yet another boom period and once again is attracting people of a like mind that want to get away from what they knew and are excited to start a new life. Atlin is once again attracting families, artists, entrepreneurs and free spirits, although it continues to exist because of its bedrock, gold mining, and it is also still proudly anchored by its big game guides, fishing guides, saw millers and trappers.

It doesn't shock me in any way the number of people that call Atlin home; all you have to do is look at their online profiles to see Atlin listed as hometown. No matter how short the stay, people are defensively proud of their time there.

My mom was a great historian. The North in general, gold rushes, arctic exploration and Atlin in particular were her fields of expertise. She was a talented archivist who dedicated herself to preserving Atlin's vibrant past. She started the Atlin Museum and was a founding member of the Historical Society. She made certain the Old Government Building and the *M/V Tarahne* ended up preserved. She co-wrote with Christine Frances Dickinson the quintessential history of Atlin, *Atlin: The Story of British Columbia's Last Gold Rush*. All these deeds stitched her to the fabric of the community.

Like so many people past and present, she dedicated thousands of hours to the community she loved and asked nothing in return. Whether serving on one board or another, attending copious meetings, working in the museum archives, sewing dresses for the men of town at Fun Days, painting signs, drawing plans, writing for the various newspapers, or putting together *A Guide to Atlin's Historic Buildings*, her accomplishments were impressive. She exemplified the Atlin spirit.

A true renaissance woman, an accomplished artist in multiple mediums, an award-winning author, a businesswoman, an explorer, a craftsman, a historian, and a consummate volunteer and single mother, she went about them all with the same confidence and resolve.

With all her accomplishments, I could never get her to see that she was history and, together with her fellow citizens, was laying the foundation for future generations, much like, and as importantly as, the earliest pioneers and Atlin's oldest families did before her. I consider her a modern pioneer and I believe she became one of the intrepid individuals she idolized from an early age. Always making her own way through life, she followed that path right to the end, calmly making her final decision—choosing death rather than "life" connected to a machine away from the place she loved.

Dogs were her constant companions. When she moved back to Alaska briefly in the 1980s for work, she brought two Malamutes with her, long-time mates Knik and Disco, short for Discovery. When Disco disappeared off the leash one night and was never found, Knik passed away a couple weeks later of a broken heart. Soon after, Mom adopted an old stray and provided a nice home for him until he died of old age. Upon returning to Atlin, she got another Malamute, Willow, who was with her until she passed away in 2003. At that time, Willow was old and incontinent, and friends and neighbors suggested I have her put to sleep, which I did.

Forever humble, her final request to me was not to make a fuss over her passing. She made me promise not to bury her or mark her grave, preferring her accomplishments be her mark, and instead asked me to spread her ashes across the land and before the scenery she worshiped. Together with her last dog, Willow, she rests in just such a place, on a sun-drenched, wildflower-strewn hillside overlooking Pine Creek, in view of her favorite mountains, beloved lake, and the home she loved.

> *We leave something of ourselves behind when we leave a place; we stay there, even though we go away. And there are things in us that we can find again only by going back there.*
> Pascal Mercier

These have been my recollections, observances and embellishments of an integral part of my life. With keen research, a great memory for all things old and moldy, and recollections of oft-told stories, I have put together this narrative for entertainment purposes and nothing more. I wave the flag that is a writer's prerogative.

Mom sitting with Cassiar, our lead dog, and Chilkoot, our wheel dog. They came with us from Juneau in 1967 when they were puppies.

Diane Solie Smith

Diane Solie was born in Washington State, December 6, 1930. She led an independent childhood, and with her first dog, Lucky, she explored the shores of Puget Sound, where she learned to fish, hunt and sail and ski. A consummate adventurer, she moved to Alaska in her mid-thirties where she met and married Ed Smith. Now Diane Solie Smith, in the summer of 1967 with her new husband and son, two-year-old Brad, she moved to Atlin, British Columbia, Canada, an isolated gold-rush era, semi-ghost town in the Northern wilderness.

Diane fell immediately and permanently in love with the history, the people, and the stark beauty of the land. With Ed, she started the Atlin Museum, and she was a founding member of the Atlin Historical Society. She coauthored the quintessential history, *Atlin, the Story of British Columbia's Last Gold Rush* with Christine Frances Dickinson. She authored articles, pamphlets and studies, notably *A Guide to Atlin's Historic Buildings* and *The Legend of*

Lillian Alling, the Woman Who Walked to Russia. She was intimately involved with the preservation of many of Atlin's historic buildings.

Diane was a business owner. She founded and owned The Discovery Shop, a craft store that sold many of her own creations as well as providing an outlet for Atlin's artists and crafters to sell their wares. She was an accomplished watercolorist and carver, selling hundreds of paintings and carvings.

She was a dog owner and lover throughout her life. At one time she owned close to thirty dogs. Diane was a proficient musher and she created a bustling dog-breeding operation.

Diane became a part of the history she adored and valued highly. She became an indelible part of Atlin's fabric, a cornerstone of Atlin's second boom, and an integral cog in the works that shaped today's Atlin.

She was an engineer, a draftsman, a sign painter, an artist proficient in several mediums, an esteemed historian and archivist, a published author, a journalist, a teacher, mentor, single mother and champion of everything Atlin, British Columbia.

Diane passed away March 7, 2003. With her last dog, Willow, she rests on a wildflower-strewn hillside overlooking the town, the lake and the Mountain she fell in love with that long ago, summer day in 1967 when she rounded the final corner on the Atlin Road where she first witnessed the unparalleled scenery that would become the magnificent backdrop for the rest of her life.

Mom with her last dog, Willow, in her flower garden in Atlin, 2001.

References

Atlin-The Story of British Columbia's Last Gold Rush—Christine Frances Dickinson and Diane Solie Smith

A Guide to Atlin's Historic Buildings—Diane Solie Smith

Atlin News-Miner Newspaper—Stories by Diane Solie Smith and general reference

Atlin Claim Newspaper—general reference

Atlin Rag Time Newspaper—general reference

The Whitehorse Star-Newspaper—Bob Elum's story about Lorrina Price

Index

About the Author

Bradford Smith grew up an only child amongst a household of huskies and Malamutes, and at times, he thought they were his siblings. From the age of two he lived in Atlin, British Columbia, Canada, a historic gold mining town nestled deep in the wilderness. It was a town without a sewer or water system, and most households burned wood for heat. People ate moose meat and lake trout and grew their own vegetables. He led life with an independent and creative spirit in Atlin. Without television, radio or video games, his imagination was fertile and his curiosity intense.

He trapped by dog team with his dad and hunted grouse and picked berries with his mom. He fished and snared rabbits and searched abandoned gold mines with his friends. Like many of his peers, he was sawing and splitting the winter wood supply by the age of ten. He ran a small team of dogs at nine and he fought his first forest fire at sixteen.

The author now splits his time between working in Arctic Alaska and his home in Northern British Columbia, Canada, where he lives with his wife and their dogs.

www.bradfordsmithauthor.com

CPSIA information can be obtained
at www.ICGtesting.com
Printed in the USA
BVHW091750150222
629082BV00004B/171